M.Lilla

VICO REVISITED

VICO REVISITED

**Orthodoxy, Naturalism and Science
in the *Scienza Nuova***

GINO BEDANI

BERG

Oxford / Hamburg / Munich

*Distributed exclusively in the US and Canada by
St. Martin's Press, New York*

First published in 1989 by
Berg Publishers Limited

—Editorial Offices—
77 Morrell Avenue, Oxford OX4 1NQ, UK
165 Taber Avenue, Providence R.I. 02906, USA
Westermühlstraße 26, 8000 München 5, FRG

© G. L. C. Bedani 1989

British Library Cataloguing in Publication Data

Bedani, Gino,
Vico revisited: orthodoxy, naturalism and
science in the Scienza nuova.
1. Historiology. Philosophical perspectives.
Vico. Giambattista 1668–1744. Scienza
nuova. Critical studies
I. Title
901

ISBN 0–85496–266–2

Library of Congress Cataloging-in-Publication Data

Bedani, Gino,
Vico revisited: orthodoxy, naturalism, and science in the Scienza
nuova / Gino Bedani.
Bibliography
Index.
ISBN 0–85496–266–2 : $40.00 (U.S. : est.)
1. Vico, Giambattista, 1668–1744, Principi di una scienza nuova.
2. Philosophy. 3. Social sciences. 4. Poetry. 5. History-
-Philosophy. 6. Law. 7. Religion. I. Title
B3581.P73B43 1989
195—dc 19

Printed in Great Britain by Short Run Press Ltd, Exeter

Contents

Acknowledgements

Most of the problems discussed in this book first came to my attention in the course of my work for a doctoral thesis on Giambattista Vico. I have also benefited greatly over my years of teaching through discussions with students and colleagues. I cannot name all those who have incited my curiosity, raised questions, shaken my complacency and urged me to face awkward issues.

I wish to thank Professor Leon Pompa for some helpful observations at an earlier stage of my research. I must pay special tribute to his scholarly generosity in suggesting ways in which my argument might be strengthened even where our interpretations differed. During the same period I received many helpful critical comments from Professor W. H. Walsh.

Mention must also be made of Dr Robin Attfield for many constructive suggestions on specific matters. Valuable comments of both a particular and general nature were kindly offered by Dr G. Tagliacozzo who perhaps has done more than any other scholar to further the study of Vico in the English-speaking world. Professor S. Gamberini first interested me in the study of Vico, and our frequent discussions helped me overcome initial hesitations in challenging prevailing and well-entrenched interpretations.

I have been particularly fortunate in being able to rely upon the assistance of Professor F. J. Jones at every stage of preparation of this work. Hardly a page of this book has not benefited in argument, presentation or content from his critical attention. His genial and enduring readiness to read and re-read one draft after another, to discuss, listen and argue has been a continual source of support and encouragement. I am also very grateful to Geraldine Stoneham who has applied her considerable editorial and stylistic skills with great energy to improving the entire manuscript. All the faults are my own responsibility.

I am thankful to the Accademia dell' Arcadia for permission to use the portrait of Vico by Francesco Solemina for the cover design. The photograph was by Signor Lupi.

Finally, I must express my grateful thanks to Vivien, my wife, who over the years of preparation of this work, faced not only the very strenuous demands of her own profession but also accepted more than her fair share of parental and domestic responsibility. Together with my children Carl, Ivanna and Francesca, she has lightened the burden of a demanding task.

Chapter I of my book has previously been published in *New Vico Studies* 4 (1986) and chapter 13 has drawn on material from an article in *Italian Studies* 43 (1988). Thanks are due to the editors of these journals for permission to use this material.

Note on Translation

Throughout this study, an attempt has been made to meet the needs of the specialist while presenting a readable account of the *Scienza nuova* for the student and the interested layman. Accordingly, although a number of academic references have been retained, a knowledge of Italian has not been assumed. In quoting from the *Scienza nuova* (*SN* followed by paragraph number), I have used *The New Science of Giambattista Vico*, translated by T. G. Bergin and M. H. Fisch (Cornell University Press, 1968), occasionally departing from their translation when the sense of Vico's original seemed to me to require it (an asterisk indicates where this has occurred). The paragraph numeration follows that normally used in standard Italian editions. I have also referred to *The Autobiography of Giambattista Vico*, translated by M. H. Fisch and T. G. Bergin (Cornell University Press, 1963). For the 1725 version of the *Scienza nuova* (SN1a) and for some of the minor works I have consulted the extremely useful *Vico: Selected Writings*, edited and translated by Leon Pompa (Cambridge University Press, 1982), and also Giambattista Vico, *On the Study Methods of Our Time*, translated by Elio Gianturco (Bobbs. Merrill, 1965), although the cited passages are my own translations. In quoting from Italian scholars and from original Italian and Latin sources, I have tried where possible to use existing translations. Where none exist, or where they are unsuitable, I have provided my own.

I am grateful to the following for permission to use such translations: Cambridge University Press, for passages from G. S. Kirk and J. E. Raven, *The Presocratic Philosophers* (1963), and Origen, *Contra Celsum*, translated by Henry Chadwick (1953), 1980; Oxford University Press, for passages from *From Alexander to Constantine: Passages and Documents Illustrating the History of Social and Political Ideas, 336BC–AD337*, translated by Ernest Barker (Clarendon Press, 1956), and *The Republic of Plato*, translated by F. N. Cornford (Clarendon Press, 1961); The Loeb Classical Library (Harvard University Press and William Heinemann Ltd) for passages from Seneca, *Naturales Quaestiones*, translated by Thomas H. Corcoran (1971–2). Use of *The New Science of Giambattista Vico*, translated by T. G. Bergin and M. H. Fisch (copyright 1948 by

Introduction

In recent years, widespread interest in Vico has been shown by a variety of scholars often working in totally unrelated subject areas. Students of disciplines as far apart as, for example, linguistics and child psychiatry have regarded him as a thinker of remarkable originality who has made valuable observations in their respective fields of study. And while some commentators are content simply to note striking parallels with subsequent discoveries in their own specialized areas or to indicate seminal ideas, others use Vico as a starting point for rather more speculative and discursive reflections.

All this is made possible by the fact that Vico does indeed touch upon a wide variety of topics in the *Scienza nuova*. It is not surprising, therefore, that his work should receive such diversified treatment and that he should frequently be cited as a 'forerunner' of subsequent movements or theoretical trends. On closer inspection many of these claims seem open to question, but they can in part be attributed to the *Scienza nuova*'s thematic complexity and its frequent presentational ambiguity, which make it difficult for the reader to grasp Vico's work as a whole.

We must also consider some questions concerning Vico's theoretical priorities. Which of his numerous areas of discourse contain his fundamental points of reference, and which are merely subsidiary to them? Is there a nucleus of ideas holding together the entire structure, or are his disparate lines of investigation no more than a gratuitous assemblage of discrete theoretical compartments?

The answers to these questions are neither simple nor straightforward. I hope in the course of this book to demonstrate that Vico was in the first place concerned to produce, as the title of his work suggests, a new science. The problem of scientificity, and all that this entailed in terms of epistemological priorities, remained central to all his thinking – on myth, language, religion, civil institutions, and so on. In many respects criticism of Vico has remained wedded to questionable assumptions, such as the alleged centrality of the 'verum factum' principle to his epistemology. I shall question both the assumption and many of the conclusions which flow from it, and shall highlight elements of Vico's theory which have been obscured by those assumptions. But while the *Scienza nuova*'s

1

epistemology will receive specific and detailed attention, it will also provide a frame of reference for those other areas of Vico's thought mentioned above. This will be one way of showing how the diverse aspects of his work relate to each other.

Similarly, Vico's 'naturalism' will be treated in both a specific and general manner. Although the importance of this aspect of his philosophy has long been acknowledged, particularly by Italian commentators, its implications for his thought as a whole have not so far been systematically examined. My hope is that this book, seeking as it does to remedy this situation, may act as a stimulus to further research. While I have discussed certain fundamental concepts, such as historical cycles and providence, very specifically in relation to Vico's 'naturalism', it is also a constitutive element of his philosophy and pervades the treatment of many other aspects of the *Scienza nuova*.

A third feature of the *Scienza nuova*, which is important in a different sense, is the question of its relation to Catholic orthodoxy. This is a contentious issue, and although it gives rise to sharp differences among scholars, it has not yet received the analysis it merits. A central aspect of this study will be to suggest that in certain places and in this respect we need to read between the lines of the *Scienza nuova*. The idea that this was necessary did not, I must confess, have an immediate or striking appeal. It was tempting to suppress a growing conviction which promised to lead into problematic and uncharted territory. Although its implications for Vico's ideas has not been systematically examined, the proposition that certain aspects of his work need to be 'demystified' is neither historically new nor today an isolated view of my own. In *The Political Philosophy of Giambattista Vico*, Frederick Vaughan has argued[1] that Vico's ambiguous and tortuous style of writing was partly the product of a surreptitious attempt to undermine the traditional Christian view of history. Whilst this suggestion requires considerable modification, the value of Vaughan's work is that it pinpoints a number of areas of religious tension which Vico seems to have tried deliberately to conceal.

Indications of this problem are not difficult to find in the text of the *Scienza nuova*. But the idea that Vico's discomfort is relevant to our reading and understanding of the *Scienza nuova* has never been easy to establish, given the reluctance of commentators to question his own claim that he was contributing to the integrity of Catholic teaching. Thus, to mention only one of numerous scholars, Paolo

---

1. See especially pp. 19–53.

Rossi interprets important elements of the work in this light, even arguing that Vico used anti-Christian ideas in Christianity's defence.[2]

Whilst there seems to me to be insufficient evidence to argue, as Vaughan does, that Vico was deliberately attacking the teaching of the Church, it seems equally misguided to see him, as do Rossi and others, as a committed defender of the Faith. It is clear that Vico wished to avoid conflict with ecclesiastical authorities, and for good reason. One can therefore understand that he should take steps to do so. But it is equally the case that he could not always contain the thrust of his ideas within the confines of the highly contingent orthodoxy discussed below. Moreover, although Vico was sometimes aware of the risks that he was taking, he did not always perceive the threat that his philosophy presented to orthodox teachings. He was not, after all, a theologian. Nor, despite the claims of some of his interpreters, was he concerned with doctrine beyond what was either of scholarly interest to him or necessary to create a certain impression of orthodoxy.

These problems are not, however, of purely historical interest because, as has already been suggested, they impinge upon our interpretation of the *Scienza nuova*. Though I do not claim to be a theologian, my years of study as a Dominican left both sufficient interest and instinct to generate a certain unease at Vico's protestations of orthodoxy. For some time I was prepared to overlook what seemed like an eccentric use of the notion of 'divine providence'; doctrinal inaccuracies in non-theological works are usually insignificant. But it became increasingly difficult to ignore Vico's somewhat insistent and seemingly gratuitous statements on 'grace' and 'free-will'. Closer inspection eventually revealed a definite pattern of contrivance which reached, in varying degrees, into many aspects of his work. Thus a new dimension was added to my study of Vico.

There are, of course, numerous other theoretical problems and tensions in the *Scienza nuova* which are unrelated to religious issues but are straightforward consequences of Vico's ambitious project. This is not surprising, for few thinkers have sought to weave a tightly knit series of interrelationships between such a wide range of apparently dissimilar and autonomous areas of study. This poses a particular set of problems for anyone attempting to give a clear account of Vico's ideas. The overall structure of his system is not easily reducible to the dimensions of a neatly unilinear, deductive

---

2. P. Rossi, *The Dark Abyss of Time: The History of the Earth and the History of Nations from Hooke to Vico.* See especially pp. 251–66.

argument. The exposition is to some extent forced to reflect the organic complexity of the *Scienza nuova* itself. Thus while, for instance, his concept of 'natural signification' will be dealt with in an early chapter on his philosophy of language, its full significance cannot be grasped without an understanding of his philosophy of nature, which in turn relates directly to his theory of history, both of which are dealt with at later stages in the book. One is therefore obliged to steer a precarious course between the related risks of sounding repetitious or of making inadequate connections between the various elements of his system.

Finally, since it is nowadays impossible for one individual to achieve complete mastery over the range of topics into which the reader of the *Scienza nuova* is drawn, I must hasten to acknowledge the limitations of my own expertise in many of the areas to which I need to refer. I do not think, though, that unfamiliarity with the details in the development of all these fields makes it impossible to grasp the fundamental principles lying behind them which were utilized by Vico. If it did, we would almost all be disqualified from ever attempting to discuss the interrelation of the various elements in the *Scienza nuova*. Yet a grasp of these interconnections remains fundamental to an understanding of Vico's overall project.

Part I
The Problem of Orthodoxy

1
The Historical Setting

The picture of Vico as a genius, rising so far above his contemporaries that he really belongs intellectually to later times, has been gradually eroded with increasing research into the cultural activity of his native city. The Naples of the late seventeenth and early eighteenth centuries, the Naples of Tommaso Cornelio and Leonardo di Capua, of Valletta, Caravita and Porzio, Francesco D'Andrea, Costantino Grimaldi and Pietro Giannone could hardly avoid being a centre of powerful new ideas. Academies and meeting places were formed to discuss the scientific ideas of Galileo and their relationship with the new physics of Descartes, the philosophies of Bacon, Hobbes, Leibniz, Spinoza, the atomism of Democritus, Epicurus and Lucretius, new theories in jurisprudence, 'natural law', and so forth.

It would be a mistake, however, to infer from the existence of such vigorous intellectual currents that they were the products of open, unrestricted debate as we understand it today. Every one of the leading Neapolitan intellectual figures just mentioned either experienced directly or else wrote about conflict with the ecclesiastical authorities over certain of these ideas. Nor is this simply a matter of historical record, of passing interest in intellectual history. It is vitally important for the student of the history of ideas, when faced with theological statements, to know whether these are questions of theoretical claims of some consequence, of straightforward professions of faith, of ritual repetitions of a casual or mechanical kind, or merely statements intended to appease a censor.

Vico's own life-span coincides almost exactly with a period of difficult relations between groups of intellectuals and the ecclesiastical authorities in Naples. Contemporary statements about the vitality of intellectual life in the city can mislead the modern scholar if he forgets that it was precisely an abundance of new ideas which caused the problems with the Church. The very year of Vico's birth, 1668, when the Church succeeded in having the Accademia degli Investiganti closed, witnessed the delivery of a heavy blow against a group of scientists and mathematicians who were to become central figures in Vico's intellectual development. And, as Costantino Grimaldi recounted in some detail,[1] although such moves did not prevent the dissemination of the ideas of Borelli, Cornelio, or di Capua, the very mention of suspect names in medical, let alone theological works could still cause an author difficulties in obtaining the Imprimatur or ecclesiastical seal of approval as late as the 1720s.

From the early 1690s Vico took part in discussions hosted by Valletta and Caravita, in which many of the new ideas were debated. But even within the confines of the households of such distinguished men of letters, the participants could never feel entirely secure. A number of Vico's friends during this period, the most notable being Giacinto de Cristofaro, were imprisoned and tried by the Inquisition. There were numerous complaints that one could be accused of heresy simply for showing an interest in the 'new philosophy'. Lucantonio Porzio wrote of the gravity of a situation in which the most serious and distinguished scholars could be persecuted in this way.[2] Luciano Osbat concluded from his detailed study of the problem, that in the case of the lower social strata it was sufficient to have heard mention of 'the word atomism or the name of Lucretius to infer that whoever had pronounced them had lost his faith and had succumbed to atheism'.[3]

We can appreciate the flavour of the period by considering, against this background, the treatment of someone like de Cristofaro who was quite a distinguished lawyer. Although proceedings, based on secret evidence, were begun in 1688, no concrete action was taken against him until August 1691, when he was imprisoned with nine others to await trial. The customary search of his dwellings then revealed the works of prohibited authors. During his imprisonment before the trial – a period of six years – de Cristofaro repeatedly asked in vain to be allowed to face his accusers. According to traditional practice, however, their identity remained secret. Such lengthy periods of imprisonment whilst awaiting the formal commencement of the trial were not uncommon. In the course of them, unsuspecting 'witnesses' were called before officials of the court and asked whether the accused had ever shown signs of being an atheist, or had expressed opinions on a wide range of topics, such as the immortality of the soul, atomism, the existence of men before Adam, the validity of the sacraments, or had even mentioned authors such as Democritus, Lucretius, Spinoza or Des-

1. C. Grimaldi, *Memorie di un anticurialista del Settecento*, p. 46.
2. See L. Amabile, *Il Santo Officio della Inquisizione in Napoli*, vol. ii, 64.
3. L. Osbat, *L'Inquisizione a Napoli. Il processo agli ateisti 1688–1697*, p. 198.

cartes. The accused knew little or nothing of such a gradual accumulation of evidence against him, unless faced with it during regular bouts of questioning, and then only at the discretion of the officials conducting the proceedings and in whatever terms they chose to present it. Often such evidence would emerge fresh and unchallenged as part of the general condemnation.

The result was often a public pronouncement of condemnation, accompanied by a special ritual, which was commonly felt to act as a deterrent. The cases of two of de Cristofaro's companions, for instance, were brought to a relatively speedy conclusion in such a fashion. In February 1693 Carlo Rosito and Giovanni de Magistris were both made to renounce their atheism before a full congregation in the cathedral, and after an appropriate sermon followed by general absolution they were publicly condemned to ten years imprisonment and obliged to perform regular penitential and devotional duties.[4] We know from Amabile that these humiliating scenes of retraction followed by a solemn condemnation continued well into the late 1740s. Other sentences included house imprisonment, banishment and, for clerics, perpetual confinement in a religious institution. The latter, moreover, were not treated with any particular regard for their positions. In one celebrated case a priest, Antonio Nava, was imprisoned in 1741 and his trial begun on 15 April of that year. Then a second and quite separate set of proceedings were set in motion against him on 30 May 1742, based on information obtained from a prison companion, even though the initial accusations of heresy, sorcery and apostasy were already regarded as sufficiently serious for the prosecutor to demand the maximum penalty of life imprisonment. The case and its consequences for Nava, described in full by Amabile, was not finally concluded until 1746.[5]

Outside the archdiocese, the accused was usually at the mercy of the local bishop who frequently imprisoned suspects with a view to transferring them to Naples for more formal proceedings to be initiated. There were many instances of ill-treatment, including some where prisoners were simply left to languish indefinitely in provincial dungeons. When informed of such incidents, Neapolitan officials sometimes intervened, as in the case of a certain Michele de Donatis, a parish priest in the diocese of Nusco, who was imprisoned in 1743 by his bishop and kept in captivity for eight months before being flogged and tortured with reeds thrust under his

4. Ibid., pp. 190–1.
5. See Amabile, *Il Santo Officio della Inquisizione*, vol. ii, p. 86.

fingernails. The bishop was forced to release the prisoner and have the case referred formally to Naples.[6] This is not to say, however, that official ecclesiastical proceedings were always humane. Torture, threats and bribes were frequently used to extract confessions or produce evidence.[7] Promises of leniency sometimes produced results, and deals of various kinds were common. A fair amount of bargaining seems to have accompanied the proceedings against two more of the debating companions of the younger Vico, Basilio Giannelli and Francesco Manuzzi. Both men confessed to having read and debated such authors as Democritus, Lucretius, Gassendi, Descartes and others; but they claimed to have done so in the company of many others, and it is hard to imagine that Vico would not have been found among that company. Another member of the group, Filippo Belli, confessed to having defended heretical ideas,[8] but does not seem to have turned informer, at least not on the scale of Giannelli and Manuzzi, who were both crucial witnesses in the more important case against their former friend, de Cristofaro.[9]

The secret nature of such proceedings was exploited to encourage defendants to become informers. It was therefore more dangerous to discuss suspect ideas even amongst friends because, under pressure, today's accomplice could become tomorrow's accuser. It was widely believed in one notorious case, for example, that the provision of a list of companions in heresy, more than seventy in number, accounted for the lenient treatment received by Abate Antonio Giliberti in 1739.[10] The mere suspicion of the existence of such lists must have proved a powerful inhibiting factor with many intellectuals and writers. More commonly, though, defendants protested their faith and denied all knowledge of the existence of persons professing heretical ideas. In this regard, the modern reader should remember that the criminality of atheistic and heretical belief was often so solidly built into the public ethic of Catholic countries that professions of faith were a stock response on the part of those wishing to avoid condemnation or even suspicion. Even to withhold knowledge of anyone proclaiming heretical ideas was a punishable offence. It is almost amusing to read de Cristofaro's depositions to the Holy Office, in which he indignantly denies uttering the 'scandalous, impious and heretical propositions' put to him by his prosecutors,[11] and asserts that if he had heard anyone

6. Ibid., p. 87.
7. Osbat, *L'Inquisizione a Napoli*, p. 251.
8. Ibid., pp. 240ff.
9. See ibid., pp. 64ff., 71ff., and 134ff.
10. See Amabile, *Il Santo Officio della Inquisizione*, vol. ii, p. 84.
11. See Osbat, *L'Inquisizione a Napoli*, pp. 276–80.

claiming that there were men before Adam – men, apparently, composed of atoms – then 'I would have come to report it to the Holy Office . . . I have never stated such a proposition, for I know very well that it is a heresy'.[12]

While in general terms the Inquisition in Naples (either as a section of the Holy Office or under the authority of the local ordinary) never ceased to function during the whole of Vico's productive life as a scholar and writer, the avoidance of its scrutiny was not the immediate problem for most thinkers of independent mind and originality. From the point of view of the Church, Inquisitorial proceedings were simply a part of the *pathology* of cultural and intellectual life, to be invoked only when its own overall and daily function as sole teaching authority in matters of faith and morals was threatened. For the most part, therefore, this meant avoiding direct challenges to the exercise of this function. More specifically, for writers, it meant submitting their work to the office of the ecclesiastical censor whose duty it was to grant the Imprimatur before publication. This, as we shall see, could generate considerable problems for particular authors.

It must not be imagined that the Church in Naples sought at all times to impose, through its censors, a rigid and inflexible orthodox line on every conceivable topic. To begin with, a high proportion of the educated population consisted of clerics who were well aware of the value of learning. Ecclesiastical careers, moreover, were frequently pursued in a worldly and ambitious manner, with little concern for strictly theological or spiritual matters. And although censors were appointed from amongst the more doctrinally reliable of the clergy, they varied greatly in their severity and were even sometimes helpful in suggesting alterations which could overcome difficulties raised by unsuspecting or theologically inexpert laymen.

There were other factors in the equation which should also briefly be mentioned. Throughout the period, the degree of religious tension which existed depended on the changing and sometimes difficult relations between the local ecclesiastical hierarchy and the Holy Office in Rome. The latter never ceased to doubt the former's ability to contain the threat posed by the new atheism and naturalism of the modern philosophy. Both wished to be in charge of Inquisitorial proceedings. Temporal rulers, Spanish and Austrian in turn, had to preserve good relations with both the local

12. Ibid., p. 172. For de Cristofaro's defence see appendix, pp. 305–9. For the ideas condemned and the sentence see pp. 243–6.

clergy and the Holy Office and at the same time demonstrate to their subjects that they were not puppets of either. These rulers were frequently called upon to protect their subjects from ecclesiastical threats. It is not by chance that a high proportion of those threatened were lawyers, teachers and administrators seeking to promote the idea of a clearer separation between temporal and ecclesiastical powers, or an end to many arbitrary privileges enjoyed by the Church. This 'ceto civile', with which Vico had strong links, tried not surprisingly to exploit the differences between the various religious and temporal authorities to its own advantage. It was more than possible to do so, given that the social and professional lives of many of the individuals concerned necessitated daily contact with members of the clergy. Thus relationships were readily formed and deliberately cultivated in a world in which, for instance, it could be extremely useful to have a friend or two with access to ecclesiastical censors. In a city like Naples, a wide circle of friends amongst the clergy was generally accepted as offering considerable social and professional advantages. Naturally, it was particularly advantageous for the doctrinally suspect to be able to move in such circles. One must be careful, therefore, concerning inferences about any particular author's orthodoxy based on connections with the clergy, since such contacts were often unavoidable and were even sought precisely as a form of protection against charges of heresy.

In the light of these remarks we are in a better position to define the parameters within which manoeuvre was possible. There was a core of doctrine, authorities and even traditions which it was dangerous to challenge. Although a certain latitude would frequently be allowed to the professional theologians who chose to raise sensitive issues in these important areas, this could hardly be extended to the layman, who would be regarded as at best ill-equipped to deal with such problems and, at worst an inevitably pernicious influence. So, if a challenge to orthodox teaching were felt to have been made knowingly or wilfully, condemnation inevitably followed.

However, the human failings and limitations of the censors themselves produced inconsistent results. Trivial matters were sometimes seized upon and pursued ruthlessly while, by contrast, serious theological errors could pass quite unnoticed. And although those writing upon such subjects as human nature, the various theories of history, ethics, and so on, were most likely to offend, a combination of camouflaging skills and technical discourse could sometimes be used to great effect to avoid censure. The histories of philosophy by Vico's older contemporary and friend Valletta stand as a monument to the exercise of this particular art.

There were, as we shall see, other tactics which the writer could also employ, but their effectiveness tended to fluctuate with changes in the religious climate and the distribution of power between the various ruling sectors, both religious and secular. With the support of Charles VI of Austria, the new ruler of Naples, for example, it became possible in 1708 for Costantino Grimaldi, Gaetano Argento and Alessandro Riccardi to launch a coordinated offensive against ecclesiastical fiscal and other privileges on economic, legal and ethical grounds.[13] Yet similar assaults some fifteen years later by Pietro Giannone forced him to flee Naples. Giannone tells us himself about his tactical reasons for holding back publication of the first volume of his *Istoria civile*; for he says that, if it had been allowed to circulate too early, 'I would certainly have been prevented from bringing out the second, let alone the third and fourth'.[14] The storm which followed the publication, in 1723, of the *Istoria civile*, indeed marked the beginning of its author's life-long exile, and also caused further problems for those left behind. One of these, Vico's contemporary Grimaldi, focused on precisely these problems in his *Memorie di un anticurialista del Settecento*, and provides an instructive first-hand account of what it meant to publish in Naples in Vico's day. A brief consideration of some of the matters to which he refers will therefore be illuminating.

After the period of intense repression in the 1690s, during which de Cristofaro and others were tried by the Inquisition, the 'moderni' began to fight back. Grimaldi's earliest excursions into print occur at this point when, in 1699, he published his first work in defence of modern philosophy against the attacks of the Jesuit Benedetto Aletino. Grimaldi's work was presented in the form of a defence of *theology*. He attempted, that is, to turn the tables on Aletino by arguing that modern philosophy provided a better foundation for Catholic doctrine than traditional Aristotelianism, to which the Church had become espoused. Nevertheless, in spite of this alleged orthodox intent, he felt it safer to publish the work anonymously through a contact in Geneva.[15] A second work on the same theme was published in Germany in 1702 and a third in Naples in 1703, although the imprint or 'data' (the contemporary term used to indicate the *place* of publication, rather than the date which the Italian word suggests) given for the latter was

13. See Grimaldi, *Memorie di un anticurialista*, pp. viii–ix.
14. P. Giannone, *Vita scritta da lui medesimo*, p. 60.
15. See Grimaldi, *Memorie di un anticurialista*, pp. 15–16.

Cologne.[16] Since the Imprimatur was frequently granted more easily, and often not required at all, in some European cities, this form of deception was often used by authors who anticipated problems in obtaining it in their home town. The frequent use of such imprints (whether fictitious or authentic), however, could itself arouse suspicion by suggesting that an author had something to hide in not publishing at home.

Grimaldi's authorship of the above-mentioned works soon became common knowledge. Many of the local clergy even defended his sincerity in wishing to base the Church's teaching on a firmer philosophical foundation. During this period, Giuseppe Valletta was also engaged in a cultural campaign, ostensibly for the same purpose but in reality to promote and legitimize the new philosophy in its own right. The arrival of the new Austrian rulers in 1707 gave fresh hope to these free-thinkers. Shortly after taking power, for example, Charles VI ordained that ecclesiastical proceedings on matters of faith should be conducted not by Roman delegates but under the authority of the Archbishop of Naples and the local ordinaries, as was the practice in his other domains. Somewhat optimistically, this was felt at the time to be an important liberalizing move. Many were encouraged by such moves, and thought and spoke more freely. In his *De Antiquissima* (1710), Vico mentions his association with the condemned de Cristofaro and other 'fellow citizens illustrious in doctrine'.[17] Grimaldi even managed to arrange for his own chosen theological experts to read his works in order to fight off any attempt to have them condemned.[18] It is within this context that the contemporary historian Muratori referred to the freedom of expression enjoyed in Naples.[19]

As a result of the increased confidence produced by this relaxation of censorship, Grimaldi published his writings in defence of the rights of temporal rulers over Church property and land under his own name. He was also an important member of the judiciary and of the local administration, and there was reason to suppose that Charles VI had something to gain in protecting him. Nevertheless, he never ceased to fear that Rome, either directly or through pressure on the local clergy, would at some more propitious time proceed against him. He knew that the changes which

---

16. See ibid., pp. 18ff.
17. *Opere filosofiche*, p. 60.
18. See Grimaldi, *Memorie di un anticurialista*, pp. 22–3.
19. See B. Croce, *Storia del regno di Napoli*, p. 158. We must, however, take account of Muratori's somewhat restricted conception of religious freedom: See E. Garin, *Storia della filosofia italiana*, vol. iii, pp. 901–6.

had taken place represented, for the most part, mere temporary swings of the general temper and mood, whereas the considerable formal powers and substantial popular moral hegemony enjoyed by the Church remained fundamentally intact.

By the early 1720s the counter-offensive which Grimaldi had feared was already underway. Rome had applied considerable pressure from various directions on Charles VI, and the appointment in 1722 of Cardinal d'Althann as Austrian viceroy in Naples signalled the final success of its strategy. Shortly after Giannone's flight from Naples, Grimaldi's attempt in 1725 to publish his *Discussioni istoriche teologiche e filosofiche*, an updated collection of his earlier writings, resulted in their being sent to Rome by Cardinal d'Althann, and their placing on the Index of proscribed works in 1726. It is interesting to note that Vico's first statements concerning his intention to use his own works to further the greater glory of the Church date from this period.

Subsequently, for more than twenty years Grimaldi attempted in vain both to vindicate the sincerity of his faith and to have his writings removed from the Index. Moreover, matters certainly did not improve with the arrival in 1735 of the new rulers under Charles Bourbon, who enjoyed papal support. In 1735, Grimaldi was dismissed from his post and two years later submitted to a painful retraction in order to have his proscription downgraded from first to second class.[20] After a short period of imprisonment in 1744, the year of Vico's death, Grimaldi – feeling by this time that he had little to lose – began work on a history of the Inquisition in Naples. In 1747, he reflected that 'no greater disaster or misfortune, no more cruel calamity can befall a man than being caught in the wretched snare of the Inquisition'.[21]

Grimaldi's case illustrates a number of important points. First, he could not rely on being protected by his considerable social and professional status, even though he enjoyed a wide circle of contacts and friends among the clergy, and seems to have been able to find numerous theologians to comment sympathetically on his work.[22] Secondly, the practice of dedicating one's work to an eminent ecclesiastic, quite apart from helping one to obtain the necessary finance for publication, could also be used both to reduce the Imprimatur to a mere formality or in some cases to avoid submitting the work to the censor altogether. However, Grimaldi was guilty of a major miscalculation in seeking to dedicate his

20. Grimaldi, *Memorie di un anticurialista*, p. xvii.
21. Ibid., p. xx.
22. Ibid., pp. 45ff.

Discussioni to the viceroy Cardinal d'Althann, and in securing its publication under the false Luccan imprint.[23] While this was a courageous gamble, in the end d'Althann's adverse reaction to the subterfuge made matters worse for Grimaldi.

Given that the publication of a work in Naples without the Imprimatur incurred automatic excommunication,[24] Grimaldi's recourse to the formal device of a fictitious imprint was understandable; and it was not, after all, an uncommon practice. As for the author's desire to circumvent the censor, he knew that attempts had already been made in the past to have some of the writings he was seeking to publish proscribed. In addition, these writings contained arguments about the dubious legality of the Imprimatur itself, arguments which had been used also by other suspect writers including the exiled Giannone.[25] The use of these tactics also entailed obvious risks for the printer, and many proved reluctant to publish under such circumstances. Thus authors who could secure the necessary equipment were sometimes reduced to printing their works in the secrecy of their own homes. Grimaldi himself asked to borrow equipment from his printer when the latter ceased printing because of the risks entailed.[26]

D'Althann, however, was able to respond to such 'abuses', and justify the success of his strategic appointment. He protected the interests of the Church by using his secular position as Austrian viceroy to declare illegal, in a decree dated 24 May 1725, both private printing without an official licence and the publication in Naples of books with fictitious imprints.[27] The penalty of excommunication for publishing without the Imprimatur remained in effect. If these, then, were the conditions under which thinkers like Vico had to work and publish, a few brief words should be said about the nature of the threat as perceived by the Church, and what it was seeking to protect.

Although much work still remains to be done, present-day scholarship has clearly established that during the period in question Naples was becoming increasingly receptive to new currents in European thought, and as a consequence was arousing alarm and opposition in ecclesiastical circles. Salvo Mastellone, for example, has shown that the ideas which the cultural 'libertini' were importing, often from Protestant sources, were seen not simply as bring-

---

23. See ibid., pp. 48ff.
24. See ibid., p. 49, fn 1.
25. See ibid., pp. 44–5.
26. See ibid., p. 47.
27. See ibid., pp. 55–7.

ing into question individual articles of faith but as undermining the whole basis of Catholicism.[28] Clearly, within such a context some ideas were more destructive than others. Let us take an example. A standard form of defence used by individuals to protect themselves against accusations of heresy was to employ the argument of the 'double truth'. According to this theory, first given serious theoretical currency in the Middle Ages by Siger of Brabant, it was possible to arrive at strictly *philosophical* conclusions which were irrefutable on grounds of reason, but which were nevertheless at variance with *revealed* truth taught by the Church. A believer did not deny his faith by engaging in such philosophical speculation. The argument of the 'double truth' was by this time, in Naples at least, regarded with suspicion, and formed the basis of one of the accusations against de Cristofaro. Traditionally, the unity of philosophy and theology meant the subordination of the former to the latter, at least when a choice between the two had to be made. Increasingly, the use of the 'double truth' argument came to be seen as an assertion of the essential independence of secular ideas, and as such was a 'death sentence on at least ten centuries of Christian civilization which had developed and strengthened itself precisely on the unity of the two spheres'.[29] Whereas in the Middle Ages the idea was the product of speculative theologians, a device for coming to terms with seemingly irreconcilable difficulties within a strictly Scholastic framework, it was now being used in a different way, to promote ideas of a different order. The proponents of these new ideas (men like Borelli, Cornelio, di Capua, Valletta, Caravita, etc.) were not theologians but philosophers, scientists, historians and legal thinkers who were producing a cultural ethos, the secular thrust of which threatened further to reduce the status of theology and unseat it once and for all as the queen of the sciences. At least, this was the situation as it appeared to the Church's official theologians.

As soon as the influence of the Neapolitan 'Investiganti' began to be felt towards the end of the seventeenth century, Rome became convinced that Naples was turning into 'a breeding ground of heresy, the direct consequences of which endangered the safety of the Catholic faith'.[30] This is why Osbat speaks of a kind of ideological cultural trial, preceding the activities of the Inquisition in Naples, 'which had taken place within the congregation of the

28. See S. Mastellone, *Pensiero politico e vita culturale a Napoli nella seconda metà del Seicento*, pp. 131ff.
29. Osbat, *L'Inquisizione a Napoli*, p. 95.
30. Ibid., p. 112.

cardinals in Rome, against everything in the modern philosophy which questioned the eternal certainties of Thomist theology, and its foundations, Aristotelian philosophy'.[31] The proceedings of the Inquisition, therefore, while always specifying the doctrine attacked by the accused, in reality represent an ideological struggle to eradicate, in the words of Biagio de Giovanni, 'an intellectual movement which vigorously challenged the old Scholastic hegemony'.[32] Rome was never convinced that the Neopolitan hierarchy was capable of containing such a challenge; this is why the Holy Office, even after Charles VI's ruling on the extension of the powers of local ordinaries in his territories, continued in its efforts to put the control of Inquisitorial proceedings into the hands of its own delegates. From about 1734 onwards, in preparation for the advent of the new ruler Charles Bourbon, the ecclesiastical appointees renewed the pressure to establish Roman control with letters and complaints to the Holy Office expressing dissatisfaction with the ineffectiveness of the local ordinaries and censors in dealing with delinquent authors, publishers and readers.[33] It is doubtful whether the latter, having been at the receiving end of local ecclesiastical offensives, would have endorsed this assessment of the situation in Naples.

Something should now be said about the kind of Catholicism to which Vico and other writers of the time were expected to subscribe. As we have seen, Osbat and De Giovanni have suggested that what the Church saw as being at risk was its Aristotelian and Thomist Scholastic tradition. There is no doubt that within the Church as a whole professional theologians had certain room for manoeuvre, and were free to draw upon the numerous currents and traditions encompassing its doctrinal history. There were thus debates, disagreements and differences, some of which were quite sharp and even bitter. Many theologians, for example, made liberal use of the Greek and Latin Fathers. Serious attention might be given to the more analytic writings of such authorities as Augustine, Bonaventure, Scotus, Ockham and others, on important issues in dogmatic or moral theology, while the use of Patristic sources tended to be somewhat impressionistic and decorative.

But having said this, it is also important to bear in mind that high-powered debates amongst specialists – which are for the most part the only sources readily available for the historian of ideas – do not paint an accurate picture of the general tenor of the faith of the

31. Ibid., p. 251.
32. B. De Giovanni, 'Cultura e vita civile in G. Valletta', p. 20.
33. See A. Melpignano, S. J., *L'Anticurialismo napoletano sotto Carlo III*, pp. 24ff.

clergy of the time, let alone that of the laity. Theological training as such, in seminaries and religious orders, remained firmly within a Scholastic framework, with strong Aristotelian foundations. No other tradition could seriously compete with it in terms of providing an intellectually well-integrated and unified body of teaching which was readily transmissible in a cogent theoretical form. The Catholicism of the popular clergy and thus of the mass of the faithful was accordingly more uniform and simplistic than that of theologians engaged in polemical debate. It was against the yardstick of the former that suspect writers tended to be measured, since it was the simple faith of the masses which the Church in Naples sought jealously to protect against the pernicious influence of such groups as the 'moderni' and 'ateisti'.

There were, of course, numerous believers, particularly among the lay intelligentsia, who were hostile to the intellectual sterility of Scholasticism. Although this opposition seems to have been far stronger in France, it was by no means absent in Italy. If we turn to Naples, however, we find that it mattered little whether a critic claimed to be a believer or not; any attacks on Aristotle were seen as assaults on the Faith itself.

The offensive against the Neapolitan 'moderni' was led by the Jesuit Benedetto Aletino who published *Lettere apologetiche in difesa della teologia scolastica e della filosofia peripatetica* (1694). It was in response to this, and to a subsequent work by Aletino, that Grimaldi published his anonymous writings, between 1699 and 1703, in which he argued that Aristotle was the true enemy of religion. Valletta and others took up the same theme, always claiming, of course, that they were defending the Faith from the pernicious influence of peripatetic philosophy. There was no doubt in Grimaldi's mind, as he wrote more than thirty years later in his memoirs, after spending a lifetime in this struggle, that the common culture of the time was 'immersed in Scholastic absurdities'.[34]

Within the overall Scholastic framework under attack there was a place of special importance for the theology of Thomas Aquinas. 'Thomism', V. I. Comparato asserts, 'was by that time one of the theological foundations of Catholicism and to reject it was to place oneself definitively outside the Church'.[35] That this was so is illustrated in the treatment of Aquinas by even such implacable opponents of Scholasticism as Valletta and Grimaldi. Valletta, as De Giovanni points out, was careful to show great respect for

34. Grimaldi, *Memorie di un anticurialista*, p. 5.
35. Ibid., p. 52, eds fn 1.

Aquinas, using him as an authority on 'natural law',[36] while V. I. Comparato has shown that 'the St Thomas of Valletta is no longer an Aristotelian, but a theologian who simply uses a few of the Stagirite's opinions, with the intention of correcting the rest'.[37] Such an attempt to drive a wedge between the two thinkers who in popular theological thinking had become an indissoluble partnership was, in effect, a response to Aletino's charge that to reject Aristotle was to reject Aquinas.

Grimaldi, although cautious, went as far as to criticize St Thomas. The Angelic Doctor, he argued in his 1725 writings, did his best to remedy the corruption of Scholastic theology, but ultimately remained too close an adherent of Aristotle's to succeed.[38] He was to pay dearly for this criticism. On being questioned by d'Althann and accused of 'undermining the whole basis of Catholic theology', he replied that he had always shown the greatest respect for St Thomas as the 'healer of the deformed and corrupted Scholasticism of his time', and had even wanted 'the *Summa* of St Thomas to be taught in the schools, without the slightest departure from his arguments'.[39] Unfortunately for Grimaldi, this did not quite square with the somewhat harsher judgements he had earlier passed on Aquinas, which were by that time in print. Many authors, including Vico, learned from Grimaldi's experience that it was safer to be silent than critical of this pillar of orthodox theological teaching. We should not judge such attempted deceptions as Grimaldi's too harshly. He knew well what was at stake. In a letter to Muratori he gives three main reasons for his condemnation in 1726: his attacks on Scholasticism, on ecclesiastical discipline, and finally his 'having criticized certain defects in St Thomas'.[40]

It is partly to compensate for the scanty and even doubtful information from Vico about his own dealings with ecclesiastics and publishers that I have attempted, in this brief historical survey, to convey some idea of the atmosphere in which he worked. It is only too easy for the modern scholar to read the writings of Vico and some of his contemporaries in the light of quite unrealistic assumptions about the circumstances under which they were produced. To adopt a critical posture *vis-à-vis* important teachings of the Church then required considerable courage, and certain camou-

36. See De Giovanni, 'Cultura e vita civile', pp. 5–6.
37. V. I. Comparato, *Giuseppe Valletta, un intellettuale napoletano della fine del Seicento*, pp. 209–10.
38. See V. I. Comparato, 'Ragione e fede nelle discussioni di C. Grimaldi', 55ff. and 76–7.
39. Grimaldi, *Memorie di un anticurialista*, p. 52.
40. Ibid., p. xiv. For the text of the Decree of condemnation see pp. 68ff.

flaging tactics, deceptions of one form or another, or the help of influential contacts.

So the fact that some such writings were published should not lead us to infer that a free and easy intellectual climate prevailed in Naples. Cardinal Belluga's demands, in 1734, for more effective repressive measures must be seen as an indication of the success of Neapolitan authors in the use of such expedients. Vico and other intellectuals were accustomed to living in a society in which criticism of the Church's teaching was regarded as a subversive activity. Even Grimaldi's criticisms of the Inquisition were limited to the manner in which its proceedings violated natural justice. Few dared to question the institution as such or the right of the Church to indict and censor on matters of faith. Given this situation, no critical reading should take at face value every statement of a religious nature or every profession of orthodox intent which one finds in the literature of the period. Nor should it surprise us, under such circumstances, to encounter in particular authors considerable undercurrents lying below the surface of the discourse.

2

Preliminary Indications of a
Problem in Vico's Work

In 1725, as part of a project to publish the autobiographies of leading Italian thinkers, Vico was invited by Count Gian Artico di Porcía to contribute his own personal history. The project was primarily pedagogical in intent, and the authors were asked to outline the course of their intellectual development. It is not surprising, therefore, that indications of Vico's unease over religious matters should appear in his *Autobiography* (1725).

In this work he informs the reader that his 'four authors' – supposedly the four major influences in his ideological formation – were Plato, Tacitus, Bacon and Grotius. He is clearly not at ease at having to acknowledge his indebtedness to such pagan and Protestant sources, and thus frequently tells the reader that his intention is to press the ideas of these writers into the service of his Catholic religion.[1] Moreover, as he reconstructs his intellectual itinerary in the *Autobiography*, Vico considerably underplays his earlier involvement in highly suspect and unorthodox currents of the cultural life of Naples.[2] Some scholars have argued that perhaps the *Autobiography* pre-dates his rejection of ideas from such sources, presenting these early contacts as no more than youthful extravagances. Such a picture is not, in my view, entirely satisfactory. It overlooks the fact that certain ideas and perspectives which he derived from these sources were never abandoned by Vico. Indeed,

---

1. Frederick Vaughan is one critic who is not prepared to accept such a claim at face value: 'It is almost comic the way Vico parades his faith throughout the Autobiography and to a lesser extent the *New Science*. He never tires reiterating his intention to turn all his scholarly efforts 'to the use of the Catholic religion'. We will recall that this is the way Vico pays his debt to Plato, Tacitus, Bacon and Grotius.' *The Political Philosophy of Giambattista Vico*, p. 28.
2. Bruce Haddock has recently drawn attention to the problem of accepting the *Autobiography* as a historically accurate account of Vico's intellectual development. See B. A. Haddock, *Vico's Political Thought*, pp. 9ff, where there is also an interesting discussion of how we should interpret Vico's claims regarding Plato and Tacitus as major influences, that is, 'as idealized representatives of distinct modes of discourse' (p. 10) rather than as 'influences' in the ordinary sense. In the case of Plato, however, there are rather more specific points of reference, which I indicate in Chapters 17 and 18 below.

they form a considerable and enduring part of his mature outlook.

We have already seen that some of Vico's friends and acquaintances had been condemned by the Inquisition for having embraced, amongst other ideas, those of Epicurus, Lucretius and other pagan writers. The *Autobiography* was, however, written in the Naples of d'Althann's viceregency, when Giannone was escaping to safety and Grimaldi was being questioned by the Cardinal about his attacks on Scholasticism and St Thomas. It is hardly surprising, therefore, that at such a sensitive time Vico should have been careful to minimize his own debt to Lucretius. Referring to his early reading of the Latin author, he wrote: 'This is a philosophy to satisfy the circumscribed minds of children and the weak ones of silly women.' And Lucretius' epistemology contained, according to him, 'a thousand inanities and absurdities to explain the operations of the human mind'.[3]

In the *Autobiography* Vico dates this reading of Lucretius – by which time he has allegedly already rejected the pagan thinker – to 1686, two years after his departure from Naples as tutor to the Rocca family. It is certain, however, that his Lucretian-inspired *Affetti di un disperato* was written no earlier than 1693. So on this score alone there is doubt concerning the validity of his claims in the *Autobiography*. And, more fundamentally, if we examine his major work carefully we find a number of important areas in which he continued to make use of Lucretian ideas.

For instance, his 'uomini – bestie' (man – beast) theory concerning the origins of humanity bears more than a casual resemblance to ideas put forward in Lucretius' *De Rerum Natura*. Vico's frequent assertions that man in his bestial state desires only his own welfare and that the first partnerships originated with violent males dragging the females into caves, are expressed in strikingly similar terms in the Latin poet's work, as indeed are references to the great strength and size of these early creatures. The gradual civilizing effects of such unions, the building of huts, the mellowing and softening of both temper of mind and physical robustness, and the gradual formation of primitive social alliances are all similarly explicit in Book V of Lucretius' work.[4]

Again, Vico's discussion of the role of nature, of necessity and utility in producing the first forms of speech, and even of the importance of simple gestures as presentiments of spoken language, probably owe a great deal to Lucretius.[5] There are still more

3. *The Autobiography of Giambattista Vico*, pp. 126–7.
4. See Lucretius, *De Rerum Natura*, Bk V, ll. 955–68 and 1011–20.
5. Ibid., ll. 1028–32.

striking parallels to add to these. Even Vico's ingenious descriptions of the invention of the gods bear a remarkable similarity to Lucretius' treatment of the same subject,[6] although perhaps for Vico the single most fertile passage from Book V of Lucretius' work is to be found in its final fourteen lines, where we find four of the most celebrated Vichian 'discoveries'. There Lucretius puts forward the idea of the gradual evolution of the written word; the even more important heuristic principle, utilized and extended by Vico, of the historical importance of the oral tradition in poetry; the proposition that early developments can be uncovered by later generations by means of an acquired capacity to reason is likewise adumbrated; and finally, the idea of the growth of the arts as a reflection of the human mind as it struggles towards the perfection of its mental powers.[7]

So, although Vico adapted, elaborated and transformed such notions, the evidence in support of the claim that Lucretian ideas were an important source of his inspiration appears quite substantial. Yet while it is interesting to trace possible sources in this way, it cannot be claimed that they necessarily enhance our understanding of the *Scienza nuova*. Indeed the 'continuist' assumptions underlying a great deal of research concerned with discovering 'influences' tend to produce regressive frameworks of interpretation which underplay the innovative thrust of new ideas. Therefore, whereas I do not think Lucretius can teach us a great deal about the theoretical substance of the *Scienza nuova*, the affinities we have noted are nevertheless important for indicating general areas where its author felt caution was required. Given that Vico was a scholar accustomed to acknowledging important sources and using corroborative authorities from antiquity, he could have been expected to make the most of these affinities. Yet not only does he conceal them, but he actively misleads the reader by subjecting to ridicule those aspects of Lucretius' philosophy for which he finds no use.

The idea of there having been religious problems associated with Vico's work is by no means new, although modern scholarship may well have underrated the importance of the question and thus not paid sufficient attention to such suggestions in early critics of Vico's work. We have already seen that the period in which the *Autobiography* was being written was a particularly troubled one. But it was also the period during which Vico was trying to publish

6. Ibid., ll. 1161–1240.
7. Ibid., ll. 1444–57.

the shorter first edition of the *Scienza nuova* 'in negative form', whatever he may have meant by this ambiguous description of the work. His own acount of his writing and re-writing of this work can be found in the *Autobiography*.

That Vico's narration of events may well have omitted to mention difficulties over religious matters was certainly the conviction of the Neapolitan economist Antonio Genovesi, his pupil and friend, and a frequent visitor to the home of the philosopher. The account which originated with Genovesi, and which is repeated in other important eighteenth-century students of Vico's Naples such as Galanti and Vincenzo Cuoco,[8] sees the re-writing of the *Scienza nuova* and all the subsequent problems connected with its publication as having been occasioned by the bout of restored ecclesiastical vigilance following the stormy Giannone affair. That there were grounds for witholding permission to publish was undoubtedly the impression of certain less than sympathetic critics. Damiano Romano, in a series of short essays published between 1736 and 1744, made numerous objections to theories of language, myth and primitive humanity in the *Scienza nuova*, pointing out the incompatibility of these ideas with the Bible.[9] Similar objections were made by others, including Giovanni Lami, Giovanni Donato Rogadei and Francesco Colangelo. There were even those, like Cataldo Jannelli[10] and later Cesare Marini,[11] who noted, but this time without censure, the ambiguity and seemingly heterodox nature of Vico's use of basic concepts such as 'providence' and the origins of religion. The nineteenth-century critic Baldassare Labanca, who reviewed the eighteenth-century religious reaction to Vico, was in no doubt about the problematic nature of the *Scienza nuova*, even asserting that the withdrawal of Cardinal Corsini's financial backing for the publication of the 1725 edition was due to his being informed of the suspect nature of this and earlier works by Vico.[12] Labanca's claim, however, that Vico's attempt to find himself an ecclesiastical protector thus ended in failure may not have been entirely correct since Vico let the dedication of the work to Corsini stand, and while he was re-writing his work to be published as the 1730 *Scienza nuova seconda* the Cardinal was elected to the papacy. Vico was thus acle to dedicate the later version of his work to Pope

---

8. See F. Nicolini, 'Il Vico e il suo censore ecclesiastico', pp. 281ff. Also, Nicolini, *La religiosità di G. B. Vico*, pp. 36ff.
9. See Garin, *Storia della filosofia italiana*, vol. iii, pp. 1018ff.
10. Ibid., pp. 1016 and 1021.
11. C. Marini, *Giambattista Vico al cospetto del secolo xix*. See especially pp. 37, 41, 42.
12. See B. Labanca, *G. B. Vico rispetto ai suoi contemporanei*, p. 11.

Clement XII.

The suspicions and assertions of contemporaries and later critics, a sample of which we have seen above, have been made more substantial by the work of Fausto Nicolini. It was he who discovered an annotated edition of the 1730 *Scienza nuova* with suggested corrections by Vico's friend, the censor Giulio Torno,[13] and indeed who first alerted us to the important role played by this ecclesiastical contact in obtaining publication of his works, from the *Diritto universale* (1720–2) onwards.[14] In Nicolini's view, the major areas in which the *Scienza nuova* conflicted with the teachings of the Church were those dealing with the ideas on the beast-like qualities of primitive men, their creation of religion, and their invention of language. Not surprisingly, Torno was not slow in pointing out the danger of expressing ideas for which Vico's associates had earlier been condemned by the Inquisition,[15] although his suggested solutions, according to Nicolini, were at times 'the most illogical and contradictory one could possibly imagine'.[16] Nevertheless, Torno was able to help his friend in his official capacity since, as Nicolini points out, the authorities would sometimes accept a censor at the suggestion of the writer himself, and he, 'naturally, would choose his Cerberus from among his friends, and from among the most accommodating of his friends'.[17]

In support of Nicolini's observations on the suspect orthodoxy of the *Scienza nuova*, there is, moreover, the most sustained of all the attacks on the work, written by the eighteenth-century Dominican theologian Bonifazio Finetti. This vigilant and assiduous friar, himself a Venetian censor, produced a veritable catalogue of theological infringements to be found in the *Scienza nuova*, ranging from its 'eccentric' use of the concept of 'providence' to its alleged defence of 'free-will'. Finetti did not fail to notice the undeclared similarity of some of Vico's ideas with those of Lucretius,[18] and he linked these with the Neapolitan's thesis concerning the primitive or feral origins of humanity. He also drew out the moral and doctrinal implications of these ideas with a detailed demonstration

---

13. Nicolini's detailed examination of these notes was first published in *La Critica* 39 (1941), 302–9.

14. See Nicolini, 'Il Vico e il suo censore ecclesiastico', pp. 282ff.

15. See *Processo contro G. De Cristofaro*, cited in Giuseppe Valletta, *Opere filosofiche*, p. 39.

16 Nicolini, 'Il Vico e il suo censore ecclesiastico', pp. 292ff.

17. Nicolini, *La religiosità*, p. 58.

18. See B. Finetti, *Difesa dell' autorità della Sacra Scrittura contro Giambattista Vico*, p. 84. The original title of Finetti's work, published in Venice in 1768, was: *Apologia del genere umano accusato d'essere stato una volta una bestia: parte prima, in cui si dimostra la falsità dello stato ferino degli antichi uomini.*

of the theological errors into which Vico was forced by his attempt to square them with Holy Scripture.[19] 'Fine words', he called Vico's claim to be demonstrating the course of providence in history, 'but too perversely belied by his system of general dehumanization whereby the whole of mankind is thrust into a bestial state'.[20] Only through a mental aberration, he claimed, could the author of the work have failed to be aware of such contradictions.[21]

Finetti was not impressed by a reply from one of Vico's supporters, Emmanuele Duni, who pointed out that the *Scienza nuova* had received the approval and even the praise of the ecclesiastical censor Torno. Finetti, too serious and critical a scholar to be blown off-course by the 'excessive praise' of the author's friend responded to Duni's claim that Torno was a 'true' theologian with the observation that such characterization in terms of 'true' and 'false' is beside the point: 'only the heretical are false theologians; the ignorant are not theologians at all, neither true nor false'.[22] Nor does Finetti, on these maters of faith, cast in the balance against Torno simply his own reputation and experience, but rather 'the authority not merely of a true theologian, but of the prince of theologians and great Doctor of the Church, St Thomas Aquinas'.[23]

Benedetto Croce, whose *La filosofia di Giambattista Vico* (1911) first directed the attention of students of the history of ideas to the *Scienza nuova*, initially accepted at least the subjective intention, if not the objective results, of Vico's self-declared orthodoxy. But, as he himself explained many years later, subsequent reflection on Nicolini's findings and research caused him to change his mind even on the question of Vico's real intentions.[24] Finetti's detailed elaboration of numerous points of doctrine denied by Vico's system must also have played its part in this change of mind; and indeed, Croce edited the modern-day 1936 version of Finetti's work. He thus became convinced that early accounts of Vico's difficulties in this regard could not be discarded. Rather, they began to seem more plausible. For example, the idea that the *Scienza nuova* 'negativa' had been re-written because it was too flagrantly

19. For Finetti's initial summary of these doctrinal errors (he lists a total of 23), see *Difesa dell' autorità della Sacra Scrittura*, pp. 27–30.
20. Ibid., p. 69.
21. Ibid., p. 25.
22. Ibid., p. 73, Cf. Rossi's account of the exchange in *The Dark Abyss*, pp. 257–60. Rossi's defence of Vico's orthodoxy seems to limit itself to repeating some of Duni's rejoinders, which do not really meet the substance of Finetti's critique.
23. Finetti, *Difesa dell' autorità della Sacra Scrittura*, pp. 75–6.
24. Croce's revised opinions are contained in a gloss to the fourth edition (1946) of his *La filosofia di Giambattista Vico*, but also earlier in an appendix to *Difesa dell' autorità della Sacra Scrittura*, pp. 111–18.

unorthodox had been a difficult thesis to sustain while scholars thought that Vico had already obtained the Imprimatur *before* re-casting the work. Croce pointed out that this was not strictly correct. The re-writing, 'from beginnng to end' in fact took place 'when the work had been "revised" by Torno (which is not quite the same as "approved")'.[25] Bearing in mind that Torno was Vico's friend, such a 'revision' could well have been a useful prelude to subsequent discussions with Paolo Mattia Doria and others which, according to Genovesi's account, were decisive in persuading Vico to continue with his project, though with greater circumspection.[26] And since, as Croce pointed out, Vico's explanation in the *Autobiography* contains 'only what seemed to him expedient', does it not seem natural to ask whether 'the reasons for the re-shaping of the work were those given by Vico, or were there other reasons?'[27]

Gradually, the evidence which Croce began to piece together produced an impression of a psychologically more complex figure than he had hitherto imagined. In reviewing those comments and letters in which Vico touches on his own feelings about religion, Croce began to see Vico as being 'one would say, fearful, circumspect and cautious', rather than ingenuous and sincere.[28] We have seen in Chapter 1 something of the conditions which would have contributed to the shaping of such mental habits, and would also have induced Vico to engage in the social practice of cultivating friends among the clergy 'which was not without effect if it helped to allay suspicion'.[29]

Vico, Croce observed, did not have the heroic will or combative spirit of a Giannone; rather 'by temperament and because of his living conditions, he felt crushed by the sheer power, political and social, of the Church, before which he behaved diffidently'.[30] But the timidity which Croce saw in Vico rendered 'all the more admirable his preservation of that fundamental liberty of mind',[31] and bestowed on the achievement of the *Scienza nuova* a heroism of its own. Croce may have overstressed as a personal quality what was after all a fairly standard reaction among intellectuals and

25. Finetti, *Difesa dell' autorità della Sacra Scrittura*, p. 113.
26. Doria was by his own account accustomed to employing a variety of techniques of evasion, such as when he 'wrote according to the sense of Plato, and not my own in order to avoid the censorship of Holy Church'. (Cited in N. Badaloni, *Introduzione a Vico*, p. 29)
27. Finetti, *Difesa dell' autorità della Sacra Scrittura*, p. 113.
28. Croce, *La filosofia*, p. 10.
29. Finetti, *Difesa dell' autorità della Sacra Scrittura*, p. 115.
30. Ibid., p. 117.
31. Ibid.

writers of the time to a set of problems they all faced. Whatever the case in this respect, there can be little doubt that the continual revision and re-publication of his major work required a certain courage and tenacity of purpose, for it won him few friends in his lifetime. Referring to his 1725 version, he wrote to a friend:

> I avoid all public places, so as not to meet the persons to whom I have sent it; and if I cannot avoid them, I greet them without stopping; for when I pause they give me not the faintest sign that they have received it, and thus they confirm my belief that it has gone forth into a desert.[32]

Another notable early student of Vico's thought, Antonio Corsano, concluded that the Inquisition's proceedings against his friends caused Vico to abandon the philosophical currents then in vogue and to take refuge in the study of the 'humanist' tradition, subsequently undergoing a kind of conversion and embracing a more flexible type of religious belief.[33] Vico was certainly acquainted with 'humanist' writings and with the classics of the Christian tradition, such as St Augustine's *City of God*. These were after all part of the culture of the well-informed and literate scholar, of which Vico was a supreme example. Nevertheless, the passage of time has weakened some of Corsano's basic assumptions. We now know that Vico wrote his famous Lucretian poem *after* the proceedings against his friends, and not before as Corsano mistakenly supposed. We also know that he did not, in fact, abandon his free-thinking friends at the first sign of trouble; nor did he cease to frequent the Accademia degli Uniti. He even enjoyed a certain reputation for anti-clericalism. He is referred to in such terms in an anonymous pamphlet directed against the feudal dominion of the Holy See in Naples, a work published in the closing years of the eighteenth century, and one in which it is claimed that not even the great power and influence enjoyed by the Jesuits in Naples 'could destroy the fruitful seeds sown by Vico and Giannone'.[34]

The mention of Vico alongside Giannone is by no means as surprising as we might at first think, for until the appearance of the latter's *Istoria civile* in 1723, Vico's *Principum Neapolitanorum Coniuratio* was one of the few works in which harsh criticism of the Neapolitan clergy could be found. This work was written, with some encouragement from within government circles, in 1703 or 1704, that is, some twelve to thirteen years after the Inquisition had

---

32. Introduction to *The Autobiography of Giambattista Vico*, p. 14.
33. This position is argued in both of Corsano's works, *Umanesimo e religione in G. B. Vico*, and *G. B. Vico*.
34. Cited in Nicolini, *La religiosità*, p. 35.

commenced its proceedings against his friends. As we have already suggested, a major change in the ideological balance of power occurred in the early 1720s in Naples; a change which seems to have dramatically intensified existing religious tensions and which might go a long way towards explaining the sudden appearance, in Vico's 1725 writings, of his orthodox assertions.

Perhaps the most important corroborating evidence of an 'intended obscurity' to come to light in recent years is contained in a series of letters discovered by Nicola Badaloni. Antonio Conti, a contemporary philosopher, who had sought to have the work published in Venice, saw in the latter's philosophy of history 'the secularization of a prophetic scheme'.[35] Conti tried to spread its influence abroad, particularly in France, where it seemed relevant to existing debates. After the re-writing of the 1725 edition Conti, in correspondence with his friend, the free-thinking philosopher Duc de Larochefoucauld-Liancourt, summarized the development of Vico's thought as it had appeared in the post-1725, expanded version of the work. Since we do not possess Conti's original letters, his assessment can only be inferred from Larochefoucauld-Liancourt's recently discovered replies. What interests us is the unmistakable indication that Conti had discussed problems relating to the ecclesiastical approval of the work, and had suggested that Vico had encountered difficulties in expressing his true opinions:

> You greatly arouse my curiosity to see Mr Vico's book . . . I am not surprised that man's natural curiosity has always alarmed those who wish to rule, and that attempts have been made to stifle it either by punishing it with death or by over-indulging it. . . . However, I believe we would more or less know the position if, instead of obscuring the ideas in order to obtain permission to print his book, there could be a sincere effort made to clarify them as far as possible, without anything to fear from the Inquisitors. I would be pleased if you could tell me more about it before it is printed, which seems to me will not be easy to achieve, however much obscurity is introduced into it.[36]

Such evidence adds considerable weight to the arguments of those who claim that there is 'deliberate obscurity' in the *Scienza nuova*, although it tells us little about the extent of camouflaging activity, which must be adduced from textual evidence. It does, though, cast suspicion on Vico's bizarre explanation, in the 1731 addendum to the *Autobiography*, that he had demanded the return of the manuscript of his post-1725 revision from the Venetian

35. N. Badaloni, 'Vico nell' ambito della filosofia europea', p. 255.
36. Cited in Appendix II, 'Vico nell' ambito della filosofia europea', p. 266.

engraving ?

publishers on the grounds that he resented their growing assumption that they possessed sole rights to print his work. 'Instead', Badaloni suggests, 'the real reasons seem to have been the delay or indeed the veto on the work by the Inquisition in Venice'.[37] It is more likely, therefore, that Vico, who had been keeping his publishing options open, withdrew his material from the Venetians when the publishers in Naples – after his friend Torno's examination had obtained ecclesiastical approval – were free to go ahead and print.

There is, consequently, a considerable amount of extra-textual evidence for suspecting deliberate ambiguity in the writing of the *Scienza nuova*. Evidence of this kind can nevertheless do little more than alert the reader to an additional dimension in the already complex task of interpretation. It can perhaps even go so far as to suggest specific areas where the reader should be especially vigilant, as is the case, for example, of the possibility of a Lucretian-type 'naturalism' in the text. It cannot, however, replace the more important task of textually validating any claims we may make regarding Vico's difficulties with religious doctrine.

One further piece of evidence, although textual, should be mentioned at this point since it is not really theoretical in nature and therefore remains external to the substance of Vico's arguments. Frederick Vaughan has drawn attention to *SN* 425 in which Vico argues that the figure of Aesop was a product of the popular imagination of the heroic era in Greece. Vico quotes a passage from the prologues of Phaedrus' *Fables*, ostensibly in support of this argument. Phaedrus is quoted as saying: 'I will now explain briefly how the fable genre arose. Confined to servitude, the slaves dared not say what they thought, so they expressed their true feelings in fables. I am extending what Aesop did . . .'*

The passage certainly illustrates that Phaedrus was familiar with the art of literary subterfuge; indeed he actually attributes its practice to Aesop. But Vico's concept of 'poetic creation', as we shall see, would not have permitted him to attribute such a deliberative intent to the poetry of this period. Since poetry, at this stage of development, was a popular and not an individual creation, he in fact rejected any such interpretation of Aesop's aims. So what is the purpose of the passage? It certainly draws our attention rather obviously to the predicament of those who cannot express their true opinions. Vico may well be asking the reader, argues Vaughan, 'to read the *New Science* in the light of these lines'.[38] The

37. Ibid., p. 258.
38. Vaughan, *Political Philosophy*, p. 28.

31

fact that he is prepared to quote at length (it is the second longest quotation in the entire work) a passage so much at variance with his own interpretation of early fables and their function certainly lends a degree of plausibility to Vaughan's suggestion that it contains a concealed message.

Given the evidence in support of the claim that Vico experienced problems regarding religious teaching, it may seem suprising that this question has not received more attention. Modern critics are perhaps not easily drawn into problems relating to theological orthodoxy, and this is understandable if it is assumed that such problems do not affect the theoretical substance of the *Scienza nuova*. Unfortunately, the question is not quite so simple. There are some aspects of the work which presented no problems from the religious point of view. There are others, however, which did, and not in an entirely peripheral manner, for the theoretical substance of a system of ideas cannot be grasped in isolation from the manner of its expression. For this reason, as we examine the work we shall find that we are regularly drawn into doctrinal issues, and sometimes in the most unexpected places.

Part II
Language, Poetry and Myth

3
The Origins of Language, 'Natural Signification' and 'Onomathesia'

The 'naturalness' of early language

'Poetry' and 'myth' in the *Scienza nuova* are concepts which describe *necessary* forms of primitive linguistic and mental processes. These terms are anthropological/historical rather than 'aesthetic' categories; that is, they describe forms of language and thought characteristic of early historical epochs. The idea of linguistic development corresponding to specific epochs is a central theme of the work, with a wide variety of implications. As far as the 'poetic' era is concerned, this means that those characteristics, such as versification, the use of figurative language, the mythological description of events, which we find in early 'poets' like Homer, were not the products of individual writers deliberately employing the conventions and artifices of certain art forms. They were, rather, the natural, spontaneous forms of expression and thought of primitive man. It was narrative prose which had to be painfully acquired; the rhythms of early speech were patterns of repetition similar to those whereby children are taught to memorize and then to understand words and concepts. An important difference is that in the case of early man such patterns grew 'naturally' out of his initial dumbness and stupidity. Thus versification was part of his struggle towards articulate language. The modern reader must, therefore, reverse his usual terms of reference: 'poetry' was for Vico an earlier, more primitive and rudimentary form of language than 'narrative prose'.

Moreover, the 'poetic' form of early man's language was not for him, a matter of choice. He was incapable of any other form of expression. At that stage, all forms of human activity were largely instinctive, part of the 'world of nature': in Vichian terms, governed by the 'necessity of nature'. Accordingly it was natural and spontaneous for early man to speak in verse; and likewise he thought 'naturally' in fables. Thus, the idea of thunder and lightning expressing divine displeasure was not the metaphorical product of an artistic mind, but the literal belief of primitive and unintelligent creatures. In this way, the contents of early myths are the instinctive or 'natural' expression of early man's primitive understanding of the world he inhabits. Thus in the early years of humanity man was 'naturally' a poet, or , as Vico puts it: 'the first gentile peoples, by a demonstrated *necessity of nature*, were poets who spoke in poetic characters.'[1]

For early man, all knowledge proceeded by way of the instinctive mechanics of myth-creation, so that the inexplicable or unfamiliar was understood or interpreted in terms of the familiar. Primitive man, in his ignorance and inability to see or understand anything beyond his immediate concerns, and incapable of conceiving a world of events or phenomena governed by principles outside his experience, reduced the world to his own primitive perspectives: 'Because of the indefinite nature of the human mind, wherever it is lost in ignorance man makes himself the measure of all things'.[2] Early man, in short, interpreted the unknown through a process of anthropomorphism: 'When men are ignorant of the natural causes producing things, and cannot even explain them by analogy with similar things, they attribute their own nature to them'.[3]

The importance of this principle lies in the instinctiveness or, in Vico's terms, the 'naturalness' of myth-creation. While it tells us little of the phenomena or events which early man interpreted, it reveals a great deal about his state of understanding and manner of experiencing life. Thus the philological deciphering of myth and its language can be utilized in reconstructing early man's rudimentary thought processes and lifestyle.

This does not mean that the discovery of increasing numbers and varieties of myths and fables leads to ever more disparate and fragmented lines of enquiry, for Vico's method of analysing such phenomena is underpinned by an almost Chomskyan linguistic 'deep-structure' in which a wide variety of linguistic and mythical patterns can be reduced to a limited, uniform number of mental constructs:

> There must in the nature of human institutions be a mental language common to all nations, which uniformly grasps the substance of things feasible in human social life and expresses it with as many diverse modifications as these same things may have diverse aspects. A proof of

1. *SN* 34. Italics mine.
2. *SN* 120.
3. *SN* 180.

this is afforded by proverbs or maxims of vulgar wisdom, in which substantially the same meanings find as many diverse expressions as there are nations ancient and modern.[4]

It is not necessary therefore to embark on endless searches for influences of one tribe upon another or of one civilization on another, since 'uniform ideas originating among entire peoples unknown to each other must have a common ground of truth'.[5] In Vico's view, the historical elaboration of ideas is a direct expression of the development of human institutions: 'The order of ideas must follow the order of institutions'.[6] The deciphering of myth, in other words, is not undertaken simply as an end in itself, or as a means of understanding primitive ideas, but in order to uncover the human institutions and practices of which they are the necessary expression.

This strict correlation between language, ideas and institutions leads Vico to propose that a common pattern of mental and linguistic development for all nations implies a parallel common pattern of historical development: 'Thence issues the mental dictionary for assigning origins to all the diverse articulated languages. It is by means of this dictionary that the ideal eternal history is conceived, which gives us the histories in time of all nations'.[7] In Vico's 'ideal eternal history', the specific features of the development of different nations follow a common and recurrent pattern of change, which is determined by a shared inventory of instinctive attitudes and forms of consciousness impressed on the human race by 'providence'.[8] This shared aggregate of instincts, attitudes and forms of consciousness is described by Vico as a 'senso comune' (a 'common sense') which he further defines as 'judgment without reflection, shared by an entire class, an entire people, an entire nation, or the entire human race'.[9]

This common base of instincts, feelings and thoughts is not simply limited to broad general features. To function as a methodological instrument for historico-linguistic research, its manifestations must be more specific and distinct. As we see from the following passage in the 1725 *Scienza nuova* – convenient to cite for the clarity with which the idea is expressed – there is, in the earliest

---

4. *SN* 161.
5. *SN* 144.
6. *SN* 238.
7. *SN* 145.
8. See Ibid. This concept will be discussed at a later stage.
9. *SN* 142. Given the quite different connotations of the English 'common sense', the original Italian 'senso comune' will be retained throughout this study.

periods of human history, an identity in the smallest details of linguistic expression. This is what Vico calls

> an etymology common to all native languages. Since the principles of things are those from which their composition begins, and also into which they finally resolve themselves; and since we have demonstrated above that the first words spoken by the Latins must all have been of one syllable, the origins of native languages must everywhere follow this pattern and be found in such monosyllables.[10]

The rather rigid and inflexible scheme of linguistic development visualized by Vico thus reduces the problem of comparative studies to an exercise in which the varied forms of development are retraced to a single and uniform pattern for all languages. His idea of a 'dictionary of mental words common to all nations'[11] implies the empirical principle that the elements of language (e.g. parts of speech) develop in a uniform manner in all cultures. Thus the successive appearance of interjections, pronouns, prepositions, nouns and verbs, for example, proves to be the same in all languages.[12] But even more importantly, these parallel linguistic developments mirror an identity in patterns of mental development, so that, for example, the first noun in all languages is the name of Jove. From the rudimentary beginnings of monosyllabic utterances, and in response to a variety of climatic and geographical conditions (which explain the superficial linguistic differences superimposed on the common mental substructure of all languages), early men, after the manner of children, developed their linguistic and mental apparatus, so that:

> at the same time that the divine character of Jove took shape – the first human thought in the gentile world – articulate language began to develop by way of onomatopoeia, through which we still find children happily expressing themselves. By the Latins Jove was at first, from the roar of the thunder, called *Ious*; by the Greeks, from the whistle of the lightning, *Zeus*; by the Easterners, from the sound of burning fire, he must have been called *Ur*, ...[13]

Linguistic differences, therefore, are accounted for by contingent factors. But the 'common mental language' underlying such differences ensures that once the language of myth has been deciphered, the historian holds the key to the 'ideal eternal history' or pattern of

10. *SN1a* 381. Passages from the 1725 edition have been translated from *La Scienza nuova prima*.
11. *SN1a* 387. See also *SN* 145, 161, 354–5.
12. See the section *SN* 445–55.
13. *SN* 447.

development which underlies the histories of *all* nations.

At the heart of Vico's conception of human development we find the idea that early man's major energies were spent on the basic problems of survival. All his activities revolved around acquiring or responding to what Vico called the 'necessities' and 'utilities' of human life. This, as we shall see, is one of the many aspects of the 'naturalism' of the *Scienza nuova*, in which 'necessity' and 'utility' are constant points of reference. Thus, in his attempt to explain the existence of a variety of vulgar languages, he writes:

> How is it that there are as many different vulgar tongues as there are peoples? To solve it, we must here establish this great truth: that, as the peoples have certainly by diversity of climates acquired different natures, from which have sprung as many different customs, so from their different natures and customs as many different languages have arisen. For by virtue of the aforesaid diversity of their natures they have regarded *the same utilities or necessities of human life* from different points of view, and there have thus arisen so many national customs . . .'[14]

But early man did not simply confront the 'necessities' and 'utilities' of his existence as if they belonged to a world of nature from which they had to be wrested. He did not possess the kind of detachment from the world of nature that this would imply. His own existence forms part of the terrain of the 'necessity of nature' in which his responses are governed more by instinctual requirements than by self-conscious 'choices'. It is within this world of 'natural' and instinctual forces that early man *of necessity* expresses himself in poetry. In his 1725 elaboration of first principles concerning the origin of languages, Vico states that the first one 'is that song and verse have arisen through a necessity of human nature, not through choice and fancy. Moreover, through thinking them to have arisen through choice and fancy, many foolish things have been said, even by the most serious of thinkers . . .'[15]

The general reluctance to acknowledge the full force of Vico's oft-repeated phrase 'necessity of nature' is part of a tendency amongst critics, dating from Croce's major work on the *Scienza nuova*, to play down the historical/anthropological context of his notion of 'poetic' man. A significant number of critics are still loath to abandon 'aestheticist' interpretations of this concept, and for these it becomes necessary to make light of Vico's frequent reminders that 'it was by a necessity of nature that the first nations spoke

14. *SN* 445. Italics mine.
15. *SN1a* 374.

in heroic verse'.[16]

An important part of the theoretical boldness and originality of the *Scienza nuova* lies in its total inversion of traditional conceptions. Early man – stupid, brutal, violent and ignorant – was nevertheless endowed with strong passions and the powerful senses which enabled him to survive in the cruel world of nature. Such qualities endowed his 'poetic' language with that power, strength, vividness and passion (which Vico calls 'sublimity') later unattainable by civilized man.[17] This is why the proposition 'that in the world's childhood men were by nature sublime poets'[18] implies, in the *Scienza nuova*, the primacy of the historical over the epistemological element. It is the contrast Vico makes when he states that 'imagination is more robust in proportion as reasoning power is weak'.[19] He goes on to insist that figurative forms of expression – all reducible to metaphor, synecdoche, metonymy and irony – originated among primitive men not in order to embellish or adorn their ideas, but as *necessary* means of expressing the practical problems they encountered in establishing primitive institutions and organizing their existence.[20] He then concludes: 'From all this it follows that all the tropes (and they are all reducible to the four types above discussed), which have hitherto been considered ingenious inventions of writers, were *necessary* modes of expression of all the first poetic nations, . . .'[21]

Early language was thus part of an expressive system governed by the immediacy and directness of the 'natural' needs of early man, and not the product of self-conscious, reflective beings. Vico makes a sharp distinction between an early period which is all instinct or 'naturalness' and a final one characterized by human reason and choice. These are two essential polarities or opposites within his theory. Hence he repeatedly contrasts the instinctual or 'natural' patterns of early language with linguistic behaviour in the later period which is governed more by convention, agreement or choice. Thus 'philologians have all accepted with an excess of good faith the view that in the vulgar languages meanings were fixed by convention. On the contrary, because of their natural origins, they must have had natural significations'.[22] Those interpretations,

---

16. *SN* 833.
17. See the section of the*Scienza nuova* dealing with the origins of poetic style, 456ff., and the section on the 'Discovery of the True Homer', 879ff. See also 821.
18. *SN* 187.
19. *SN* 185.
20. See *SN* 404–11.
21. *SN* 409. Italics mine.
22. *SN* 444.

therefore, which play down this opposition create serious distortions of Vico's thought. It is important to grasp the idea of 'natural signification', especially in relation to other concepts within his 'naturalistic' problematic, since it becomes a fundamental component of the methodology he constructs for interpreting early poetry and myth.

What Vico argues in his theory of 'natural signification' is that in the language of rational man the relationships between words and the ideas they signify are governed entirely by convention, so that men have a measure of control over their speech. New words can be introduced into language, and different individuals can even mean slightly different things when using the same words. This is because there is no *necessary* relationship between any particular word and the object signified – any linguistic expression will do, provided that its meaning is agreed or accepted by convention. It is this element of choice and discrimination which is absent in early language. That is, the relationships between words and the ideas they signify are governed, in early language, by a fixed correlation which excludes the flexibility of later linguistic behaviour. This correlation is part of the 'necessity of nature' in which early language 'must have begun with signs, whether gestures or physical objects, which had *natural* relations to the ideas (to be expressed)'.[23]

There are, as we shall see later, certain problems latent in the opposition Vico sets up between 'natural' and 'conventional' signification. As I have already suggested, however, the notion of 'natural signification' is part of a deliberately constructed methodological strategy, which will be discussed more fully at a later stage. But Vico tells us that early man is incapable of deception; only with the acquisition of reason and deliberation does this become possible in human behaviour. Thus, 'natural signification' in language is part of an early instinctual pattern of natural responses uninhibited and unobscured by the later mediatory processes of deliberation, reflection and choice, that is, by those faculties which introduce diversity of meaning and expression into human language. It thus becomes the guarantee that early poetry and myth are the most reliable sources possible for historical documentation. This is why Vico calls his discovery that 'poetry' was early man's 'natural' form of expression the 'master key' to his new science.[24]

23. *SN* 401. Italics mine.
24. See *SN* 34.

'Natural signification' and 'Onomathesia'

The process of 'natural signification', according to Vico, must have begun well before the arrival of any alphabets, which already contain a substantial element of convention. Before this, he observes in a passage similar to the one just cited, 'Mutes make themselves understood by gestures or objects that have natural relations with the ideas they wish to signify'.[25]

From such a notion he immediately concludes: 'This axiom is the principle of the hieroglyphs by which all nations spoke in the time of their first barbarism'.[26] Hieroglyphs, therefore, are a form of communication which preserves the natural relation or likeness to the object signified.

Given that Vico's account of the origins of both speech and writing involved a radical theoretical break with the most respected contemporary opinions, it is noteworthy that he does not avail himself of a supportive and prestigious figures such as Francis Bacon. It has been shown convincingly by De Mas[27] that there can be no doubt of Vico's familiarity with Bacon's contention that 'it is evident . . . that hieroglyphs and gestures carry a certain likeness to the signified object'.[28] In view also of Vico's open references to the English philosopher as one of his 'four authors', such an omission in his discussion of the origins of letters requires some explanation.

Reference to Bacon's *De Dignitate et Augmentis Scientiarum* reveals striking similarities with Vico's theory:

> Signification of objects, which is either without aid or by means of words, is of two kinds; of which the first kind relies on a congruity or likeness. The other signifies by convention. Hieroglyphs and gestures belong to the first whilst the others are what we call letters or words.[29]

And further:

> The use of hieroglyphs is an ancient and venerable practice. It was especially widely used among the ancient Egyptians; so much so that hieroglyphs seem to have been an early form of writing and to have provided the first elements of letters – except perhaps in the case of the Hebrews.[30]

---

25. *SN* 225.
26. *SN* 226.
27. E. De Mas, *Bacone e Vico*.
28. F. Bacon, *De Dignitate et Augmentis Scientiarum*, vol. 6, ch. 1, p. 281.
29. Ibid.
30. Ibid. In his authoritative and detailed study of Vico's ideas on language, *Mente corpo linguaggio: Saggio sull' interpretazione vichiana del mito*, Gianfranco Cantelli

Vico echoes the Baconian thesis even to the point of excluding the Hebrew language from his scheme of development.

Vico's account of early language conflicted with the traditionally approved theological version of the 'invention of letters'. Here we may have the reason for Vico's 'oversight'. For, while to acknowledge one's indebtedness to a Protestant author on literary or scientific matters might well pass without comment, openly to espouse his ideas when they could be seen as a threat to the scriptural account of the 'invention of letters' was quite another matter. As we shall see, in order to incorporate such ideas on language into the general thrust of his historical scheme (while at the same time avoiding arousing ecclesiastical suspicion), Vico had to be ingenious.

The problem of hieroglyphs and the origins of the letters of the alphabet is, of course, only part of the wider question of the origin of language. It was within this general context that Vico was first faced with the problem of coming to terms with the scriptural tradition. In explaining the nature, origins and diversity of language, he could not indeed avoid a confrontation with orthodox interpretations. It is important to appreciate the weight of religious and theoretical pressure brought to bear by the general consensus of theological opinion. Fausto Nicolini has observed that during the period when Vico was writing,

> there was not a single Christian, be he Catholic or Protestant who, in investigating the nature of language did not find before him [the doctrine of] 'divine onomathesia' and the miracle of the confusion of tongues. These, like high mountains, rose up before him as if to obscure the view of what it was possible to see beyond such obstacles.[31]

When Vico was preparing his major work, there were two contending views amongst theologians concerning the diversification of language. Broadly speaking, these rival accounts depended on whether the focal point of interpretation was based on Genesis 10:45 and 32 or on Genesis 11:1–9. In verse 5 of Genesis 10 (Revised Standard Version) the prophet writes: 'These are the sons of Japheth in their lands, each with his own language, by their families, in their nations', which verse 32 simply reiterates via the 'spread of nations' under the families of the sons of Noah after the flood. Although such passages seem compatible with the thesis that geographical and social differentiations are sufficient to account for

---

argues that hieroglyphics are for Vico the first form of 'language' rather than 'writing' (see pp. 19ff).

31. Nicolini, *La religiosità*, p. 134.

the diversity of linguistic development, the different languages are still envisaged as corruptions of the God-given Hebrew language which continues to be the 'model' language. It is also the medium, via the prophets, through which God spoke to his people.[32] Genesis 11:1–9, by contrast, deals more specifically with the confusion of tongues, and was the point of reference favoured by the Catholic Church. According to this account, 'the whole of the earth had one language and few words. And as men migrated from the east, they found a plain in the land of Shinar and settled there' (verses 1–2). Men, the passage continues, decided to build themselves a city with a tower reaching into the heavens. Such an achievement, they thought, would ensure their renown. This presumption was judged harshly by God:

> And the Lord said, 'Behold, they are one people, and they have all one language; and this is only the beginning of what they will do; and nothing that they propose to do will now be impossible for them. Come, let us go down, and there confuse their language, that they may not understand one another's speech'. So the Lord scattered them abroad from there over the face of all the earth, and they left off building the city (verses 6–8).

As a Catholic, Vico would have been expected, in so far as his theories touched on such matters, to subscribe to three major propositions: namely, that before the construction of the Tower of Babel all men spoke one universal language – Hebrew; that the confusion of tongues was a more or less instantaneous event occurring in one place; and that there was a subsequent dispersion of peoples. Speaking of the confusion of tongues, he writes:

> The confusion of tongues came about in a miraculous way so that on the instant many different languages were formed. The Fathers will have it that through this confusion of tongues the purity of the sacred antediluvian language was gradually lost. This should be understood as referring to the languages of the Eastern peoples among whom Shem propagated the human race. It must have been otherwise in the case of the nations of all the rest of the world; for the races of Ham and Japheth were destined to be scattered through the great forest of this earth *in a savage migration of two hundred years*. Wandering and alone, they were to bring forth their children, with a savage education, *destitute of any human custom and deprived of any human speech, and so in a state of wild animals.*[33]

32. See M. Papini, 'La Babele delle umane lingue', in *Arbor Humanae Linguae*, pp. 205ff. Papini also discusses the question in relation to St Augustine's *City of God*, of which Vico was aware when using passages from Genesis.
33. *SN* 62. Italics mine.

On close inspection this passage from the *Scienza nuova* can be seen as a truly audacious theoretical manoeuvre. Vico simply takes the orthodox biblical account and uses it as the starting point for his own account of human development. He utilizes the biblical 'dispersion' by converting it into a process of 'bestialization' through which all nations, except the Jews, lose all vestiges of humanity and revert to a state of primitive bestiality, dumbness, violence and stupidity – a state from which his scheme of human evolution can then begin. In this way the biblical account is left intact, or so the ecclesiastical censor is meant to think. But in effect there is no genuine theoretical integration between Vico and the orthodox view.

In Vico's chronological table the dispersion is dated at 2128BC. The process of bestialization then takes place over a period of two hundred years (one hundred years in the case of the sons of Shem) ending at a point Vico assumes to be the one from which all human development (apart from that of the Jews, that is, sacred history) begins. Throughout the *Scienza nuova* Vico repeatedly alludes to this exception of the Jews with respect to the natural course of development he describes for the rest of humanity. Unperturbed by the lack of empirical evidence for his suppositions, he makes no attempt to justify them, nor to describe, beyond the briefest assertion, this extraordinary process whereby the whole of Gentile humanity loses its capacity to think, speak and associate, reverting to the primitive barbarity of beast-like cave-dwellers within the short space of two hundred (and one hundred) years. Yet such a device does enable him to start his account of the civilizing process in which one might well suspect he really considered the whole of humanity to have had its beginnings, that is, with primitive, beast-like creatures.

Having thus seen how Vico utilizes the biblical account to his own ends, we must add a few words about his awareness of the theologically unorthodox nature of such a manoeuvre. In the passage we have just read, Vico states that the confusion of tongues should be understood as applying only to Shem, that is, the progenitor of the Semitic race, including the chosen Jewish people who are the subjects of sacred history. Noah's other two sons, Ham and Japheth, are the progenitors of the degenerate and bestialized races from which an evolutionary linguistic process began. But how legitimate was it to place this dispersion of the races *before* the biblical confusion of tongues, and to restrict the latter to the descendants of Shem?

Vico was in fact fully aware of the dangers of such an interpretation, for in the 1730 edition of the *Scienza nuova*, he qualifies his account of the two hundred years of feral wandering before the confusion of tongues by stating that it

> seems, however, contrary to what Holy Scripture states in Genesis. Because, otherwise, if the dispersion had taken place before the confusion [of tongues], the following profanity would ensue: namely, that Noah's sons having separated on the face of the earth two hundred years earlier, . . . the impious races of Ham and Japheth would have avoided the divine punishment, and only the race of Shem, which was godly, would have been punished . . .[34]

Nicolini has shown that this qualification was almost certainly due to the intervention of Torno,[35] as was in all probability the similar qualification in the following paragraph, on the same topic, where he restates the idea that the dispersion took place before the confusion of tongues which, however, 'one is not allowed to say, because it is clearly contrary to what is stated in Genesis'.[36]

The use of such qualifiers was a time-honoured device – a variant of the 'double truth' escape route – employed by such thinkers as Bruno, Campanella, Galileo and many others. It enabled the writer to express his true opinions while being able to argue, if ever questioned on the offending ideas, that they were simply being put forward as hypotheses. The Dominican Finetti, who scrutinized both of the later editions of the *Scienza nuova*, did not fail to notice the disclaimer and asked,

> But if 'one is not allowed to say it', why has he stated it so clearly in the places I have shown? . . . Why has he not corrected it anywhere? Why has he repeated it [the idea that the dispersion took place earlier than the confusion of tongues] in the third and last edition, even concealing the conflict [with Scripture] so clearly recognized and admitted in the second edition?[37]

In answer to Finetti's question, it is likely that the insertion of the qualifiers was the price for Torno's approval of the work, and its omission in the final edition seems to confirm this because by that time he was no longer Vico's censor. The reason for Vico's boldness, moreover, was that the disclaimed ideas came closer to the demands of his theory.

Vico was hostile to theories which implied an ability to reason in

---

34. *La Scienza Nuova Seconda*, par. 1146, p. 177.
35. For a discussion of this see F. Nicolini, *Saggi vichiani*, pp. 281–95.
36. *La Scienza Nuova Seconda*, par. 1147, p. 178.
37. Finetti, *Difesa dell' autorità della Sacra Scrittura*, p. 48.

early man. As has already been suggested, this opposition to reason-based activities such as the shaping of linguistic conventions or the deliberate 'naming' of objects was nurtured by his reading of such authors as Bacon and Lucretius. Vico took the opposition much further than his sources and produced a convention/nature antithesis in which, for example, the 'lingua muta' or language of gestures of early man became essentially an instinctual expression of natural requirements. Within such a pattern of behaviour the idea of 'naming' objects as currently understood by his contemporaries was quite absurd. Early man lacked the intelligence necessary either actively to engage in such a naming process or meaningfully to endorse it. In other circumstances *De Rerum Natura* would have provided Vico with a useful precedent from classical antiquity in support of this contention. Lucretius had written that, 'to suppose that someone on some particular occasion allotted names to objects, and that by this means men learnt their first words, is stark madness'.[38]

Given the orthodox view, based on Genesis 2:9, that God supervised Adam in the naming of objects, we can hardly be surprised that Vico does not draw attention to what would have been seen as a direct affront to scripture. In so doing, he would only have highlighted the pagan affinities of his theories on language and at the same time possibly alerted the ecclesiastical censor to his numerous other classical sources.

The centuries-old belief in divine onomathesia entailed the further idea that Adam's 'names' for all the objects he signified mirrored their 'essence' or 'nature'. While this is, of course, a notion far removed from Vico's own theory of natural signification, he nevertheless makes obeisance to the orthodox doctrine.[39] Given that Jewish history is, according to Vico's thesis, subject to separate (divine) laws of operation, his acceptance of the orthodox doctrine need not go beyond a simple and concise statement of mere acknowledgement.

The ingenuity of Vico's theoretical manoeuvre in equating the dispersion of the nations with the beginning of the 'feral wandering' means that he is able to use the notion of a distinct sacred history as a method of theoretical disengagement from uncongenial doctrines. Everything that happens within the domain of sacred history is governed by a special dispensation from those laws of development he feels free to expound for the 'natural' course of

---

38. Lucretius, *De Rerum Natura*, Bk V, ll. 1041–3.
39. See *SN* 401 and 430.

events. Vico's treatment of 'onomathesia', therefore, underlines the important function of some of his intermittent statements of belief.

Vico was, of course, touching upon a sensitive area with his suggestion that in the theological and heroic epochs early men created and named their gods; for, as the Dominican censor Finetti noted, this argument could equally be applied to Christianity itself. He had, therefore, to distinguish between the pagan gods and the God of the Judaeo-Christian tradition, by saying that

> that first language, spoken by the theological poets, was not a language *in accord with the nature of the things it dealt with* (as must have been the sacred language invented by Adam, to whom God granted *divine onomathesia, the giving of names to things according to the nature of each*), but was a fantastic speech making use of physical substances endowed with life and most of them imagined to be divine.[40]

He thus differentiates between the 'natural signification', so to speak, of sacred history in which the naming process (onomathesia) reflects *the essence or nature of the objects* and a 'natural signification' in which the natural correspondence is between the names and *how the objects are pictured in the primitive mind*. There is no claim in the latter case that the conception or idea of the object corresponds to its 'essence'. This is why Vico is careful to stress that his 'mutes' express themselves through objects or gestures which have a natural relation 'with the *ideas* they wish to signify'.[41]

Once again the ideas of 'onomathesia' and a separate course of sacred history are introduced in a way which neutralizes in advance any possible opposition to Vico's ideas. Naturally, he assures his readers, the imaginative process whereby primitive men name their gods cannot be likened to the biblical process of naming. In the latter, the names reflect the true nature of what they signify. While primitive Gentiles invent names to denote their false and illusory gods, the name of Yahweh points to the one true God of the chosen people. Vico's reference to 'onomathesia' in this way reassures the authorities that his own theory does not challenge an accepted Christian idea in its own sphere.

If we consider for a moment the doctrine of 'onomathesia' within the overall context of Vico's treatment of language in the *Scienza nuova*, a further antinomy emerges. The doctrine proves to be a typical product of the essentialist tradition so central to western, and particularly Catholic, thinking, in defining objects in terms of

40. *SN* 401. Italics mine.
41. *SN* 225. Italics mine.

'essences'. Although there had been challenges to this tradition, the strongest having been the Nominalist movement associated with the name of William of Ockham and his followers, it is nevertheless true to say that the dominant practice in Catholic theology at the time was still to teach that objects consist of an essence identifiable in terms of one or more quintessential, permanent and immutable qualities. The rational human soul, which constitutes the underlying essence of man, is perhaps the prime example of such an essentialist definition. Therefore, if there was one single element of the western philosophical tradition above all others which the *Scienza nuova*, with its thoroughgoing historicism, sought to destroy it was this one. There can be little doubt that the doctrine of 'onomathesia' must have been totally repugnant to a thinker whose work consisted of a running battle with traditional essentialist definitions. Vico was indeed quite explicit in articulating this historicist and evolutionist conception of the 'nature of things' according to which objects are not identified in terms of eternal 'essences' but in accordance with their changing and evolving existential settings: 'The nature of things is nothing other than their coming into being at certain times and in certain guises. Whenever the times and guises are such and such, so and not otherwise are the things that come into being.'[42]

But 'onomathesia' is only one of a number of religious concepts which seem to exist on a separate, theoretically non-functional level in the *Scienza nuova*. Vico more than once specifically proclaims his faith when he does in fact appear to be placing some item or other of Catholic doctrine in jeopardy. If this is so there are grounds for suspecting that the function of such formal declarations might well be to divert attention from the religious implications of the ideas he is putting forward.

Despite his apparent efforts to guard against possible charges of heterodoxy, there is, in connection with the question of the origin of written communication, an unwitting lapse on Vico's part. Moreover, in this case it cannot be remedied by recourse to his usual technique of 'disengagement' from sacred history. The passage in question is one in which Vico argues that certain art forms belong properly to a rational stage of human development and cannot be ascribed to earlier, non-rational and primitive stages of humanity. He writes that 'painting abstracts the surfaces absolutely, and this is a labour calling for the greatest ingenuity. Hence neither Homer nor Moses ever mentions anything painted, and this

42. *SN* 147.

is an argument of their antiquity.'[43] In coupling Homer and Moses Vico was, in fact, echoing a comparison frequently made by scholars of the time. He was, however, raising enormous issues in this passage, and it is difficult to know whether he did so in innocence of the implications of his comparison or whether he hoped such problems would pass unnoticed.

According to the terms of Vico's philosophy, to accept the idea of Moses' authorship of the Pentateuch would be to imply a high level of cultural, rational and literary ability on his part and that of his readers. In such a cultural environment, again according to the terms of Vico's theory, paintings could have been produced. But the passage in question not only denies their existence but clearly associates the Old Testament prophet with that lack of rationality and intelligence characteristic of the Homeric era. In fact, Homeric man is described by Vico as stupid, barbarous, violent and bestial,[44] which is why Homer never mentions art forms which clearly require a higher form of intelligence. By implication Vico also extends all this to Moses and the Jewish people of the time. Moreover, he frequently emphasizes that in Homer's time letters had not yet been invented,[45] implying that Moses, too, was a fictional symbol of an unlettered, primitive, ignorant and violent people, incapable of the forms of social and moral activity described in the Old Testament. Such an idea was clearly unacceptable to any Catholic interpretation of scriptural inspiration, since the extension of such primitive circumstances to Moses' time reduces his authorship to a cultural fiction and the contents of the sacred books to a collection of orally transmitted legends.[46]

This was, of course, perfectly consistent with Vico's theory of early literature, although he could certainly never have openly expressed such a view.[47] The 'onomathesia' he elsewhere professes to accept, on the other hand, would render both Moses and the Jewish people capable of meaningful linguistic, social and moral

43. *SN* 794.
44. See, for example, *SN* 787.
45. See *SN* 66 and 429.
46. This is what Vico argued in the case of the Homeric epics. Even today Catholic teaching requires belief in a 'real author' or group of authors composing either at the time of the events described or at least from living memory.
47. Spinoza, whose works Catholics were forbidden to read, had expressed views similar to these. As we shall see, Vico was familiar with Spinoza's theories of primitive literature as applied to Scripture. On the question of Homer and the Bible see the comments by Peter Burke who notes that 'one is left wondering whether in private Vico ever considered the Bible as a corpus of myth' (*Vico*, p. 67). See also pp. 39–54 of this work for an excellent brief survey of sixteenth- and seventeenth-century debates and discussions on language and myth which may have influenced Vico.

activity – yet this would in turn make nonsense of the Homer/ Moses parallel in *SN* 794. In what was possibly an unguarded moment, therefore, Vico produced a theoretical contradiction of the 'onomathesia' he elsewhere professed to believe.

So far we have gained an initial indication of the methodological importance to Vico of the notion of 'natural signification' in language. We have also touched on the religious problems associated with this idea. Similar problems will recur in relation to other aspects of his thought. But there are also issues of a straightforward theoretical nature arising out of his linguistic philosophy, and to these we shall now turn our attention.

4
The 'Vera Narratio' as Historical Method

Vico did not conceive of 'poetic' language as a 'higher', aesthetic form of expression. Its figurative forms, for example, similes, metaphors, circumlocutions, are not artistic creations but rather are 'born of the grossness of the heroic minds, unable to confine themselves to those essential features of things that were to the purpose in hand, as we see to be naturally the case with the feeble-minded and above all with women'.[1] He thus compares the mental processes of the early poets with those of idiots and women, the closest approximation he could conceive of, by way of illustration, in his own age of fully developed humanity. This comparison was made with the intention of undermining the existing wide-spread belief that the 'poetic' language of ancient myths and fables was rich in allegorical, symbolic and learned significance.

Many writers of the late sixteenth and seventeenth centuries accepted the Neoplatonist and Hermetic idea that the ancient wisdom of the Greeks and Egyptians was expressed in poetry and hieroglyphs, in order to conceal from the common people the profound secrets of divine wisdom. Paolo Rossi has argued that the inspiration behind Vico's innovatory attack on the idea of myth as 'profound wisdom in allegorical form' derived from his desire to combat the anti-Christian implications of this long-standing Hermetic/Neoplatonist tradition. Having allegedly perceived a threat to Christianity in it, Vico attacked those of its defenders (Marsham, Spencer, Van Heurn) who argued that Egyptian civilization was more ancient than, indeed the source of, Hebrew civilization.[2] Such a view clearly reduced the status of sacred history to just one of a number of civilizations and deprived the Scriptures of any claim to theological or moral pre-eminence. Ficino, for example, had even asserted the possibility of the temporal precedence of Hermes Trismegistus over Moses. Vico's

1. *SN* 457. See also *SN* 456.
2. P. Rossi, *Le sterminate antichità: Studi vichiani*, pp. 133–64; *The Dark Abyss*, pp. 176ff.

attacks, therefore, are seen by Rossi and others as a defence of the Judaeo-Christian tradition and as a refusal to bring together sacred and profane history into a single scheme or perspective.

There are, however, a number of difficulties associated with Rossi's argument. While Vico did most decidedly reject the arguments of Marsham, Spencer and Van Heurn regarding Egyptian influence on Hebrew culture, he made no mention of the orthodoxy which Rossi insists he was defending. His failure to do so is quite consistent with what seems to me his fundamental lack of interest in theological issues beyond what was necessary to protect himself against possible charges of heterodoxy. Vico's reason for rejecting the conclusions of these scholars regarding Egyptian and Hebrew civilization is, in fact, central to his whole theoretical enterprise.[3] Their reasoning, he argues, is a typical product of what he calls the 'conceit of the learned', a point Rossi also makes. Their crime lies in assuming that all men, at all times, have always displayed the same rational capabilities; and that similarities in diverse cultures must be accounted for in terms of 'influences'. Vico's primary concern is with defending his 'primitive' interpretation of ancient (including Egyptian) writings against the Hermetic interpretations of a 'concealed wisdom' such as were suggested by these scholars' anachronistic readings. Also, his 'polygenic' view of parallel patterns developing in *all* cultures was opposed to their tendency to propose 'influences' as explanations for the frequent emergence of similar linguistic or mythological patterns. For this reason Vico attacked those who asserted a necessary 'influence' of Egyptian upon Hebrew culture. The Hermetic/Neoplatonist tradition, in other words, proved irreconcilable with his conception of the primitive nature of the early poets.

Vico's attack on interpretations of 'ancient wisdom' in early poetry is determined by the internal requirements of his own theory, which we shall now examine a little more closely. As indicated earlier, he in fact found among the 'thousand inanities and absurdities' of Lucretius' writings a few key ideas whose source he preferred not to declare. One of these was undoubtedly Lucretius' reference to the time when 'poets began to hand down the deeds of men in verse'.[4] For Vico, this insight was to become a major heuristic principle because the poems of the ancient world were the true source of historical knowledge for the periods they describe.

Let us reconstruct his argument in a little more detail. Early man,

3. See *SN* 44, 58–9, 66, 93, 100.
4. Lucretius, *De Rerum Natura*, Bk V, ll. 1444–5.

he argues, lacks the ability to conceptualize or form abstract relations between objects. His communicative patterns are determined by 'natural' and 'necessary' responses to his surroundings, because, 'the first men, the children, as it were, of the human race, not being able to form intelligible class concepts of things, had a *natural necessity* to create poetic characters . . .'*[5] and because of the 'natural' correspondence or 'adequation' of the poetic image to its object, 'we assert that poetic speech, in virtue of the poetic characters it employs, can yield many important discoveries concerning antiquity'.[6] The 'natural' correspondence between poetic image/ myth and early man's understanding of reality is what makes his poetry an accurate and 'true' recording of his structures of thought and feeling. This 'true' and accurate recording of his mental state under conditions and constraints of 'natural necessity' is what Vico calls 'true narration' or 'vera narratio' in early poetry.[7] There is to him an infallible connection of 'necessity' between the conditions of existence and the beliefs of these early men on the one hand, and the *literal* (not symbolic) expression of these conditions and beliefs in mythical form on the other. Myth is a symbolic fiction to us; to early man it was the *literal* expression of his mode of perception. Nor is there any possibility of deception in the 'vera narratio' since, as we have already indicated, deception requires powers of reflection beyond the capabilities of such primitive creatures:

> Here emerges a great principle of human institutions, confirming the origin of poetry disclosed in this work: that since the first men of the gentile world had the simplicity of children, who are truthful by nature, the first fables could not feign anything false; they must therefore have been, as they have been defined above, true narrations.[8]

The process of myth-creation by 'natural necessity', together with the principle of 'natural signification', guarantees a reliable pattern of correspondences between primitive mental and linguistic processes and the objects imagined or signified by them. The ensuing 'vera narratio', moreover, is free from the distorting effects of deliberation. We shall see later how Vico arrived at this idea of a stable pattern of relationships in early structures of thought and feeling. For the moment it is sufficient to note that it is the basis of his claim that early man was a 'poet' and thus a kind of historian by nature.

5. *SN* 209. Italics mine.
6. *SN* 413.
7. See *SN* 401.
8. *SN* 408.

Given the originality of this approach to interpreting early poetry, it should not surprise us, when we examine Vico's own application of the system, if we come across certain factual errors which critics have emphasized in his etymological conclusions. But a more important question, it seems to me, is whether or not there are rational deficiencies in the various aspects of the theory which may be producing these empirical 'lapses'. It seems, in fact, that he was himself aware of certain difficulties. The problem relating to the 'vera narratio' is twofold – theoretical and methodological – and, whereas Vico explicitly indicates a methodological difficulty, though without giving it formal recognition, he seems not to have been aware of any serious conceptual shortcomings.

The methodological problem arises because, whereas for Vico early poetry and myth present infallible pictures of primitive mental and social conditions, the evidence upon which such correlations are to be established is never transmitted incorruptibly:

> The fables, which at their birth had come forth direct and proper, reached Homer distorted and perverted. As may be seen throughout the Poetic Wisdom above set forth, they were all at first true histories, which were gradually altered and corrupted, and in their corrupt form finally came down to Homer. Hence he must be assigned to the third age of the heroic poets. The first age invented the fables to serve as true narratives, the primary and proper meaning of the word *mythos*, as defined by the Greeks themselves, being 'true narration'. The second altered and corrupted them. The third and last, that of Homer, received them thus corrupted.[9]

So, although Vico frequently writes of Homer as an expression of the development of the Greeks throughout the whole heroic period, as we can see from this passage he associates him more specifically with the final phase of the era, the period in which the pre-existing fables were actually recorded. Yet the *actual recording* of the fables required a certain reflective capacity, and therefore took place at a time when the human mind had already sufficiently evolved to be able to produce at least some of the distorting effects of artifice and deliberation. He makes the point just as clearly elsewhere when he states that the Greeks imputed their own dissolute and corrupt practices to the gods in an attempt to justify themselves. In this way the original fables had 'lost their original meanings and were altered and obscured in the dissolute and corrupt times [beginning] even before Homer'.[10]

9. *SN* 808. See also *SN* 81, 814.
10. *SN* 221.

It is clear that this important factor in the recording of fables threatens to undermine the stability of the entire naturalistic framework of Vico's 'vera narratio'. Yet in spite of this serious deficiency he suggests no method of discriminating between those elements of the fables which can be taken as truly 'natural' expressions of human 'necessities', mental processes and institutions and those that have undergone post-reflective corruption during the process of transmission. In fact, many of the methodological advantages provided by the 'vera narratio' seem to vanish when we consider that there is no logical reason for supposing that the whole corpus of the epic tradition was not affected by the 'corrupting' influence which he mentions. This being the case, without adequate discriminatory instruments independent of the recorded fables themselves the concept of 'vera narratio' is gravely weakened as an investigative principle. Moreover, in the absence of such validatory processes the feasibility of the concept as an adequate description of the real evolution of myth lies well beyond the bounds of verification. In the light of these limitations it has to be admitted that many of Vico's mythological interpretations in the *Scienza nuova* seem to display a somewhat unwarranted definitiveness.

It seems to me necessary, therefore, to note these methodological problems, for Vico's achievement must after all be set against the claims he makes for his work. In the opening section of the *Scienza nuova*, entitled 'Idea of the Work', he claims that the heroic fables 'were true stories of the heroes and their heroic customs, . . . so that the true poems of Homer are found to be two great treasure houses of discoveries. . . .'[11] The 'vera narratio' as expressed in the 'true stories' or histories referred to is part of Vico's attempt to effect a wholesale cultural transformation by means of which history is delivered from its Cartesian subordination to abstract and anachronistic systems of thought. His historicization of the study of myth is, in short, meant to produce a more methodologically secure science for uncovering the facts of humanity's infancy, for 'by virtue of new principles of mythology herein disclosed . . it is shown that the fables were true and trustworthy histories of the customs of the most ancient peoples of Greece'.[12] Vico's originality, therefore, at least in his own view, does not consist simply of perceiving in greater depth than anyone had done before him the relation between ancient literature and concrete historical practices and institutions; instead, this general perspective is advanced in

11. *SN* 7.
12. Ibid.

terms of certain definite propositions about 'natural necessity' and 'natural signification' determined by specific conditions of barbarity and reflective incapacity. He is making, in other words, a series of highly specific and distinct assertions, not merely advancing a generalized insight, a fact which I do not think has so far been adequately stressed. The value of the particular heuristic principles he puts forward, moreover, depends upon the degree of 'natural correspondence' that can be demonstrated between ancient myth, language and fables, on the one hand, and the primitive needs and institutions they are meant to express on the other.

We have already seen that even in Vico's own terms there can be no recorded history before the phase of reflective corruptibility. So, on the basis of mythological evidence alone Vico can never guarantee the reliability of his conclusions. This means, in practice, that he is unable to take historical validation beyond the limits of a more or less inspired or perceptive historical impressionism.

The problems we have noted so far arise from within the theory itself. The very recording of the evidence Vico requires implies a 'corrupting' process which neutralizes the natural signification which gives the original fables their quality of a 'vera narratio'. But an even more crucial problem in a sense is the fact that the process of natural signification itself remains an unsubstantiated hypothesis. It is not simply that the recording operation obscures an earlier 'vera narratio' which was thoroughly reliable. Vico in fact proposes no independent means of demonstrating that his hypothesis concerning 'true narration' has any sound historical basis at all. It remains, at best, sheer conjecture. Inspired it may well be, even brilliant; but his apparent indifference towards validatory criteria is no minor defect. In fact, as we shall see in later chapters, this fault was determined by a series of insoluble problems arising out of the magnitude of the theoretical task he had set himself.

If the methodological consequences of the 'vera narratio' prove to be problematic, this is no less true of the concept itself and of its underlying basis, the doctrine of 'natural signification'. Vico created a theoretical opposition between the notion of natural signification and that of the meaning of language established by convention. He sees the latter as more appropriate to rational man. Its absence is important, by contrast, in early man's creation of fables, since it guarantees the purity of the 'natural' process, untainted by the distorting effects of reason. The overall naturalistic framework within which the 'vera narratio' is cast thus demands an opposition between nature and convention.

But there are problems in postulating such a polarization. The language of gestures created by early man, argues Vico, was created naturally by a creature incapable of reflection. This being so, it could not have been the result of agreement or convention. It is not at all self-evident, however, that conventions are incompatible with the world of instinctual and natural expression. The animal world, for instance, is full of highly 'conventionalized' instinctual behaviour. One could indeed argue that there is an even greater need for convention at the level of natural existence, since the very regularity and reliability of instinctual behaviour patterns are basic to survival. So there is, it seems, a greater interpenetration than Vico allowed between so-called natural expression and conventional structures.

To illustrate the argument, Vico was fond of imagining a world in which primitives must first of all have communicated through gestures which bore a natural resemblance to the idea being expressed. For example, gestures resembling three scything movements were a 'natural' expression of the idea of three years, that is, three cycles of the seasons.[13] But the association or connection that Vico suggests requires much more mental abstraction than he supposed. First of all the ability to conceptualize a cycle of seasons, and then to associate a simulated scything movement with such a concept are highly complex associative processes. Besides, the quantification of such movements, in order to signify a given number of years, is hardly natural in Vico's sense of the word. One could conceive of a number of equally plausible 'natural' symbols signifying a year: for example, gestures, depicting the various activities connected with harvesting, collecting of bundles during the early gathering of crops, and so forth. It is difficult to see, moreover, how one particular gesture could be selected from amongst all the other conceivable ones except on the basis of some form of agreement or convention.

Had he been less hostile to the conventionalist thesis and seen it less as an adjunct to the anachronistic 'rationalist' interpretations of myth to which he was opposed, Vico might have incorporated an element of choice or selection into his description of early linguistic development. He would undoubtedly have had to sacrifice something of the heuristic force he attempted to bring to the 'vera narratio', but since its power is largely destroyed in any case by the difficulties we have discussed above, he would have lost nothing in

13. See *SN* 431. Vico's choice of scything movements as an example of the pre-reflective language of gestures among primitives is open to question. The use of such an implement suggests a variety of rational skills associated with its construction and use, a certain organization of labour, and so on.

real terms. On the contrary, he would have drawn a less implausible divide between the all-truthful early period of pre-reflective poetic creation and the appearance of a later 'falsifying' period of reason.[14] Likewise, without diminishing the impact of the highly original historicist dimension he had brought to the deciphering of early forms of expression, he might well have tempered some of his more fanciful and extravagant claims, based as these often are on the highly dubious etymologies he professed to found on relations of 'natural necessity'. Writing of the use of hieroglyphs – the first graphic form of expression – Vico states that

> it was by a common *natural necessity* that all the first nations spoke in hieroglyphs. . . . In northern Asia, Idanthyrsus, king of Scythians . . . used five *real words* to answer Darius the Great, who had declared war on him. These five were a frog, a mouse, a bird, a ploughshare, and a bow. The frog signified that he, Idanthyrsus, was born of the earth of Scythia as frogs are born of the earth in summer rains, so that he was a son of that land. The mouse signified that he, like a mouse, had made his home where he was born; that is, that he had established his nations there, etc. . . .[15]

One may well be willing to concede a certain ingenuity in Vico's interpretation of the symbols used in this passage. But to characterize the relationship between signifier and signified as one of 'natural necessity' strains our credibility to a considerable degree. It is mistaken, therefore, to pass off the etymological absurdities noted by linguisticians such as De Mauro as empirical errors.[16] They are not simply the products of unsound methodology, but are in large part conditioned by an inflexible *theory* of the 'naturalness' of the linguistic, imaginative and mental practices of early man.

Fortunately, Vico's historicization of the concept of myth survives the deficiencies we have noted. It is true that he was frequently indebted to earlier scholars and thinkers, even though he did not always feel free to acknowledge their influence. Bacon, for instance, had written of primitive forms of graphic expression, while Spinoza had spoken of Scripture as a collection of stories suitable for primitive minds. Vico was also heir to the remarkable

14. For a detailed discussion of this problematic transition from early to late linguistic and mental forms, see Cantelli, *Mente corpo linguaggio*, pp. 152–62; 231ff; 255ff.

15. *SN* 435. Italics mine.

16. Tullio De Mauro, 'From Rhetoric to Linguistic Historicism' makes the following observation, in which is included Leibniz's etymological explorations: 'Vico and Leibniz will not arouse any deep interest in the historians of linguistics. When they engaged in etymological research the results were absurd; thus, in that respect, they deserve a negative verdict or a compassionate silence'. (p. 284.)

achievements of etymologists such as Lorenzo Valla in the field of historical linguistics. Yet none of these scholars had drawn together the various strands of these insights into an evolutionary scheme. It is the very range and boldness of the enterprise that in part at least produced the theoretical ambiguities we have noted. For the moment, however, there are further aspects of his conception of language which require examination.

5

Linguistic Creativity and the Anomaly of the Third Epoch

The concept of the three ages or phases of human development is a commonplace in Vichian studies. Its epistemological corollary is that humanity's mental capacity moves from a predominantly 'sense'-oriented understanding during the age of the gods, through a phase which is dominated by a vigorous 'imagination' during the age of the heroes, and then on to a final 'rational' stage which he calls the age of men. There is a tendency in the critical literature to assert that Vico conceived of the mental characteristics of the earlier phases as being carried over into the later ones. While this may indeed seem a reasonable assumption at first sight, it is hard to square with what Vico actually says. It is, however, a widely argued view among a substantial number of scholars, and its major elements require some discussion and scrutiny.[1]

The main features of this interpretation can be summarized as follows:

(*i*) that the mental forms of the first two periods of humanity (i.e. of the gods and of the heroes) constitute a generalized or single 'poetic' frame of mind;

(*ii*) that this stage of development and expression does not result from any deficiency or poverty of linguistic capacity in early humanity;

(*iii*) that this early 'poetic' capacity lives on into the final stage of development as humanity's aesthetic faculty.

Plausible though these propositions may seem, Vico seems to me to deny them as such. Briefly, from (*i*), the conflation of the early periods into a single type of poetic mentality or language is somewhat problematic. The stages are, in fact, distinct and early man's linguistic and 'poetic' production are explicitly related to his

---

1. A more detailed argument against this interpretation can be found in my 'The Poetic as an Aesthetic Category in Vico's *Scienza nuova*'. For arguments in its favour cf. particularly D. P. Verene, 'Vico's Science of Imaginative Universals and the Philosophy of Symbolic Forms'. By the same author see also *Vico's Science of Imagination*.

changing forms of mental operation: 'Men at first feel without perceiving, then they perceive with a troubled and agitated spirit, finally they reflect with a clear mind'.[2] What I think misleads some critics is the fact that Vico often conflates the two early phases in his purely descriptive characterizations of primitive man. This is because he had not worked out all the empirical or historical details implicit in the distinction; but such a fact cannot be used to deny that he had made the distinction in the first place. Furthermore, his use of the descriptive term 'imaginative universal' to describe the mental products of both periods should not be used to imply an *identity of form* in the mental processes of both periods, any more than terms such as 'mental image' or 'emotive construct' – which can be used to denote very different conceptual or affective experiences ranging from those of primitive cave-dwellers to those of modern man – imply that such experiences were identical. Vico's failure rigorously to maintain his tripartite distinction at all levels of his historical and descriptive discourse must not then lead us to suppose that he had abandoned it at a fundamental theoretical level. Those who doubt this should refer to Book 4 of the *Scienza nuova*, where his description of the 'course of nations' in all their forms of development – languages, customs, laws, etc. – follows a rigorous tripartite scheme.

But while the interpretation which conflates the first two periods of his evolutionary scheme can be based in a certain way on ambiguities or empirical conflations in the text, it is however harder to justify (*ii*), namely, that 'poetic' expression is not born of inexperience and poverty of language. It is enough to recall just one of the many occasions on which Vico stresses precisely this point: 'In this way the nations formed the *poetic language*, . . . *It was born entirely of poverty of language and need of expression*'.[3] As is made clear in this passage, and other similar ones, not to mention the whole context of the discourse, Vico's concept of early man's 'poetic' language is totally bound up with the latter's inarticulate, violent and passionate nature. The term 'poetic' is not, in other words, an 'aesthetic' concept in the *Scienza nuova*.

In response to (*iii*), therefore, there seem to be good grounds for asserting that there can be no continuity in Vico's scheme between such a 'poetic' process and the 'arte poetica' he distinguishes as characteristic of the final, 'rational' stage of human development. One can, in fact, go further than this and argue their fundamental

2. *SN* 218.
3. *SN* 456. Italics mine. See also *SN* 453–4 and the whole section *SN* 456–72.

incompatibility, for 'it has been shown that *it was deficiency of human reasoning power that gave rise to poetry* so sublime that the philosophies which came afterward, *the arts of poetry and of criticism*, have produced none equal or better, *and have even prevented its production*'.[4]

There is a further difficulty, however. Closely related to the view we have just been questioning is the thesis of the 'contemporaneity' of the three forms of language. This idea has been powerfully argued and ably utilized by the distinguished linguistician and Vichian scholar A. Pagliaro.[5] Without denying the historical thrust Vico gives to his linguistic insights some commentators argue that there are textual, and indeed, conceptual grounds in the *Scienza nuova* for the asertion that the basic linguistic forms characteristic of each epoch do in fact overlap or even coexist. This argument, if correct, gives substantial support to the idea that one can find the basis of an aesthetic theory in Vico. If this is not the case, how is one to understand *SN* 446, where he writes that 'as gods, heroes, and men began at the same time (for they were, after all, men who imagined the gods and believed their own heroic nature to be a mixture of the divine and human natures), so these three languages began at the same time, each having its letters, which developed along with it'. Whichever way one looks at the question, there are ambiguities in Vico's remarks at this point. The problem is initially one of deciding whether the difficulties are conceptual or linguistic. The contemporaneity thesis, which assumes that there is a conceptual problem to explain, involves the difficulty of explaining what Vico can mean by stating that forms of language which are characteristic of and develop in successive periods also begin at the same time. One can clearly assume in one way or another, as do the scholars I mentioned, that linguistic forms which evolve out of each other must have a common source of origin. This is a strong point, and one can argue an explanation around such ideas.

My own reading of the passage is different, and I think the problem is linguistic and not conceptual. In other words Vico could have been clearer, more explicit, in a manner which would have removed the difficulties surrounding this otherwise puzzling passage. If we take *SN* 446 in the total context of the paragraphs which precede and follow it we find that the overall concern of these

4. *SN* 384. Italics mine. See also *SN* 821–2.
5. See A. Pagliaro, *Altri saggi di critica semantica.* See especially 'Lingua e poesia secondo G. B. Vico' (pp. 299–444), where he deals more particularly with the question of 'contemporaneity' from pp. 411ff. See also A. Battistini, 'Gli studi vichiani di Antonino Pagliaro' for a fuller bibliography of Pagliaro's writings.

passages is to reconcile the phenomena of different languages with Vico's postulated uniformity of linguistic development in all nations. In *SN* 445 he asks 'How is it that there are as many different vulgar tongues as there are peoples?' The linguistic differences between the nations (which are explained in terms of factors such as climate), however, conceal common clusters of ideas and experiences, because 'evident confirmation of this is found in the proverbs, which are maxims of human life, the same in substance but expressed from as many points of view as there are or have been different nations'. Continuing in *SN* 445 Vico refers next to the idea of a mental dictionary common to the languages of all nations 'reducing them all to certain unities of ideas in substance' though expressing them in different forms. A few sentences further on he refers to Thomas Hayne's writings on the 'harmony' of various languages. Throughout, Vico's major preoccupation remains that of fitting the reality of different nations into his scheme of linguistic development, and this overall concern stays with him through *SN* 446, 447 and 448.

In *SN* 446 Vico assumes that the reader is still with him, still alert to his concern with the question of *different nations*. When, therefore, he states that the three epochs and the three corresponding forms of language began 'at the same time', he does not mean at the same time *as each other* but rather at the same time or point *in (the histories of) the different nations*. Given his train of thought it is easy to see why Vico omits a further specification he does not see as necessary. He is concerned at this point to stress the fact that the gods – heroes – men pattern of development *common to all nations* (i.e. begins at the same point *in each of them*) gives rise to a corresponding common pattern of linguistic development. He then continues, in the same vein, to explain in *SN* 447 that the order and succession of gods is the same in all nations while the names are different, and in succeeding passages performs the same exercise for the common order of development of the parts of speech in all nations. Essentially, therefore, the problem facing the reader of *SN* 446 is a choice of qualifier for the phrase 'at the same time', that is, a choice between *as each other* or *in different nations*. Whereas the former perhaps springs to mind more readily, it seems to me that the sense of the section as a whole requires the latter.

Vico's statement in *SN* 412 (and a similar one in *SN* 629) to the effect that 'poetic speech which our poetic logic has helped us to understand continued for a long time into the historical period, much as great and rapid rivers continue far into the sea, keeping sweet the waters borne on by the force of their flow . . .' has also been taken to suggest a degree of contemporaneity of linguistic forms. Strictly speaking, in this passage we are dealing with overlaps rather than contemporaneity, and Vico seems to be justifying exceptional 'survival' of characteristics from the earlier period rather than theorizing a total integration. The surviving characteristics are carried along by their natural power and momentum 'for a long time' – which implies that it is neither a permanent nor strictly schematically normative state of affairs.

The tendency of some critics is to see in the existence of links, overlaps and even coexistence between the different linguistic moments of Vico's philosophy the basis of a conception of artistic creativity. By contrast, it can be argued – and this is indeed my own persuasion – that the points of separation between the linguistic moments are functional, indeed part of a 'naturalistic' philosophy which inverts our normal assumptions. I think it is mistaken, therefore, to dilute the tension which exists between the phases in Vico's historical periodization. For example, rationality, philosophy and the 'poetic arts' actively prevent the production of 'poetic' language of the sort to be found in the early Greece of Homer. The language and poetry of Homer, argues Vico in *SN* 785,

> is certainly not characteristic of a mind chastened and civilized by any sort of philosophy. Nor could the truculent and savage style in which he describes so many, such varied, and such bloody battles, so many and such extravagantly cruel kinds of butchery as make up all the sublimity of the *Iliad* in particular, have originated in a mind touched and humanized by any philosophy.

Vico's concept of poetic 'sublimity' is indeed difficult to interpret, and, as we can see, is in total conflict with that which is ascribed to him by those who aestheticize his thought. It arises out of primitive brutality, and out of those violent passions and uncontrolled feelings which are the direct antithesis of the characteristics we usually associate with the production of 'sublime' art.

This use of 'sublimity' in the *Scienza nuova* is by no means an isolated eccentricity. It forms, in fact, part of Vico's wholesale reversal of a long-standing intellectual tradition whereby man's rational faculty is assumed to be the constitutive principle of all his creative and inventive powers. As the problem appeared to him, human rationality implied within this tradition a transcending of man's 'nature' in such a way as to reduce the latter to the status of a collection of more or less regrettable, even if necessary, instincts and tendencies, all linking him with the lower orders of animal

existence. Vico attempts, therefore, to reinstate the 'natural' order
at the centre of man's creative capacities. The reader should bear in
mind the shift in conceptual associations Vico is trying to bring
about in his descriptions of early man. As will become increasingly
clear, even his references to early man's primitive and savage
customs are part of his attempt to assign to this more 'naturalistic'
phase of human evolution a creative power we habitually associate
with later, more civilized periods. By noting this tendency we
make more sense of that inversion of certain elements of discourse
in Vico which the modern reader finds so puzzling and is tempted
as a consequence to ignore.

When Vico speaks of early man's creative or inventive powers he
is not thinking, therefore, in terms of a well-developed faculty of
reflection. On the contrary, such creative capacities as he envisages
are the stronger the more man is immersed in the world of natural
or instinctual responses. This is why he argues that in its early
phases of development human nature 'was a poetic or creative
nature'.[6] And it is in this initial stage of language development that
man is linguistically at his most creative, that is, in accordance with
the process of 'natural signification'. That process is governed, in
its turn, by the requirements of 'natural necessity'. Hence Vico
frequently reminds the reader that poetic speech arose as a 'necessity of human nature'.[7]

The early, creative phase of man's existence is the one in which
he developed his skills for surviving in the natural world. As such,
it lent an immediacy and urgency to his expressive requirements.
'Natural necessity', in other words, largely dominated the process
of linguistic construction. We have seen, in a different context, that
Vico characterized this process as one of 'natural signification'. We
have also seen that he defined linguistic signs as having a certain
natural or necessary relationship with their object. On the other
hand, the fixed nature of the relationship excluded the possibility of
consciously elaborated variants or linguistic superstructures until a
later stage. Consequently, in the production of signification during
this whole period, there is a markedly unilinear principle of linguistic evolution.

For Vico, the unidimensional relationship described between
signifier and signified is a necessary part of primitive symbolism,
and proves to be an important argument in his polemics against
'concealed wisdom' and 'allegorical' theories as interpretations of

6. *SN* 916.
7. *SN* 460. See also *SN* 409, 435, 833.

early myth. As Nancy Streuver has stressed,[8] he argues for a 'univocal' as opposed to an 'analogical' etymology as the key to understanding the symbolic forms of early language. 'Poetic' man, according to Vico, did not possess the discursive and reflective abilities to invent the analogical patterns of discourse necessary for the construction of allegorical meanings. The meanings of the symbols of his 'poetic speech' were 'univocal', literal, fixed. It is only in the 'vulgar speech' of later, more literate man that one finds analogical modes of discourse. Behind the apparent allegories of 'poetic' man's myths, therefore, 'must be the etymologies of the poetic languages, which would make their origins all univocal, whereas those of the vulgar languages are more often analogical'.[9]

If on the one hand Vico's 'naturalism' imposes on early language a rigid pattern of evolution which seems at first sight at variance with accepted notions of human creative capacities, there is on the other a sense in which it provides such notions with a firmer base in material reality. It does so by relating the concept of 'creation' less to mental activity than to the 'necessity of human nature', which for Vico embraces all aspects of early man's struggle to survive. The starting point of human language is thus to be found in the efforts of mute-like, stammering creatures to produce articulate sounds. The cadences and rhythms of early verse were formed in this way: 'Concerning song and verse, since men are shown to have been originally mute, they must have uttered vowel sounds by singing, as mutes do; and later, like stammerers, they must have uttered articulate consonantal sounds, still by singing'.[10] Even the physical inflexibility of the vocal cords of these early men was an important 'natural' determining factor: 'Again, this first song of the peoples sprang *naturally* from the difficulty of the first utterances, which can be demonstrated both from cause and from effect. From cause, since in these men the fibers of the organ for articulating sounds were quite hard, and there were very few sounds they could make . . .'[11]

The negative aspect of Vico's 'naturalism' points to early man's natural incapacity and physical limitations. There is a positive feature, however, in the fact that the need to construct words, concepts and images correponding to emergent social needs was accompanied by a highly fertile imagination. Thus early man invented gods to sanction certain institutions and practices. But it must not be forgotten that this 'creative' activity, and the strong

8. N. S. Streuver, 'Vico, Valla and the Logic of Humanist Inquiry'.
9. *SN* 403.
10. *SN* 461.
11. *SN* 462. Italics mine.

imagination which underlies it, were inevitably accompanied by primitive ignorance:

> but they, in their robust ignorance, did it by virtue of a wholly corporeal imagination. And because it was quite corporeal, they did it with marvelous sublimity; a sublimity such and so great that it excessively perturbed the very persons who by imagining did the creating, for which they were called 'poets', which is Greek for 'creators'.[12]

These early 'poets', moreover, created their gods 'on certain occasions of human necessity or utility'.[13]

Successive commentators, in the wake of Croce, have uprooted this strong imaginative faculty from its natural habitat in the instinctive drives and emergent social impulses of Vico's primitives. They have either idealized and de-historicized, or otherwise obscured the literal effects of his statements, transforming them into expressions of an aesthetic philosophy. It is indeed tempting to absorb Vico's thought into more modern semantic patterns, but there seems to me little doubt that fidelity to the text of the *Scienza nouva* demands that this tendency be resisted.

An intensely practical creative power is thus alive in early man before the eventual development of rationality in the age of the 'filosofi'. It is, as he frequently repeats, the practical inventive capacity which, early on in man's evolution, ensures that he possesses all the 'necessities' and 'utilities' of life:

> And in those first times all things necessary to human life had to be invented, and invention is the property of genius. In fact, whoever gives the matter some thought will observe that not only the necessaries of life but the useful, comfortable, pleasing, and even luxurious and superfluous had already been invented in Greece before the advent of the philosophers.[14]

Creativity, inventiveness, genius: in the *Scienza nuova*, these interrelated qualities signify practical capacities of a pre-reflective kind. Vico insists on maintaining a clear division between the periods of 'creative', 'poetic' imagination and the epoch of rationality. 'Genius' ('ingegno') and rationality thus typify different epochs.[15]

Two further points must be made concerning the early periods of

---

12. *SN* 376.
13. *SN* 392.
14. *SN* 498.
15. Vico occasionally uses the term 'ingegno' to describe a rational capacity (Bergin and Fisch translate its use in *SN* 785 and 794 as 'mind' and 'ingenuity' respectively). Each use is, however, clear from the context and leaves the basic distinction Vico makes between 'creative' and 'rational' capacities intact.

creative capacity or genius. The first takes us back to the de-historicizing interpretations of later critics which transform Vico's imagination/reason distinction into an aesthetic epistemology. The plausibility of such interpretations is further weakened when we remember that the 'poetic' language which expresses early man's creative capacity is not the product of gifted individuals. Vico states, in fact, that the fables and myths resulting from this 'poetic' language 'must have been the manner of thinking of entire peoples, who had been placed under this natural necessity in the times of their greatest barbarism'.[16] Another reason, therefore, for rejecting the 'aestheticist' reading is that not only are the most 'creative' epochs of linguistic evolution confined to earlier phases of development, but furthermore such processes of 'poetic' invention are part of the innate creative impulse of a 'senso comune' shared by *entire peoples*.[17]

The 'poetic' language of early man had nothing to do with the free and creative urges of gifted individuals whose artistic capacity is judged precisely by their ability to *rise above* the common structures of thought and feeling characteristic of Vico's 'senso comune'. In the *Scienza nuova*, the very essence of the sublimity of the incomparable Homer lay in the faithfulness with which he reflected the feelings of those times,

> in his wild and savage comparisons, in his cruel and fearful descriptions of battles and deaths, in his sentences filled with sublime passions, in the expressiveness and splendor of his style. All these were properties of the heroic age of the Greeks, in which and *because of which* Homer was an incomparable poet, *just because*, in the age of vigorous memory, robust imagination, and sublime invention, he was in no sense a philosopher.*[18]

We recall that the 'master-key' to the *Scienza nuova* was Vico's discovery that early poetry, fables and myth could be used as raw materials for historical analysis. For this reason he invented the idea of the 'vera narratio'. We are now in a position to link this methodological aspect of the *Scienza nuova* with our present discussion, in which we have seen that 'poetic' language is the language of entire peoples. *The very essence of the 'vera narratio' demands that 'poetic' language should reflect the thoughts and feelings of an epoch and not those of gifted 'innovators'.* A theory of poetic production relying

---

16. *SN* 816.
17. Indeed Gianfranco Cantelli argues that the very term 'universale fantastico' was intended by Vico to draw attention to the collective nature of the early imagination. See *Mente corpo linguaggio*, pp. 53ff.
18. *SN* 893–6. Italics mine.

on the concept of 'gifted individuals' would, in fact, undermine the theory of 'correspondences' so essential to Vico's historicist scheme and simultaneously diminish the importance of Homer's poetry for historical research. The concept of creative imagination essential to modern aesthetic perspectives derives from the belief in the independence or transcendence of the natural order by certain individuals which carries with it a heightened capacity for artifice. In referring to the Greek epic, Vico could hardly have expressed the point more clearly than when he wrote: 'the Homeric poems, having been regarded as works thrown off by a particular man, a rare and consummate poet, have hitherto concealed from us the history of the natural law of the gentes of Greece'.[19] In other words, to attribute the Homeric writings to the pen of a gifted individual destroys the theoretical fabric of the principles of 'natural signification' and 'vera narratio' which alone make the epics reliable historical sources. The aestheticism that Vico is so frequently claimed to be promoting is thus, in reality, one of the greatest obstacles to understanding the function which 'poetic' language acquires in his system. Its creative centre is, by contrast, firmly located *within* the realm of 'natural necessity' and not *over and above* it, in a sphere of self-conscious awareness.

A second point must also be stressed concerning the early periods of creative aptitude. Robert A. Hall Jr observed long ago that Vico 'admitted the theory that language was a product of convention only for the third, or "popular", stage'.[20] In a brief description of his three linguistic phases he does indeed remind the reader that the third kind of human language was one 'using words agreed upon by the people, a language of which they are absolute lords . . .'[21] In other words, he sees linguistic conventions as part of the rational process of exercising mastery and control over language. But the most creative periods of linguistic evolution are already over by this stage. The curious effect of Vico's linguistic theory, therefore, is to produce an account of language in which *the period of least creativity coincides with the stage at which men acquire, as 'absolute lords', a capacity for choice, discrimination and innovation in linguistic behaviour.*[22]

There are clearly some serious problems in such a theory. They derive in the main from the assumptions intrinsic to a philosophy in

---

19. *SN* 904.
20. Robert A. Hall Jr, 'G. B. Vico and Linguistic Theory', p. 151.
21. *SN* 32.
22. For a study which discusses the question of Vichian linguistic 'creativity' in the context of the classical tradition of rhetoric, see the section 'Sapienza Poetica', in M. Mooney, *Vico in the Tradition Of Rhetoric*, pp. 206ff.

which nature and the world of 'natural necessity' are seen as the repositories of all creative powers. Within this naturalistic perspective rational man, in transcending and freeing his linguistic patterns from purely 'natural' requirements, tends to distance himself from his innate creative life-source. But there is in fact no valid reason to suppose, as Vico does within his evolutionist scheme, that the 'natural necessities' and 'utilities' which he sees as the mainsprings of man's creative activity should not continue to exercise the same functions in the third phase of development as they did in the previous two. Human needs may alter, become increasingly complex and varied, but they do not disappear. Vico's argument that all the great, utilitarian discoveries were made before the late Homeric period is not among the more credible of his propositions. On the contrary, there are strong reasons for arguing that man's creative efforts, in response to necessities and utilities have achieved far more spectacular results *subsequent to the Homeric period* than they ever did before it.

The epistemological separation devised by Vico between 'ingegno' (genius or ingenuity) and 'raziocinio' (rationality) is based on a view of the latter as a sterile, analytic and ratiocinatory activity. It is not the prime source of anything new. Its concern is with the utilization and deductive juxtaposition of facts, knowledge and evidence abstracted from the initial discoveries thrown up by the more creative 'ingegno'. The tendency in the *Scienza nuova* to see in the rational stage of human development a rather sharp separation and a distancing of humanity from the realm of 'natural necessity' is probably Vico's historicized solution to a problem arising from discussions in the Valletta household during the years of his philosophical apprenticeship. The problem in question concerned the relationship between 'mind', on the one hand and, 'nature' and 'matter', on the other. Hence his interest in Lucretius and the whole atomist tradition.

One of the recurring themes emerging from the writings of the Investiganti[23] was the idea of a certain type of 'wisdom' immanent in the natural world. They talked of mechanisms and principles of self-preservation in nature and in animals; and one of the dominant preoccupations of these thinkers was the relationship of such natural 'forces' (which men supposedly shared) to 'mind'. Among the developments and offshoots from such speculations seems to have been Vico's own highly historicized brand of naturalism. His

---

23. The important early study by N. Badaloni, *Introduzione a G. B. Vico*, provides an exhaustive study of these mainly seventeenth-century Neapolitan thinkers, in relation to whom Vico maintained a cautious silence.

solution was to make the natural mechanisms and instincts of self-preservation predominate in an early period of creative vitality, and to consign rationality to a later epoch when such instincts begin to weaken. This would seem to provide a plausible reconstruction of the intellectual itinerary which led him to such a problematical separation of the qualities of 'ingegno' and 'raziocinio' into distinct epochs. We shall find additional reasons for this historical dichotomy when we examine other aspects of Vico's naturalism. For the moment, we can observe another expression of this separation in the statement that providence 'aroused human minds first to topics rather than to criticism . . .' Topics, as he goes on to explain, have 'the function of making minds inventive', whereas 'criticism has that of making them exact'. Topics, moreover, came first because in the early years of the human race, as we have seen, 'all things necessary to human life had to be invented . . .'[24]

In short, Vico conceived of the 'creative' process as a practical, and socially and materially productive activity. In terms of his linguistic theory this leads to a serious conceptual incongruity: namely, that at the point when *individuals*, by virtue of their newly acquired rationality are capable of innovation, such linguistic advances as they are able to make do not qualify as creative activity.

So apparent a contradiction is a direct result of Vico's philosophy of nature. But there is one further consequence of his theory of language which also needs to be mentioned. He does seem to possess a clear grasp of the distinction between language as a socially structured system, and language as a field of individual idiosyncratic endeavour. Yet he seems to organize the significance of the two levels diachronically. In the *Scienza nuova*, linguistic development in the two phases of the 'poetic' era takes place wholly at the socially structured level. The 'senso comune' dominates the process, and individual linguistic achievement counts for little or nothing at this stage, whereas it becomes operative in the third epoch, at which time Vico permits conscious innovation. In other words, where most philosophers would regard the distinction in question as reflecting two permanently abiding levels of linguistic activity in constant interplay, Vico consigns them to distinct and successive periods. There comes a point, therefore, when basic creative activity is complete, and the 'innovations' on the individual level which then become possible through reasoned activity are simply rational 'adjustments' to what has already been created by man's primitive ingenuity operating at the social and pre-reflective

24. *SN* 498.

levels. That is to say, in conformity with other aspects of his system, just as all the practical 'necessities' and 'utilities' of life had been created before the age of reason, the same is true of the language which expresses these needs.

In conclusion, it is clear then that Vico's conception of 'poetic' language is far removed from that contained within modern aesthetic theories. Moreover, the notion of 'creativity' associated with it gives rise to anomalies which can be traced back to his 'naturalistic' philosophy – more precisely to the function of the 'vera narratio' and to the phenomenon of 'natural signification' discussed in Chapters 3 and 4. Again, while the theological problems touched upon in Chapter 3 have not arisen in this discussion, they have by no means disappeared, since the 'poetic' language we have been examining, and its 'creative' activity, found their earliest expression in the creation of gods. In this connection Vico encountered further substantive difficulties.

Part III
The Origins of Religion and the
Growth of Institutions

6
The Creation of the Gods

Natural Theogony

The process of 'bestialization', whereby man was reduced to a state of inarticulate primitiveness following the universal deluge, was partly a device for introducing into the discourse of the *Scienza nuova* the notion of linguistic barbarity. Such linguistic incapacity was only one aspect of an overall state of social and institutional savagery produced by man's degeneration. The theological problems surrounding Vico's linguistic theory naturally had implications for his overall evolutionist scheme regarding human development. The difficulties resulted particularly from the fact that the whole social and institutional texture of primitive existence was bound up, according to the *Scienza nuova*, with the capacity of the first men – the theological poets – to create their own gods. But before examining the problems Vico faced relating to the theological implications of his theory, we should perhaps, in this chapter, outline the major features of his scheme.

In the maxim: 'Jove hurls his bolts and fells the giants, and every gentile nation had its Jove',[1] Vico restates his hypothesis concerning fixed and uniform patterns of social development in the era of the theological poets. Thus Jove is the first god to be created by all nations.[2] Yet two points must always be remembered in connection with Vico's frequent use of the notion of a common pattern, whether linguistic, mental, social or legal. It was never intended to imply the contemporaneity of developments in different nations; yet it *was* intended to undermine what he saw as an obsession among scholars with the problem of tracing 'influences' from one nation or culture to another. Hence, common features in the mental, social or legal habits or customs of different peoples did not imply the lateral transmission of culture with all its attendant problems of dating and chronology.

1. *SN* 193.
2. See *SN* 392.

77

During this early period – the era of the creation of the gods – the universal mental pattern by which the divinities were invented conforms to a fixed and uniform phase in the development of human nature itself. During this initial stage of human history men were incapable of thinking in any abstract terms, since their minds 'were entirely immersed in the senses, buffeted by the passions, buried in the body'.[3] This primitive 'sense-dominated' mentality is frequently likened by Vico to the mentality of children who attribute the qualities, feelings and passions which they themselves possess to the whole world around them. Thus lifeless objects and natural phenomena are endowed with passions and feelings similar to their own or to those displayed by their parents. To primitive man, lightning and thunder, for example, are assumed to be the angry outbursts of a being of extraordinary size and power inhabiting the heavens. So, Vico writes of the first men, 'whatever these men saw, imagined, or even made or did themselves they believed to be Jove; and to all of the universe that came within their scope, and to all its parts, they gave the being of animate substance'.[4]

The divinity of Jove was the first and most powerful of these mythical creations:

> In this fashion the first theological poets created the first divine fable, the greatest they ever created: that of Jove, king and father of men and gods, in the act of hurling the lightning bolt; an image so popular, disturbing, and instructive that its creators themselves believed in it, and feared, revered, and worshiped it in frightful religions.[5]

Other gods followed, as Vico tells us, 'from time to time on certain occasions of human necessity or utility'.[6]

'Necessity' and 'utility', as we have observed, constitute a permanent point of reference in this gradual emergence of the primitive consciousness. The theological poets, therefore, created their gods under the tutelage of the same kind of 'natural necessity' as that which determined their language. The unilinear process of image or word production (which in 'poetic language' excluded the possibility of referential variants implying rational discriminatory abilities) also persisted at this level. The uniform rhythm of human

---

3. *SN* 378.
4. *SN* 379.
5. Ibid. Vico's use of the term 'fable' needs some explanation. As with metaphors and other figurative forms at a later stage of development, he regards these individual gods as 'fables in miniature' because they encapsulate the whole mental process which creates them.
6. *SN* 392.

development, which produced instinctive linguistic expressions of 'natural necessities' at fixed stages in the evolutionary scale, accordingly produced deities as expressions of equally fixed aspects of historically determined social 'necessities'. To this process, whereby the gods of primitive man are created at crucial and significant moments in his evolution, Vico gave the name 'natural theogony'. It produced, in all nations, twelve major deities corresponding to twelve stages of development:

> The *natural theogony* above set forth *enables us to determine the successive epochs of the age of the gods*, which *correspond to certain first necessities or utilities* of the human race, which everywhere had its beginnings in religion. . . . And the twelve major gods, beginning with Jove, successively imagined within this age, serve to divide it into twelve smaller epochs and thus give some certainty to the chronology of poetic history.[7]

We can see in this passage the reappearance of the methodological principle of the 'vera narratio'. The chronology of the twelve deities 'enables us to determine the successive epochs of the age of the gods'. The historian is able, in other words, to periodize the early development of a nation by the succession of its gods. Here we meet once again the optimistic faith in the scheme which we encountered in its application to the doctrine of 'natural signification' and the stages through which that particular process worked.

We recall how 'natural necessity' determines the development of language in a fixed and unilinear manner, which contrasts sharply with linguistic behaviour at a later stage. The same principle of operation applies to the invention of the deities. There are first the gods, twelve in number, created *naturally* by the theological poets of Greece:

> first there were those of the greater gentes . . . and among the Greeks their number was so well known that they were called simply 'the twelve'. . . . following a natural theogony, or generation of the gods, framed *naturally* in the minds of the Greeks, they will be set forth in this order: Jove, Juno; Diana, Apollo; Vulcan, Saturn, Vesta; Mars, Venus; Minerva, Mercury; Neptune.

These are then followed by 'the gods of the lesser gentes; that is to say, those *consecrated later* by the peoples . . .'[8] As we can see, even in the contrast between the 'natural' creation of the first gods and the 'later consecration' of the second group of deities, the latter

---

7. *SN* 734. Italics mine.
8. *SN* 317. Italics mine.

yes -
excellent
①

result from more conscious forms of mental activity. Thus the gods created by the later 'peoples', whilst reflecting human needs, aspirations and customs, do so by means of a degree of deliberation, gradually acquiring the characteristics of rationality. Such deities, therefore, no longer possess the 'natural', expressive directness of the earlier 'major' gods.

The reservations expressed earlier in relation to the opposition Vico creates between 'natural' and 'conventional' linguistic phenomena must also apply to the distinction between the gods produced by the process of 'natural theogony' and those of the later period. When we consider the question of the representational functions of the major gods, Vico's schematic division becomes something of a methodological liability. The *qualitative* difference entailed in the distinction implies that the major gods reflect certain customs and institutions according to the canons of the 'vera narratio', while the significance of the later deities is less immediate and direct, more complex and mediated. It is difficult, however, to give complete credence to such a scheme in relation to the interpretations Vico actually produces.

Juno, for instance, is associated with marriage (or rather its rudimentary cave-man equivalent);[9] Diana represents a first human need (water), and through a series of subsequent 'fabulous' associations comes to symbolize chastity;[10] Apollo is the god of divination;[11] Vulcan, Saturn and Vesta represent, respectively, the burning of forests, the sowing of fields and the cultivating of land;[12] Mars is the god of war,[13] Venus of 'civic beauty',[14] and so forth. Now the problem associated with a number of these representational functions is that Vico derives them from accepted mythology, and in order to give them a basis in the realm of 'natural necessity' associated with primitive mankind he is forced into some of the etymological absurdities referred to earlier by De Mauro.[15]

Fortunately, the socio-institutional role of the major deities is not limited to the period of 'natural necessity'. The supposition that the gods are subject to a development which is parallel with that of man himself enabled Vico to move out of the area of implausibility into which his rigid 'naturalism' had frequently drawn him. At

9. See *SN* 511.
10. See *SN* 528.
11. See *SN* 533.
12. See *SN* 564, 549.
13. See *SN* 562.
13. See *SN* 565–6.
14. See De Mauro, 'From Rhetoric to Linguistic Historicism', p. 284.

times, therefore, his interpretations of myth are charged with that rich and resourceful imagination which is his hallmark. But it is, nevertheless, regrettably true that the qualitative distinction between the twelve major deities of the early period and those of later epochs contributes little to such interesting observations as one finds in his work as a whole.[16] Indeed, there are grounds for advancing here the same critique as was put forward earlier on the more strictly linguistic level. That is to say, that even the empirical yield from his enquiry might have benefited had Vico introduced an explicit element of nascent rationality into the early period. This would have liberated his etymological investigations from the rather constricting limits of his 'natural theogony'.

The Creation of the Gods and Moral Virtue

The religious customs arising out of early man's belief in the gods set in motion the religiously orientated, civilizing process which humanity undergoes, and which the *Scienza nuova* sets out to explore, 'for the gentile nations were everywhere founded by fables on religion'.[17] An important reason why religion has this function at the dawn of history is that 'religion is the only means powerful enough to restrain the fierceness of peoples'.[18] Early man followed the dictates of his bestial nature, but at the same time the awesome and frightful deities he created in his ignorance caused him to keep such drives in check. Thus civilization seems to be the product of a constant dialectic between instinct and restraint. He illustrates the process quite explicitly when describing man's first primitive groping towards a stable union between man and wife:

> And here it is worth reflecting how men in the feral state, fierce and untamed as they were, came to pass from their bestial liberty into human society. For in order that the first of them should reach that first kind of society which is matrimony, they had need of the sharp stimulus of bestial lust, and to keep them in it the stern restraints of frightful religions were necessary.[19]

Having given such prominence to the role of a rather rigid

---

16. One notes a flicker of uncertainty about the 'twelve epochs' in *SN* 317. This need not, however, undermine the basis of his doctrine of 'natural necessity' for he could argue that the *function* of specific deities could be exercised by a greater or lesser number of gods in the conditions of different societies.
17. *SN* 362.
18. *SN* 916.
19. *SN* 554.

'naturalism' in Vico's account of early development, one might at first be tempted to interpret this passage in the same way. Thus the fear inspired by the deities of early man would become part of that same pattern of pre-reflective instinctive response to reality which created them in the first place. As is frequently the case in the *Scienza nuova*, however, no such easy solution satisfies the requirements of Vico's uneasy and searching theoretical explorations. The fear inspired by the gods is, in fact, his attempt to infuse into primitive beings a form of response which is later capable of being socially and historically transformed into that faculty recognizable as 'free-will'. This concept presented him with two distinct problems: both doctrinal and philosophical. At present we shall confine ourselves to the manner in which Vico introduces the notion of 'free-will', together with a few preliminary caveats against overhasty conclusions.

The development of man's ability to exercise human liberty is described by Vico as the emergence of a capacity for 'conatus'. The *strategic* significance of his choice of this particular term will be discussed at a later stage, but for the present it should be noted that it can be variously translated, according to context, as 'effort', 'endeavour' or alternatively 'restraint'. The complex process surrounding the emergence of 'free-will' begins, as always, with the all-important 'utilities' and 'necessities' of the early epochs: 'Hence they [men] came to imagine that all the human utilities supplied to them and all the aids provided for their human necessities were so many gods, and feared and revered them as such.'[20*] This early fear or sense of awe is transformed into an ability to exercise 'conatus' or restraint:

> Then, between the powerful restraints of frightful superstition and the goading stimuli of bestial lust (which must both have been extremely violent in such men), as they felt the aspect of the heavens to be terrible to them and hence to thwart their use of venery, they had to hold in conatus the impetus of the bodily motion of lust.[21]

In this way, Vico argues, early man abandons his promiscuous and bestial wanderings, restrains his concupiscence, drags his partner into a cave and initiates the practice of stable unions. Thus primitive men were exercising a truly human faculty because 'they began to use human liberty, which consists in holding in check the motions of concupiscence and giving them another direction . . .'[22]

20. *SN* 1098.
21. Ibid.
22. Ibid. See also *SN* 388.

Vico introduces man's apparent capacity for freedom of choice at a surprisingly early point – in fact, during the era of the gods, when man was at his most primitive and still incapable of anything resembling ratiocination. We know this because at the stage in question we are repeatedly told that he can barely stammer, that his mental processes function at a correspondingly low level, and that he has not even reached the second or middle stage of unrestrained imagination. Yet during this period of his existence, in which he is not yet capable of rising above sense-based responses and perceptions, primitive man accomplishes something for which he would seem, according to Vico's own theory, totally unprepared. He is able to infer that the deities either disapprove of his promiscuous dealings or somehow require him to limit his sexual relationships to one partner. This clearly implies some deductive ability. Vico does not, however, explicitly draw attention to the problem. He deliberately presents early man's nascent monogamy as determined by fear, intending thereby to preserve the conditioned basis of the response. But not all fear is a reflex response to physical threats. The *objects* of fear, in this case, are certain practices, customs and habits, or more exactly, the consequences of persisting in such habits, and thus displeasing the deities.

The 'fear' Vico attributes to early men, therefore, is a conflation of two different types of emotion. One is certainly the instinctive, protective response of a creature faced with what must have appeared as menacing signs of displeasure (such as thunder and lightning) on the part of gigantic beings. The other, however, which leads him to make inferences about that displeasure, would be better described as 'awe' or even 'reverence'. Vico, in his conflation of two different states within the single concept of 'fear', is attempting to provide a stimulus for civilized virtues through what we have described more properly as a separate notion of 'awe' or 'reverence', while also wishing to preserve the instinctual base of the response by using the notion of 'fear' as a conditioned reflex. The difficulty is, however, that Vico must remain consistent with other aspects of his theory in which we have seen that at this early stage man is incapable of reason. He must, therefore, exclude 'rationality' from the sense of 'awe' or 'reverence' which leads early man to infer that the gods demand certain things of him, especially that he should appropriate a single female and form a stable union.

Since Vico consistently excluded rational behaviour from early man's field of experience, he had to find a way of accounting for human 'choice' without basing it on any ability to reason in order to retain this consistency. In *SN* 388 he seems to produce precisely the kind of distinction intended to justify such a move. Here, he repeats the arguments we have seen elsewhere concerning early man's emergent 'conatus', the abandonment of his bestial wanderings and the holding in check of his licentious impulses. This ability to exercise 'freedom of choice', he notes, is the fundamental quality of human nature; it provides what he calls 'human authority'. He then proceeds to add what seems at first sight a gratuitous distinction: 'This authority is the free use of the will, *the intellect on the other hand being a passive power* subject to truth.'[23] 'Choice', in other words, belongs to man's *volitional* capacity and not to his *rational* faculty which, we recall, within his evolutionary scheme emerges at a later stage of development.[24]

The distinction Vico makes in this passage seems irrelevant to the immediate context. The need to mention 'intellect' does not arise at this point from anything said in preceding passages. The entire aside is instead intended to anticipate a problem in the mind of the orthodox Catholic reader relating to the question of 'choice' and its connection with 'reason'. It seems most likely, therefore, that Vico was himself aware of difficulties. These will be discussed more fully at a later stage, although it is clearly necessary here to introduce a brief cautionary note on the entire issue. There is little doubt that Vico's treatment of 'free-will' as an emerging capacity gives rise to major doctrinal difficulties. The principal problems (which relate to theological questions) will become more evident as we touch upon such questions later in our discussion. They will also be highlighted when we examine his 'naturalism' more closely.

The evolution of human moral and civil virtues takes place via an increasingly active role on the part of the deities in the developing practices and customs of early man. Vico discusses, for example, the sacrificing of human victims, particularly children, to the gods; also the holding of contests and duels, the outcome of which was believed to be controlled by the gods. In this way, we are told, religion transforms cruel and savage customs into elemental human virtues. But even here, if we look carefully, we can see Vico's 'naturalism' at work. The origins of the virtue of prudence, for instance, can be found in early man's savage and violent customs,

---

23. *SN* 388. Italics mine.
24. The whole thrust of Vico's argument runs counter to traditional Catholic thinking on the relation of intellect to volition as expressed, for example, by Aquinas when he argues: 'Only a subject with intellect can act with free choice.' (*Summa Theologica*, 1a, q.59, art.3, Resp.) See also St Thomas' more elaborate argument contained in question 83 of the same *Prima Pars*, where he is most careful to preserve a compatibility or parallel between volition and reason as primary human faculties.

since 'piety and religion made the first men *naturally* prudent, by taking counsel from the auspices of Jove . . .'[25]

Vico is anxious to retain the connection between incipient human virtue and what we would perhaps term man's 'baser' natural instincts. The same passage describes the manner in which the gods rendered early men just 'in that first justice towards Jove', but he adds that this early justice, 'though it appears to be justice, was in fact savagery . . .'[26] From such crude and violent beginnings, the same 'savage' piety and religion also rendered men 'temperate, content with one woman for their lifetime. And, as we shall see later, piety and religion likewise made them strong, industrious, and magnanimous'.[27] Prudence, justice, temperance, fortitude, industriousness and magnanimity are consequently the qualities required in the construction of civilization.

Yet even at this point Vico is still anxious to preserve the role of 'natural necessity'. What is more, he remains determined to keep at a distance any suggestion that these nascent qualities are ever tinged with rationality. We must not, he tells us, interpret such virtues (as we have been taught to do so by 'effeminate poets',[28] i.e. poets of the age of reason) as qualities of men endowed with reason, for in that phase of human history men were still 'insensible to every refinement of nauseous reflection'.[29] The more we ponder the virtues he lists, however, and the practices he describes as developing in conjunction with the demands of the deities, the more difficult it becomes to accept the formal division inspired by his 'naturalism' with its rather implausible exclusion of rationality from the early experiences of mankind. Yet, having suggested that nascent human virtues and 'free-will' have their origins in a pre-reflective era, he could hardly have failed to notice the problem which thereby arose. He thus produced an expedient explanation that 'free-will' (i.e. the faculty which forms the basis of all virtues) is a property of volition and not of reason.

We shall eventually appreciate more fully how Vico was led into such positions by the overall requirements of his theory. For the moment, however, we must remain with his idea that man creates his own gods and religions. This gave rise to further problems of a theological nature which he was naturally anxious to conceal, and which merit our attention.

25. *SN* 516. Italics mine.
26. Ibid.
27. Ibid.
28. Ibid.
29. Ibid.

7

The Primitive Mind, Heretical and Pagan Sources and the Question of Orthodoxy

Arnaldo Momigliano has noted that there was a tendency among seventeenth-century historians to make biblical and pagan legends coincide. This had the effect of diminishing the qualitative difference between the two kinds of narrative, and of undermining the traditionally accepted 'veracity' of biblical history.[1] The tendency was part of a wider and growing interest in the chronology of ancient history and in the mutual borrowing of myths between cultures. Foremost among the thinkers who tended to reduce the production of the biblical stories to myth-creating activities was Spinoza. Vico, we are told, was trying to re-establish, in opposition to the latter's views, a rigid separation between the laws governing sacred and profane history, and to combat the idea that Judaism (which Christianity would later bring to completion) could be reduced to a purely human artefact in the same manner as pagan religions.

Momigliano also states in support of his argument that Vico's objections to Selden (who maintained that the 'natural law of eternal reason' was taught by the Hebrews to the Gentiles), to Bochart (who believed the Gentile languages to have been deformities of the sacred tongue), and to Huet (who held the view that the pagan myths were corruptions of the biblical stories) were based on the heretical implications of their ideas.[2] The ideas in question, however, do not seem to contain doctrinal errors; at least, such views were both highly respectable and were even held by many Catholics at the time.

In reality, Vico's opposition to these ideas is implicit in the nature of his own theory. The 'natural law of eternal reason', according to Vico, grew out of the 'natural law of the gentes' which in turn

---

1. See A. Momigliano, 'Vico's "Scienza Nuova": Roman "Bestioni" and Roman "Eroi"'.
2. See ibid., pp. 10–11.

originated in the primitive sanctions of cruel and barbarous customs. Similarly, both Gentile languages and pagan myths evolved from the naturalistic process of development previously described. Vico is hostile, in other words, to theories of early cultural interchange precisely because of their pro-rationalist and unhistorical assumptions concerning the capabilities of early man, particularly his mental capacities and his institutions. This is the reason why he opposes the views described by Momigliano; in fact, if there is any suspicion of heterodoxy, it is more likely to be found in Vico's own ideas rather than in those he opposes.

We noted earlier that there is a *strategic* level of discourse in operation in the *Scienza nuova* to which the reader must attune himself. Any failure to do so entails the risk that purely defensive statements of orthodox intent, made for reasons of prudence, may then be taken as interpretative criteria and extended to all areas of Vico's work as general principles. This, in fact, seems to have been the case with Momigliano, who argues that the *Scienza nuova* was meant to be 'a powerful support for the Catholic *status quo* against wrong beliefs of Protestants and atheists'.[3] Again, Vico's 'disengagement' of sacred from profane history, which we earlier showed to be an ingenious tactical device, becomes for Momigliano 'one of the most profound attempts to reassert a Christian – or, perhaps Hebrew – dualistic vision of the world on the eve of the age of Enlightenment'.[4]

When Vico states that the 'first substance of all myths' is the creation of gods and religious practices, he is of course careful to make his usual exception regarding the one true God and the inspired religion of the Hebrews. But this he was more or less obliged to do. In fact, such theories were regarded with suspicion even when applied to pagan religions, for they were but one step from suggesting that the same process applied to Christianity. Vico was fully aware of this, so that his disclaimer should not be seen as countering the ideas of Spinoza. On the contrary, it was almost obligatory – having said what he did about the creation of gods – in order to avoid the suspicion of sharing his ideas. Indeed, as Vaughan suggests, far from opposing Spinoza, the Jewish philosopher was one of his foremost sources, and we should not be misled

3. Ibid., p. 13.
4. Ibid., p. 23. Momigliano's assertion is restated by Rossi in *The Dark Abyss*, pp. 176ff. Neither commentator seems to take account of the positive advantages to an author like Vico of being able to detach the developments within profane history from the doctrinal and other constraints imposed by sacred history. Seen in this light, their separation, far from being a defence of orthodoxy, liberates the author from its restrictions.

by the confusion created by Vico's statements of orthodoxy because

> Vico is writing under a veil of deliberate ambiguity. If the case against Vico's orthodoxy . . . is true, then Vico would have every reason to write in such a confusing and difficult manner. We must not forget that Vico was a professor of rhetoric and had read the works of Spinoza, Hobbes and Locke and knew the importance of concealing an unpopular and dangerous doctrine.[5]

Spinoza had so shocked religious opinion as to have been formally excommunicated from the Jewish faith. Nevertheless, as we shall see, it is difficult to avoid the conclusion that Vico was familiar with the contents of the *Tractatus Theologicus–Politicus*, though he never specifically mentioned the work. In 1670, for fear of persecution, Spinoza, living in Amsterdam, published his work anonymously and under a fictitious imprint, in Hamburg. This work, which denied scriptural inspiration and argued that biblical stories were products of the primitive imagination, caused a storm in theological circles. It thus achieved widespread notoriety and went through five editions in as many years. It was banned in the Dutch Republic in 1674 and condemned by both the Dutch Reformed and the Catholic churches, the latter subsequently placing the work on the Index.[6] Its real authorship soon became common knowledge, and the ideas of the 'impious' Spinoza were precisely of a kind to arouse interest in the circles in which the young Vico moved. They were also a strong reason on his part for exercising caution.

Whereas he does not follow the Jewish thinker into the outright heresy of asserting that 'the prophets perceived God's revelation only with the aid of the imagination',[7] he certainly does seem, in the *Scienza nuova*, to be echoing certain epistemological implications of Spinoza's ideas. The latter had written that 'we must indeed inquire how the prophets became certain of those things

---

5. Vaughan, *Political Philosophy*, p. 33.
6. Even before he had been won over to the idea of a 'deliberate obscurity' in Vico's treatment of religion, Croce had referred to the near certainty of his having read Spinoza's *Tractatus Theologico-Politicus*. (See B. Croce, *The Philosophy of Giambattista Vico*, p. 196.) It should also be remembered that Vico, the son of a bookseller, was aware of a variety of sales networks and was something of an acknowledged expert in the world of books. During his lifetime there was a regular shipping link betwen Naples and the Netherlands (the *Tractatus* was published secretly in Amsterdam), so he could have obtained editions of the notorious work without any great difficulty. His reputation in the world of books was such that he was asked to make the valuation for the sale of the Valletta library, reputedly the most exhaustive private collection of books and manuscripts in Naples at the time.
7. Spinoza, *Tractatus Theologico-Politicus*, ch. 1, par. 43.

they perceived through the imagination and not by the certain principles of mental operation'.[8] Moreover, the parallels are even more striking when Spinoza pursues this point to the conclusion that 'those who are strongest in imagination are less able to understand things through pure reasoning; and conversely those who are stronger in the use and cultivation of the intellect have a much more tempered and limited power of imagination'.[9]

In addition to ideas such as these, Spinoza's attack on the veracity of biblical stories contains another theme we find echoed in Vico's ideas on the Homeric epics and their supposedly concealed wisdom and knowledge: 'Those therefore who study the books of the prophets to discover wisdom and knowledge of both natural and spiritual things are completely mistaken . . .',[10] while in the chapter on the interpretation of Scripture Spinoza castigates those who 'dream that the most profound mysteries are to be found in the sacred writings, and make themselves weary investigating these absurdities whilst neglecting all that is useful . . .'.[11] Vico's polemical remarks against scholars who attempt to find a hidden and profound wisdom in ancient writings bear a remarkable resemblance to such passages in Spinoza.

This striking similarity of treatment was noted long ago by Croce, who observed:

> We might almost venture to say that it was Spinoza's Biblical criticism that suggested to Vico his criticism of the composition and spirit of the Homeric poems; but that the latter, after passing in this way from sacred to profane history, from Moses to Homer, set his face stubbornly against the opposite transition from Homer to Moses, from profane history to sacred.[12]

These words were written before Croce became convinced of the existence of deliberate ambiguity in Vico's work. The latter's ecclesiastical critic, the Dominican Bonifazio Finetti, was from the first suspicious of Vico's intentions, and was quick to spot the subversive potential of his ideas: 'Vico's manner of philosophising seems highly suited for anyone who wishes to use it to attack and cast doubt upon Holy Scripture or divine revelation'. This was especially dangerous, continued Finetti, since it was 'an easy matter for the ill-intentioned to pass from the sphere of the profane to the

---

8. Ibid., ch. 1, par. 48.
9. Ibid., ch. 2, par. 1.
10. Ibid., ch. 2, par. 2.
11. Ibid., ch. 7, par. 5.
12. Croce, *Philosophy*, p. 196.

sacred, when one can use the same manner of arguing in both cases'.[13]

On one occasion, we recall, Vico did (whether unwittingly or not) make the transition from Homer to Moses which, as Croce correctly observed, he should certainly as a Catholic have set his face against. In Chapter 3 we drew attention to *SN* 794, a passage in which he illustrated an argument concerning the difference between the primitive and the rational minds by means of a casual reference to the primitive mentality typified by the writings of Homer and Moses. We showed then, without drawing out the Spinozist echoes, how the implications of the parallels drawn between the two ancient authors (i.e. barbarity of language and non-rational mental processes; oral transmission of legends; denial of the 'real authorship' of the writers, etc.) resulted in undermining any acceptable notion of revelation or scriptural inspiration. We shall never know whether *SN* 794, with its strong Spinozist overtones, was the innocent oversight we suggested, but it certainly seems to have escaped the notice of Finetti, and his more modern commentators, including Croce.

If Vico had intended a positive defence of the Bible against the methods of interpretation then being applied to pagan myths, the most natural target for attack would have been the 'impious atheist Spinoza'.[14] In this connection it must be remembered that he could not have done so without drawing attention to the striking parallels between Spinoza's biblical iconoclasm and his own destruction of the accepted canons of Homeric interpretation, both of which were identical in method and theoretical substance.

But if Vico's failure to repudiate Spinoza's ideas does little to support the contention that he was actively engaged in a defence of the Faith, other omissions likewise serve to reinforce the suspicion surrounding his self-declared orthodoxy. We recall from Chapter 2 his highly misleading account, in the *Autobiography*, of his alleged rejection of Lucretius. We noted then how he avoided any mention of Lucretius' ideas on a whole range of topics which happened to bear a remarkable similarity to his own, and that this reticence was

---

13. These, and other comments on Vico's application of Spinoza's ideas to Homer can be found in Finetti, *Difesa dell' autorità della Sacra Scrittura*, pp. 21–4.

14. Even if Vico had not himself read the *Tractatus*, Spinoza's reputation was notorious and a frequent target of attack. In his *Lettera in difesa della moderna filosofia*, Vico's friend Giuseppe Valletta makes a number of highly opportunistic attacks on Spinoza. Hoping thereby to allay any suspicion of heresy on his part, Valletta continues this vilification in his *Istoria filosofica*, echoing the view held by believing Catholics that Spinoza was a moral degenerate who 'denied God and his Providence, the immortality of the Soul, Revelation, the Prophets, the Devil and Hell' (G. Valletta, *Opere filosofiche*, p. 325).

hardly surprising given that some of his friends were actually tried by the Inquisition for expressing such ideas.

In connection with early religious practices Lucretius *is*, in fact, mentioned, but in a manner which is calculated to divert any suspicion of dependence upon this suspect source. In the whole of the final edition of the *Scienza nuova* he makes only three cursory references to Lucretius. One of these, a classical allusion of little importance, need not detain us.[15] The two remaining citations are also, in a sense, pieces of classical ornamentation, yet they are nonetheless significant. In both instances Vico quotes an identical passage from the *De Rerum Natura*. Having occasion, in the *Scienza nuova*, to refer to Agamemnon's vow to slay his daughter, he adds to Lucretius' comment on the king's rash promise to the goddess Artemis: 'Hence we can understand how denial of providence led Lucretius impiously to exclaim upon this deed of Agamemnon: *Tantum religio potuit suadere malorum*! – "So great were the evils religion could prompt!"'[16] This rather contrived and ritual disapproval is repeated in the other passage of the *Scienza nuova* in which the story of Agamemnon is mentioned. On this occasion, however, Vico is speaking more specifically about idolatry, pagan religions and human sacrifices. He restates his idea of the gods as inventions of early man, but supports his point with a quotation from the *Thebaid* of the more acceptable Statius: 'These things give the right sense to the saying, "Fear first created gods in the world" (*Primos in orbe deos fecit timor*) [Statius, *Thebaid* 3.661]: false religions were born not of imposture but of credulity'.[17]

Leaving aside the question of Vico's indebtedness to Lucretius in other spheres, his distancing himself from the 'impious' Lucretius and his more favourable citing of Statius might appear both innocent and of little importance. But if we examine the matter a little more closely a quite different impression emerges; for on the precise points under discussion there is a remarkable parallel between the ideas of Lucretius and those consistently expressed by Vico.

Lucretius devotes a lengthy section of Book V of the *De Rerum Natura* to the question of how reverence for the gods first arose. If we allow for Vico's more historicized elaboration of the same ideas, there are times when the *Scienza nuova* appears to be almost a translation of the more ancient work. Thus, we find in *De Rerum Natura*: 'Moreover, who does not feel his soul shrink with terror of

15. See *SN* 634.
16. *SN* 968.
17. *SN* 191.

the gods; whose limbs do not shake with fear when the dried earth trembles under the awful stroke of lightning and rumblings travel across the great skies?'[18] Not only does Vico use the same examples of primitive fear of thunder and lightning, he even attributes the latter phenomena to the same cause, the 'dry earth'[19] – an idea which can be traced to the ancient Greek cosmology of which Lucretius was a major exponent. Furthermore, as we shall see in the next chapter, Vico goes to the trouble of attempting to accommodate his chronology to this kind of cosmological theory in order to allow time after the Universal flood in Genesis for the earth to become sufficiently dry for thunder and lightning to occur, thus enabling the process of god-creation to begin. The creation of gods by unintelligent mortals is a constant theme of the *De Rerum Natura*. Ignorant of natural phenomena and their causes – it could almost be Vico speaking – men create gods because 'they behold many things happening on earth and in the sky, the reason for the occurrence of which they cannot perceive, and think that a divine power brings them about'.[20]

The evidence pointing to Lucretius as a concealed favourite of Vico's is considerable and present in numerous contexts. There is, however, further evidence suggesting that Lucretius constituted both an important source and also at the same time a problem for Vico in his attempts to obtain ecclesiastical approval for the publication of the *Scienza Nuova*. Central to Vico's ideas on the development of language, on the 'vera narratio', and also on the human invention of pagan religions and their deities is the concept of the 'erramento ferino' (feral wandering). This period of feral existence is one in which man is little more than a beast, and from which Vico's anthropological/evolutionist scheme of human development begins. We know from Nicolini's studies that many of the religious objections to the *Scienza nuova* in the eighteenth and nineteenth centuries centred around the idea of the 'erramento ferino'. Indeed, the very title of Finetti's refutation of Vico contains a defence 'of human kind accused of once having been a beast', and it is for this reason that Finetti proceeds to demonstrate the 'falsity of the feral state of ancient men'. While, therefore, the 'erramento ferino' was an idea central to the whole theoretical project of the *Scienza nuova*, it also proved to be a sensitive theological one.

Giulio Torno, as we have seen, had warned Vico of the dangers of expressing this idea. In the 1730 edition of the *Scienza nuova*,

18. Lucretius, *De Rerum Natura*, Bk V, ll. 1218–21.
19. See *SN* 62, 192, 377.
20. Lucretius, *De Rerum Natura*, Bk I, ll. 152–4.

*why depend on L, when whole
17th century was debating thing ? ?*

discovered by Nicolini, are to be found a number of annotations
and comments dictated by Vico himself, in addition to the marginal
notes we mentioned earlier.[21] Among Vico's supplementary comments is one defending the concept of the 'feral wandering' against
its ecclesiastical opponents, and it refers to an ancient classical
tradition, which includes Lucretius, amongst others, in support of
the idea:

> Some wish to dismiss as a fairy-tale this dispersion of men into a wild
> and solitary state. However: 1. We have it from ancient tradition that the
> first men were born of the earth, had led a wild, rough and meagre
> existence, etc.; that they wandered about dispersed and lost (Horace. BK
> I, sat. 3; Lucretius, BK V; . . .)[22]

Not surprisingly, in the final edition of the *Scienza nuova* we find
no such reference either to Vico's opponents or to the infamous
Book V of Lucretius' work from which in fact he drew so many
ideas.

Vico's defence of the 'erramento ferino' in this lengthy marginal
note involved a refutation of the 'pagan corruption' thesis, that is,
that pagan religions were a corruption of the true religion revealed
by God to the chosen people. In other words, he wished to retain
the 'erramento ferino' and his primitive beast-like men as the real
initiators of an anthropomorphic creation of deities. He insists,
therefore, that those who suffered the process of 'bestialization'
after the dispersion of the nations gradually *forgot* their earlier
religion and started afresh. This was also the case with their
language, mental processes, and so forth. His opponents

> cannot imagine how the descendants of Noah lost all sight of religion,
> and then created a new one; *they argue, rather, that they corrupted the ancient
> and true religion.* However: 1. It is not to be wondered at that clumsy
> stupid men should think little about religion, *and indeed lose all trace of it,
> and that later, shaken by lightning and other such phenomena, should form a
> conception of Jove,* etc.; just as they forgot and lost the language of Noah
> and created new ones.[23]

The idea of a 'pagan corruption', therefore, was in direct conflict
with Vico's theories about primitive humanity and with his whole
evolutionist anthropology. Its rationalist assumptions, moreover,
undermined the centrality of the 'feral wandering'.

21. See particularly Nicolini, *La religiosità*, pp. 91–3, and his 'Il Vico e il suo
censore ecclesiastico', pp. 281–95.
22. 'Postille inedite redatte sotto la direzione dell' autore da un discepolo', in *La
scienza nuova seconda*, p. 332.
23. Ibid., 333. Italics mine.

It is quite clear from what we have seen that in Vico's mind acceptance of the 'erramento ferino' involved the rejection of the more respectable notion of 'pagan corruption'. It is consequently mistaken to suggest that he is attacking the idea in defence of orthodoxy. On the contrary, he not only refuted it in the interests of his own theory, but, as we shall see, he was actually conscious of undermining an aspect of traditional teaching.

The Jewish contention regarding pagan indebtedness to the Hebrew tradition had found its way into Christianity at least by the time of Clement of Alexandria (*c* AD 150–215). This highly cultured Greek, steeped in the philosophical and literary thought of his time, used all his academic skill to lead souls familiar with the gods of pagan religion towards Holy Scripture. A powerful apologetic device was his establishment of links between the (corrupt) gods known to his educated audience and the true God of the new religion to which they were gradually being introduced. By the time we reach St Augustine's speculation that Plato, travelling in Egypt, must either have heard Jeremiah preach or have read the Hebrew prophets,[24] the whole issue had become a theologically academic one and was no longer a pressing missionary problem. It remained, however, within Catholic opinion, a perfectly respectable and widespread idea – one which an orthodox mind would quite naturally have hesitated to reject out of hand.

When, in the final edition of his work, Vico does attack ideas of lateral cultural interchange or assertions that 'corruptions' of Holy Scripture accounted for pagan religious ideas, he does so with circumspection *and no longer with explicit reference to the 'erramento ferino'*. Indeed, it is only when we bear in mind his desire to proceed with caution and to avoid confrontation with the censor that we can make sense of certain *non sequiturs* he places before the reader, such as his apparently gratuitous assertion that the universality of the human invention of gods in all nations is a proof of the universality of the Flood which precedes their creation. Such statements, as will become increasingly evident, amount to a 'camouflaging' technique, which Vico employs when asserting a position he knows to be theologically problematic. We can see this manoeuvre at work in relation to what we are discussing at present, that is, that pagan ideas are a 'corruption' of the true religion. Vico's mode of procedure is subtle and somewhat deceptive. If we look carefully at the passage which follows, however, we shall see that

24. See St Augustine, *De Doctrina Christiana*, Bk II, ch. 27. The idea of pagan borrowing from Judaism is also echoed in the writings of other Church Fathers such as Justin, Athenagoras and Origen.

he both denies the 'pagan corruption' theory and at the same time presents this denial as a *proof* of the truth of Christianity:

> And from this there emerges a most luminous proof of the truth of the Christian religion: that Pythagoras and Plato, by virtue of a most sublime human science, had exalted themselves to some extent to the knowledge of the divine truths which the Hebrews had been taught by the true God . . .[25]

In other words, while carefully setting aside in the final edition all mention of his pagan sources, Vico rejects the idea, first suggested by St Augustine, of pagan contact with the religious world of the Hebrews. For him, pagan religious ideas evolve independently, and he tries to render the implied rejection of the 'corruption' theory more acceptable by means of a somewhat unwarranted if expedient assertion that the idea which entails this rejection proves the truth of Christianity. Moreover, having advanced this 'proof' by showing that pagan ideas about religion arise independently of the true Faith, he concludes 'there arises a weighty confutation of the errors of recent mythologists, who believe that the fables are sacred stories corrupted by the gentile nations and especially by the Greeks'.[26] We can now return to the earlier claim that Vico wished to defend a Judaeo-Christian view of history, and that he did so by refuting the 'corruption' or 'cultural interchange' theories put forward by heretical authors. In point of fact, not only did such ideas *not* represent any threat to Catholic teaching but, if anything, Vico's coupling of his denial of such ideas with an expedient show of orthodoxy which carries little conviction, illustrates an anxiety not to offend.

All this seems to reinforce the contention that it is highly misleading to give straightforward credence to Vico's remarks about sacred history or to stress the orthodox purpose behind his work. As we shall discover more and more to be the case, there are in his writings too many textual 'manoeuvres' of this kind, all centred around theological matters, for the latter not to have presented a genuine problem. We have seen Vico struggling to avoid open conflict with certain aspects of traditional religious teaching. While, therefore, one cannot endorse the argument that the *Scienza nuova* is a positive defence of the Judaeo-Christian tradition, it would seem equally misleading to present its author as relishing the contest. When he clashed with orthodox Catholic teaching, Vico probably did so with the reluctance of the scholar who wants to be

25. *SN* 95.
26. Ibid.

allowed to pursue his ideas with the least trouble from censoring authorities. For this reason, such conflicts as occur must be elicited from a reluctant and resistant text. And nowhere does he try harder to conceal his problems than in the historical accommodation of his evolutionist scheme to an orthodox biblical chronology.

8

Vico's Scheme of Development and Its Chronological Accommodation to Sacred History

In spite of its obvious unorthodox implications, the 'erramento ferino' was theoretically an essential notion in the *Scienza nuova*. Without it there could be no convincing starting point for Vico's evolutionary scheme. Whereas in the case of de Cristofaro and other condemned thinkers man's primitive state had formed part of a general corpus of unacceptable atomist and Epicurean ideas which denied such sacrosanct doctrines as the immortality of the soul, the resurrection of the body, etc., in Vico's case every effort was made to accommodate the 'erramento ferino' to orthodox requirements.[1]

In order to retain it, however, his account of man's primitive origins had to conform with Genesis and the biblical account of the beginnings of humanity. And since the 'erramento ferino' clearly could not be posited as the 'original state' of mankind without contradicting Scripture, it had to be presented as a degeneration from the original state of humanity as described in Genesis. According to Vico, it followed from this, 'that the first people of the world were the Hebrews, whose prince was Adam, created by the true God at the time of the creation of the world'. Vico is careful never to deny the temporal priority of the Hebrews. This acceptance of the orthodox position is then followed by a statement of methodological intent, in which he suggests a relationship of interdependence between what he has just said about the Hebrews and the kind of mythological enquiry he intends to undertake: '*It follows* that the first science to be learned should be mythology or the interpretation of fables . . .'.[2] In fact there is no sense in which Vico's mythological enquiries follow from his assertion of the greater antiquity of the Jews. On the contrary, in the absence of the

---

1. Cf. the discussion of Vico's chronology and other relevant points in Rossi, *The Dark Abyss*, Parts II and III. Rossi does not, however, discuss the anomalies presented here.

2. *SN* 51. Italics mine.

97

orthodox statements which he is careful to make, the cultural thrust of his theories could be assumed to be working in the opposite direction. Students of comparative mythology had already been tending to reduce the idea of the temporal priority of the Hebrews to the level of a dogmatic irrelevance. Vico's intention, therefore, in this and in similar passages was clearly to dissociate himself from such trends.

The 'tactical' nature of his religious remarks is all the more evident because such statements invariably precede or follow arguments and ideas which could raise awkward doctrinal points. On the question of the temporal precedence of the Jewish people as described in the Bible, for example, the problem was not simply that Vico could be seen to be accepting the mythological discoveries of the historians who had already undermined the Christian belief in the greater antiquity of the Hebrews; such a notion was also threatened by his own conception of the 'erramento ferino', and even by his ideas about the origins of social life and the invention of the gods. This is why, after setting out a number of theoretical and methodological principles underlying these ideas, he states once again: 'Sacred history is more ancient than all the most ancient profane histories that have come down to us, for it narrates in great detail and over a period of more than eight hundred years the state of nature under the patriarchs . . .'[3] Now, whereas under normal circumstances the type of narration involved in sacred history, being far removed from the primitive 'natural signification' of the 'vera narratio', would be considered by him as anything but reliable,[4] in the case of the Bible this narration 'proves the truth of sacred history . . .'[5]

Vico is, of course, invoking here the idea that sacred history proceeds according to separate and distinct laws of operation. He continues: 'The Hebrew religion was founded by the true God on the prohibition of the divination on which all the gentile nations arose'.[6] This in turn explains 'the division of the entire world of the ancient nations into Hebrews and gentiles'.[7] But whilst the divergence of the two spheres enables him to solve certain problems,

---

3. *SN* 165.
4. In the passage just quoted Bergin and Fisch translate as 'narrates in great detail' the Italian 'narra tanto spiegatamente'. The translation does not fully convey the sense of 'rationality' contained in Vico's 'spiegatamente'. In fact he frequently characterizes the third, rational phase of human development as that of 'ragione *spiegata*'.
5. *SN* 166.
6. *SN* 167.
7. *SN* 168.

there is little or nothing it can do to resolve other difficulties arising out of biblical chronology.

An Antediluvian 'erramento ferino' abandoned

On the face of it, Vico's insistence in the *Scienza nuova* on the universality of the flood strikes the modern reader as perhaps either of little importance or else as a curious and superfluous piece of religious posturing.[8] Neither of these is the case for a number of reasons. Perhaps the most important is the fact that the statements concerning the flood contained in the final edition of Vico's work represent his solution to the problem of an orthodox accommodation which had dogged him ever since the 1725 edition. He did not openly articulate his difficulties because it would not have been prudent to do so. But a certain amount of textual exhumation reveals that there were numerous dilemmas to be faced.

When Vico wrote the 1725 edition there was in his view a historical lacuna which needed to be filled, the gap which he referred to as 'the lengthy period of 1656 years of obscurity in antediluvian sacred history'.[9] What he is indicating at this stage, is the necessity for what he calls a 'supplimento della storia antidiluviana', or a 'supplementary' historical account of a period of 'profane' civilization *before* the flood. In other words, he wished to begin his 'naturalistic' account of human development as early as biblical chronology would allow, even earlier than the account of the Deluge in Genesis. What he does, in the 1725 edition, therefore, is to postulate a process of 'bestialization' and a period of 'feral wandering' before the flood, similar to the one we have seen him posit as occurring shortly after it.

The manner in which Vico accomplished this adjustment to Scripture is highly problematic and, as we shall see, there are a number of possible reasons why he should eventually have abandoned this pre-Deluge cycle of human degeneration, rebirth and dissolution in the final edition deciding instead to begin the whole historial process of 'profane' history immediately *after* the flood. The idea of antediluvian degeneration presents enormous difficulties, and it is precisely in order to overcome such difficulties that he utilizes, in the 1725 edition, the biblical account of the banishment of Cain.

---

8. See *SN* 169, 192, 194, 380.
9. *SN1a* 406. Vico seems to have used the biblical chronology of the Jesuit Petau.

Finally Cain, aware of the evils of vagrant and impious living, together with a number of giants born at least within two hundred years of his bestial wandering, must have founded the city, in contempt of the religion of Adam his father, *on a divination similar in kind to that of the Chaldeans* (because before his time there was no deluge, a long time after which the sky would have had to thunder, *because perhaps before the flood it never thundered*); and he brought agriculture back to them, since having been born and brought up with a clear mind in the true religion, he had already known it; but with this single important difference: namely that Adam, enlightened by the true God, immediately found himself with articulate heroic speech. *Cain, on the other hand, because he had to bring together roaming giants on the basis of the idea of a provident deity, in order to communicate with them, had to begin with a divine mute speech.* In this way we account for the lengthy period of 1656 years . . .[10]

Rossi's suggestion that Vico eventually abandoned this passage in the final edition so as not to set back further into history the fall into bestiality fails to appreciate that this is precisely what he *had* previously hoped to achieve.[11] As we shall see, it illustrates both the lengths to which Vico would go to accommodate his scheme to the Bible, and at the same time the theoretical implausibility of any such undertaking. The difficulties presented by it are far-reaching and fall roughly into three separate types of problem.

In the first place, an antediluvian cycle such as Vico proposed contains elements of non-Hebrew civilization, such as pagan deities, languages and letters, and there is no mention of these in Genesis. Moreover, by weaving strands of biblical history into the texture of his own scheme, as he does when he makes Cain the initiator of a process of bestialization, Vico imports new historical material into traditional interpretations of sacred history. Given the suspect nature of the 'erramento ferino' of which the process of bestialization forms an integral part, it is by no means likely that such novel importations would have been acceptable if their significance had been grasped, as they certainly were by Torno. But even if Cain's improbable role had been capable of reasonable accommodation, the whole thrust of the scheme would still have given rise to further problems which might well have proved even more difficult to resolve.

Although Vico eventually abandoned the attempt to integrate into his scheme an antediluvian cycle of profane history, the fact

---

10. Ibid. Italics mine.
11. Rossi, *The Dark Abyss*, p. 181. See also Nicolini, *La religiosità*, pp. 98–9.

that he took so much trouble in attempting it initially shows how anxious he was to place the beginnings of his (Gentile) human evolution as early as possible, within the constraints imposed on any believing Catholic. It is probable that he was encouraged to do so by his reading of such authors as John Marsham,[12] John Spencer,[13] and Otto van Heurn,[14] who had argued that there were civilizations more ancient than that of the Hebrews. These 'heretical' authors were not, however, simply placing the origins of pagan civilization earlier than traditional biblical exegesis would allow, but actually arguing that the Jews had obtained their ideas of divinity from earlier sources. Thus the Hebrew religion was seen to derive from Egyptian sources or even indirectly from such practices as the Chaldean oracles. Such ideas naturally undermined the Christian pre-supposition of the divine inspiration of the Hebrew prophets. They also threatened the notion of the universality of the flood. For in the first place one could not be bound by accounts which had lost their guarantee of historical truth, and in the second God's promise to destroy the earth[15] could not have been fulfilled, since in the view of these authors evidence of pre-Jewish civilization was plentiful.

Vico came closer than he realized to acknowledging his acquaintance with such ideas when he suggested, in the passage we have just quoted, that Cain communicated to the feral degenerates around him gods derived from 'a divination similar in kind to that of the Chaldeans'. In addition to this, however, Vico's acceptance of an antediluvian cycle of non-Jewish civilization not mentioned in Genesis suggests that he was prepared to use evidence which tended to undermine the authority of Scripture. It was impossible, in other words, for him to utilize such evidence for his scheme without both compromising the credibility of his proclaimed orthodoxy and without also seeming to lend support to the arguments of such scholars as Marsham, Spencer and van Heurn.

Once again, moreover, there are good reasons for suspecting that he was concealing the extent of his knowledge of suspect authors. We note, for instance, that there is no mention of the above writers in the 1725 edition of the *Scienza nuova*, that is, when he was advancing propositions which could be associated with their ideas. Yet Vico felt free to acknowledge his acquaintance with their

---

12. *Chronicus Canon Aegypticus, Ebraicus, Graecus et Disquisitiones*, London, 1672.
13. *Dissertatio de Urim et Thummim*, Cambridge, 1669.
14. *Barbaricae Philosophiae Antiquitatum*, 2 volumes, Leyden, 1600.
15. See Genesis 6: 13.

writings in the final edition of his work,[16] by which time he had decided to abandon his attempt to include any suggestion of an antediluvian process of bestialization. The reason could well be that the danger of being associated with the views of Marsham, Spencer and van Heurn no longer existed. Indeed, in the later work, any mention of these authors actually became a positive advantage, since by selecting those of their ideas to which he was opposed they could be presented as opponents.

While the factors noted so far undoubtedly exerted some pressure on him to abandon this idea, there is nevertheless a final and more fundamental type of problem which must have caused Vico to change his mind. If we look once again at the passage in question and examine the role of Cain, together with the convenient biblical niche which his banishment seemed to provide for an early 'feral wandering', serious theoretical problems are at once evident. For the fact is that each and every act of intervention by Cain in the cycle of social degeneration and reconstruction constitutes a theoretically unacceptable interference in the evolutionary process as Vico describes it elsewhere in the work. The figure of Cain *as an individual* dominates the scene. This in itself raises major problems. So that, when we consider Vico's propositions in a little more detail, we at once understand the true proportions of these difficulties.

The most strikingly anomalous feature of the whole episode is that the social evolution of the antediluvian primitives *is actively promoted by Cain himself*. This means, of course, that in order to make the story function at all, Cain has to preserve his humanity intact while his descendants have to degenerate into the bestial condition from which Vico's scheme of evolutionary development can begin. Subsequently, according to this account, in place of the usual pattern whereby early man learns to master the world on the basis of 'necessity' and 'utility', Cain unaccountably 'brought agriculture back to them'. Then, abandoning the organic or natural processes whereby these savage creatures imagine and construct their own deities out of their ignorance of natural phenomena, we find Cain deriving such gods from possibly Chaldean sources. Conscious that such an explanation conflicts with his account of how the first major divinity grows out of the response of ignorant savages to thunder and lightning, Vico attempts to cover up the defects of his account by gratuitously asserting that 'before the flood it never thundered'.

16. See *SN* 44, 58, 66, 93, 100 and 745.

Finally, we know from passages elsewhere in the *Scienza nuova* that the early epoch of the major divinities coincided with man's first groping efforts at speech. It is the period in which he makes his first, inarticulate, stammering sounds and communicates his awe-struck experiences of the natural phenomena which he mistakes for expressions of the gods through the primitive gestures of a 'divine mute speech'. This early form of communication, inspired by experience of a 'divinity', is primitive man's first 'social' experi-ence. In the passage in question its whole 'naturalistic' dimension is however replaced by the activity of Cain who 'because he had to bring together roaming giants on the basis of the idea of a provi-dent deity' was himself able 'to communicate with them' using 'a divine mute speech'. This means that he could pass from man to brutish communicator at will. In other words, Vico removes the whole 'naturalistic' dynamic of his scheme in order to introduce an active intervention on the part of a biblical figure, so offering the prospect of a patently untenable accommodation.

It is evident from what we have already said that so contrived and implausible an expedient could not be allowed to stand. At least it could not do so without reflecting on Vico's theory. Its contortions do, however, demonstrate how anxious he was to place the beginnings of humanity as early as possible while inte-grating his account with the orthodox interpretation of the Bible. Unfortunately, he could not accomplish the task with out seeming both to court heresy and to mutilate important aspects of his own theory. It is not surprising, therefore, that he abandoned the attempt and contented himself with beginning his account from the period after the Flood.[17] Thus, in the final edition of his work he asserts more forcibly than before the doctrine of 'onomathesia': that is, that the Jews obtained their language directly from God and not from other, allegedly older civilizations. He also insists upon the universality of the Flood. Little wonder, therefore, that he sees fit at this juncture to acknowledge acquaintance with the works of Marsham, Spencer and van Heurn, since their views now appear to be in opposition to his own. In the final edition we can see how in reality – despite their neglect in 1725 – these authors must have been at the forefront of his mind even then. His own chronology, he argues,

> takes a position quite opposed to that of the Chronological Canon (*Canon chronicon, aegyptiacus, hebraicus, graecus*) of John Marsham, in

17. Vico does retain a passing reference to the idea in the 1730 edition; see *La scienza nuova seconda*, par. 1308.

which he tries to prove that the Egyptians preceded all the nations in the world in government and religion, and that their sacred rites and civil ordinances, transported to other peoples, were received with some emendation by the Hebrews. In this opinion he was followed by (John) Spencer in his dissertation *De Urim et Tummim*, in which he expresses the opinion that the Israelites had taken from the Egyptians all their knowledge of divine institutions. . . . Finally Marsham was acclaimed by van Heurn in his *Antiquitates philosophiae barbaricae* . . . .[18]

Vico had, of course, long been familiar with the arguments of these authors in favour of the greater antiquity of pagan culture. But he was also very familiar with the arguments of their orthodox adversaries. And a typical response of the latter was to assert that pagan religions were, in fact, corruptions of Judaism. We have seen that this idea of 'pagan corruption' had been advanced by some of the Church Fathers for missionary purposes amongst pagans during the early years of Christianity. In Vico's time it was being pressed into service to oppose the ideas of scholars such as Marsham, Spencer and van Heurn. In the 1725 *Scienza nuova*, Vico mentions Pierre-Daniel Huet, Bishop of Avranches, as the most learned amongst those arguing for the dependence of pagan religions upon the Judaic tradition. Huet's *Demonstratio Evangelica* was printed in 1722 in Frankfurt, although his arguments were well known before that period.[19] According to J. Duchesne-Guillemin, Huet was not simply repeating the arguments of the Church Fathers, but was polemicizing against scholars who had argued that Jewish religion and civilization were indebted to pagan cultures. After presenting the general thrust of the works of Spencer and Marsham who had argued precisely along these lines, Duchesne-Guillemin concludes that it was probable that 'such were the adversaries against whom Huet wrote his *Demonstratio'*.[20] We come now to the point of this brief mention of the work of Huet. Just as Vico seemed to be deliberately and conveniently omitting the 'heretical' authors when making use of their ideas in the first edition, and citing them as opponents when it was safe to do so in the last, the process was exactly reversed in the case of Huet. When, in the final edition of his work, Vico explicitly rejects the argument put forward by the defenders of the orthodox tradition, we find no

18. *SN* 44. See also *SN* 58.
19. See *SN1a* 30. Huet's work was known to Vico before this period. He is frequently mentioned, as a respected but misguided opponent, in the defence of 'modern philosophy' written by Vico's friend Valletta a great deal earlier. A copy of the *Demonstratio Evangelica* is listed among the volumes of the Valletta library. The latter also refers to the work in an Italianized form. *Dimostrazione Evangelica*.
20. J. Duchesne-Guillemin, *The Western Response to Zoroaster*, pp. 9–10.1.

mention at all of Huet.[21] Once more, therefore, the impression is reinforced that there is a marked tendency in the work to angle and adjust citations and omissions according to what amounts, strictly speaking, to extra-theoretical considerations.

Vico's Chronological Compression

For a combination of reasons, 1725 seems to have been a crucial year and something of a turning point with respect to Vico's proclaimed religious attitudes. His decision to go for a post-diluvian point of departure for his scheme of Gentile development, whilst partly determined by the theoretical problems already described, may also have had something to do with the narrowing of religious tolerance in the wake of the Giannone and Grimaldi affairs. A post-diluvian starting point for Gentile humanity raised fewer immediate problems, and did not associate Vico with scholars who asserted that the earth was many thousands of years older than the Bible would have us believe. St Augustine, in Book XII of the *City of God*, which Vico knew well, had attacked such ideas together with Egyptian accounts of ancient monarchies (with which he was also familiar), because they contradict 'the true account of the number of years' to be attributed to the world in Holy Scripture.

But in order to give a reasonably orthodox appearance to his account in the final edition and accept the period after the Flood as the beginnng of Gentile history, Vico had to pay a price. The necessary chronological compression within which he was forced to contain his scheme of evolution seems so forced and displays such a degree of manipulation that it is difficult to accept as anything other than an attempt at appeasement. To establish this we shall have to look at the matter in some detail. His process of bestialization begins when

> the impious races of the three children of Noah, having lapsed into a state of bestiality, went wandering like wild beasts until they were scattered and dispersed through the great forest of the earth, and that with their bestial education giants had sprung up and existed among them at the time when the heavens thundered for the first time after the flood.[22]

21. In a footnote to *SN* 95 in his Ricciardi edition of the *Opere*, Nicolini states that in rejecting the 'pagan corruption' idea Vico had in mind, amongst others, Pierre-Daniel Huet. This reinforces the argument that the failure to mention Huet (and other defenders of the orthodox position) in the final edition was probably a calculated omission.
22. *SN* 195.

The gradual loss of all human faculties is thus set in motion with the three sons of Noah – Ham, Japheth and Shem. Once reduced to a bestial state of primitive barbarity, the process of re-humanization begins when these wild creatures have their first experience of thunder and lightning and invent their fearful gods.

Now if we do not feel altogether at ease with this process of bestialization followed by a reversal into a re-humanizing cycle after the experience of thunder and lightning, then the time Vico allows for it to take place is not likely to leave us any more convinced:

> Of such natures must have been the first founders of gentile humanity when at last the sky fearfully rolled with thunder and flashed with lightning, as could not but follow from the bursting upon the air for the first time of an impression so violent. As we have postulated, *this occurred a hundred years after the flood in Mesopotamia and two hundred years after it throughout the rest of the world*; for it took that much time to reduce the earth to such a state that, dry of the moisture of the universal flood, it could send up dry exhalations or matter igniting in the air to produce lightning. Thereupon a few giants . . . who were dispersed through the forests on the mountain heights where the strongest beasts have their dens, were frightened and astonished by the great effect whose cause they did not know, and raised their eyes. . . .[23]

Within this improbably short space of time, the descendants of Ham, Japheth and Shem suffer not only total social, linguistic and mental degeneration but undergo an even more remarkable physical mutation into gianthood. The reason for such chronological compression is that once Vico had taken the Flood as his starting point, his whole cycle of 'imbestiamento', age of gods–age of heroes–age of reason, had to be contained within certain fixed points. These had to start with the Flood (2328 BC) at the beginning, and had to accommodate a number of well-established historical and cultural points of reference shortly thereafter. Once he had decided to adjust his scheme to orthodox biblical criteria, Vico was thus left with a very restricted time span and, needless to say, numerous chronological tensions appeared in the *Scienza nuova*.

One example is provided by his handling of Chaldean civilization (known as Assyrian after the reign of Ninus). The latter kingdom is dated from approximately 1247 BC in Vico's chronological table. Since monarchy is to him the final and most evolved stage of development in the scheme, and since the process of bestialization could only have begun, at the earliest, around 2328

---

23. *SN* 377. Italics mine.

BC, the full course of development (including the preceding period of degeneration) had to be completed in all its phases in something of the order of 1081 years. Yet, if we piece together other elements of chronology scattered throughout the *Scienza nuova*, we find this span of 1081 years, to say the least, highly problematic.

In the first place, we recall Vico's insistence on the uniformity of the pattern of development he describes for all nations. In this respect the Chaldeans are no exception:

> Now, in virtue of the uniform course run by all the nations, which has been proved above by the uniformity of the gods raised to the stars, as brought by the Phoenicians to Egypt and Greece from the East, *we must infer that the reign of the Chaldeans in the East covered a like period of time (1100 years)*, from Zoroaster to Ninus, who founded there the first monarchy in the world, that of Assyria. . . .[24]

Vico specifies a period of nine hundred years for the age of the gods, during which time the Gentile nations traversed all the mini-epochs of the twelve divinities. This 'natural theogony', as we have seen in Chapter 5, is the same for all nations. Thus,

> the natural theogony above set forth enables us to determine the successive epochs of the age of the gods. . . . The age of the gods must have lasted at least nine hundred years from the appearance of the various Joves among the gentile nations, which is to say from the time when the heavens began to thunder after the universal flood.[25]

Out of the total span, therefore, of approximately 1081 years for the process of development up to the Assyrian monarchy, nine hundred years are taken up for the age of the gods, which means that only 181 years remain to account for the initial period of bestialization *before* the 'natural theogony' is set in motion, together with the two epochs of the heroes and of rationality after the age of the gods has run its course. It is in order to minimize the incredibility of this chronology that Vico reduces the period of bestialization for the race of Shem, from whom the Assyrians are descended, to a hundred years:

> In order to determine the beginnings of universal history, which must precede the monarchy of Ninus . . . we set up this chronological canon: that from the dispersion of fallen mankind through the great forest of the

24. *SN* 737. Italics mine. The period of time mentioned is in fact closer to 1081 years.
25. *SN* 734.

earth, beginning in Mesopotamia . . . , a span of only a hundred years of feral wandering was consumed by the impious [part of the] race of Shem in East Asia, and one of two hundred years by the other two races of Ham and Japheth in the rest of the world.[26]

In consequence, it only leaves about 81 years for the remaining two epochs.[27] Readers can judge for themselves the plausibility or otherwise of such a chronological scheme.

Nevertheless, Vico does what he can with this particular compromise to sustain the credibility of his orthodox posture. His argument, briefly, is as follows. The first monarchy to develop was that of Ninus. This indicates that the Assyrians were the most ancient of the Gentile nations. Since, however, the Assyrians were descended from Shem, the son of Noah, their claim to antiquity cannot be as great as that of the Hebrews, who can claim an unbroken line of descent from the father, Noah. Vico also claims that the inland nations were founded first, and all these arguments prove 'the antiquity of the Hebrew people, which was founded by Noah in Mesopotamia, the country farthest inland of the first habitable world; so it must have been the most ancient of all nations. And this is confirmed by the fact that the first monarchy was founded there, that of the Assyrians.'[28] In this way Vico utilizes his chronological compromise to range himself alongside the orthodox defenders of the greater antiquity of Judaism. He thus appears to reinforce his opposition to those implicitly and explicitly denying the orthodox argument: Spinoza, Marsham, Spencer, van Heurn, Peyrère,[29] and others.

The difficulties he experienced in placing the Assyrians within his scheme of human development were repeated with the Egyptians. Here the anomalies are equally, if not more pronounced. We have seen that Vico allows a period of nine hundred years for the age of the gods. In *SN* 736 he repeats this, adds two hundred years for the heroic epoch, and in the following paragraph insists upon the

---

26. *SN* 736.
27. There can be no doubt that Vico is using the term 'monarchy' in his usual manner as denoting the final phase of social development. He makes it clear in *SN* 737 that the monarchy of Ninus must have been preceded by theocratic, heroic and popular governments. This applies also to the Egyptian monarchy.
28. *SN* 298.
29. Vico was acquainted with Isaac de la Peyrère's work *Preadamite*, published in 1655, which, as the title suggests, argued that men existed before the time of Adam. As Vico states, the work also denies the universality of the Flood. See *SN* 50. Cf. also Rossi's comments in *The Dark Abyss*, pp. 132–6. Views which, on this and other related problems, differ from those of Rossi and are closer to my own can be found in N. Badaloni, *Introduzione a Vico*, pp. 48ff. See also the comments in Burke, *Vico*, pp. 65–7.

'uniform course run by all the nations'. This extends the periodization not only to the Assyrians, as we have seen, but also to the
Egyptians, 'from Thrice-great Hermes to Sesostris, the Ramses of
Tacitus, who also founded there a great monarchy'.[30] To the
Egyptian chronology of nine hundred years for the theological era
and two hundred years for the heroic we must add a further two
hundred years of bestialization following the Flood and preceding
the two eras mentioned.

Using Vico's own chronology, this means that in the case of the
Egyptians the appearance of what he calls a 'vulgar language' (i.e.
articulate, non-versified language) at the end of the heroic period
should have occurred around 1028 BC. The first Egyptian armies
should have appeared at the beginning of the heroic period two
hundred years earlier, at around 1228 BC. According to the biblical
chronology, which Vico accepts, this is many hundreds of years
later than the time when Genesis speaks of Jewish contact with the
princes of Pharaoh. We know from Genesis 12 that Abraham
conversed with the princes. The Bible also speaks, during the time
of the great Patriarch, of numerous non-Jewish kings, armies and
alliances, etc. Since the call of Abraham must be dated by Vico at
around 2000 BC we can see that the Bible refers to articulate
language and armies *at least* seven or eight hundred years before
Vico can account for their existence, since he must allow his
scheme of 'naturalistic' development from barbarity to function
before such social phenomena as articulate language and military
organization can possibly emerge.

Ironically, since it is not bound by any theory of human development, the Bible, in relation to the *Scienza nuova*, considerably
anticipates advanced forms of social and linguistic development
among the Gentile nations. At a time when, according to Vico's
scheme, the first Gentiles should still have been hunting in skins,
dwelling in caves and uttering their first barely human syllables,
Genesis speaks of highly complex and sophisticated social, linguistic and mental processes among such peoples.

There is no need to dwell on further anomalies of the type we
have described. On the basis of those we have noted we are in a
strong position to argue that *it is a theoretical impossibility* for Vico to
have believed in both the biblical descriptions of the Egyptian and
Assyrian civilizations, on the one hand, and his own periodization
of development for such civilizations, on the other. Whatever
personal or private compromise this may have involved in terms of

30. *SN* 737.

faith, *the objective contradiction subsists*. It is important, however, to clarify what the contradiction means in terms of the overall objectives of the *Scienza nuova*.

In terms of the *theory of development* the conflicts with biblical chronology are not dysfunctional. In other words, if Vico had been able simply to shift the origins of Gentile humanity to an earlier period it would have enabled his chronology to reflect in a more plausible manner the various stages of development of his theory. The problem was that he could not do so without undermining ideas such as the universality of the Flood or the greater antiquity of Judaism. We have also seen that for various reasons he was equally constrained to abandon the alternative of an antediluvian cycle of human development and corruption. Yet this further indicates that the problem of orthodoxy could well account for the numerous accommodations, omissions and seemingly 'expedient' citations and declarations of orthodoxy in the various editions of the work.

If in one sense the contradictions we have mentioned are external to the theoretical substance of the *Scienza nuova*, they do not leave its integrity wholly intact. The work argues that theories of historical development, if they are to avoid being simple mental constructs or figments, are incomplete without validation at the historico-philological level. Vico claims, moreover, that the *Scienza nuova* is itself an example of the new method it propounds.[31] His programme, therefore, consists of producing a theory of history *with the backing of historical verification*. This is the famous Vichian reconciliation of 'vero' and 'certo' (the 'true' and the 'certain') without which the *Scienza nuova* would lose much of its significance. So, in terms of the claims he makes for the work as an illustration of the method it propounds, the contradictions we have noted do not help his case. While such problems do not, as we have already stated, necessarily damage the theoretical substance of the *Scienza nuova*, they nevertheless undermine its *empirical* objectives. These difficulties, together with Vico's abandoned attempt to postulate a feral wandering and process of bestialization before the Flood, and his all too obvious and calculated management of sources, illustrate the problems confronting him in elaborating his ideas. It is unfortunate that he was sometimes forced to conceal certain things in order to maintain some semblance of orthodoxy. Yet it is important to highlight such areas of concealment so as to recognize the differences between his theoretical and his tactical propositions. Failure to do so undoubtedly distorts and impoverishes the reading of one

31. See *SN* 7.

of the major landmarks in European thought. This point is important in all areas of Vico's work, and no less so when, in the *Scienza nuova*, we come to consider the status he accords to the problems of jurisprudence.

Part IV
The Problem of Law

9

The Reconciliation of Positive and Ideal Law

Vico did not write his *Scienza nuova* for experts in the history and philosophy of law, and the legal aspect of the work is neither over-technical nor beyond the grasp of the informed layman. It is important, however, to look beneath the surface of its generalized legal discourse, and in order to do this we shall have to make some brief excursions into his earlier work on jurisprudence, the *Diritto universale* (1720–2).

As a thinker, even when he is ambiguous, Vico fortunately does try to articulate the underlying premises of his thought. This makes it easier for us to detect the general theoretical assumptions underlying otherwise inaccessibly technical discussions. In this chapter an attempt will be made to uncover certain key ideas which can be found in seminal form in his writings on law. Such ideas trace out a clearly discernible line of development from the earlier legal writings to the *Scienza nuova*. They generate, as it were, abiding 'naturalistic' and 'historicist' elements pervading Vico's entire perspective.

There is no universally recognized starting point for the dominant ideas which find their expression in the *Scienza nuova*. Vichian criticism gives the impression of a certain lack of specificity in Vico's original objectives. Hence the work tends to be seen as the product of a highly original mind which happened to be engaged in reflection upon certain problems and themes. While many of the topics he discussed had already been touched upon by others, Vico's originality is said to consist largely in his greater breadth of vision and in his truly innovative capacity, which draws together a variety of disciplines and areas of thought into a historically unified conception of human development.

All this is largely true. Nevertheless, it will be suggested here that the whole conception of Vico's major project was prompted by a more specific objective than is traditionally supposed to be the case. The philosophical and methodological problems which constitute the raw material of his reflections did not arise arbitrarily.

115

They sprang from the need to solve a problem which first arose in the field of jurisprudence. If unresolved, this problem would have threatened to undermine the very authority and rationale of legal systems.

The Two Laws

Vico, it must be remembered, was a lawyer by training. And one aspect of his work which seems to have been largely ignored is the fact that he perceived a need to provide a theoretical account of social movement and legal change with a strong *prescriptive* dimension. While he rejected traditional explanations and doctrines concerning man and history, he was vigorously opposed to any suggestion that the historical process, in any of its various forms and manifestations, could be a random affair. His legal training, moreover, led him to search for a rationale in the social order. Thus an important intention of the theory he constructed was to produce a justification for the authority of legal systems, while simultaneously allowing for their inadequacy and their subsequent revision and renewal as consequences of social change. We should not imagine that this aspect of his programme overshadowed all his other theoretical concerns. It remained, however, a constant preoccupation and partly explains what he meant when he stated, in the *Scienza nuova*, that his work amounted to a 'philosophy of authority'.[1]

In its simplest terms the problem Vico set himself was the one of reconciling 'real' (existing or past) legal systems with the conception of an ideal 'natural law' valid in all circumstances and at all times. Amos Funkenstein has observed that this problem was not invented by Vico:

> Hotman, the contemporary of Jean Bodin, denied the validity of the *Corpus Iuris Civilis*, not only because the historical conditions underlying it were unique, but also on the strength of the argument that even in its own time, the Justinian code was but an ideal – abstract, never actualized constitution. In the tedious discussions between the adherents of the *Loi écrite* and the adherents of the *coutumes* ('customs'), some of these humanists ended with the realization that there could never be an ideal –

---

1. See *SN* 7, 350 and 386–90. B. A. Haddock also rightly stresses a further aspect of the importance of problems in law, that is, as essential first steps in the development of Vico's theory of knowledge. Haddock's *Vico's Political Thought*, pp. 72–112, contains a detailed discussion of this earlier phase of Vico's intellectual development.

rational constitution, valid for every society and at all times.[2]

However, whilst such problems may have exercised the minds of some legal thinkers for many years prior to Vico, they were actually no nearer a solution when he began the *Diritto universale* in 1720.

As we have seen, the two poles of the question for Vico were 'real' existing laws on the one hand and 'ideal' or eternally valid laws on the other. His first significant innovation was to fuse the *Corpus Iuris Civilis* of Justinian and the 'coutumes' referred to above into a single category on the same side of this dichotomy. In other words they both lay for him on the *empirical* side of the 'real' versus 'ideal' divide. Now this involves a considerable realignment of traditional distinctions. Leading jurists simply tended to endorse the official ideology that the Justinian *Corpus Iuris Civilis* embodied, or at least should ideally have embodied, the eternally valid principles of natural law.[3] It thus acquired the binding force which the 'coutumes', though they were more organically linked to the societies out of which they arose, could never claim.

For Vico, however, this distinction between precepts having the force of eternally valid principles and others not possessing such authority was not the major problem. The concept of the force of law itself was at stake. This is because the fundamental distinction to be made is between laws, rules and customs which are historical products reflecting the social norms and values of their times, and those immutable principles of 'natural law' which transcend all the historical vagaries of social and moral change. Within this scheme, the *Corpus Iuris Civilis* was just as much a historical product as were the 'coutumes'. Both reflected the intrinsic limitations of contingent constructions of particular epochs. It is his unambiguous belief in the *inevitability* of such limitations in the whole of 'positive' (i.e. real or existing) law, and his determination to follow such a conviction through to its ultimate theoretical consequences, which distinguishes Vico from most of the major legal thinkers of his time.

This is not to say that such eminent jurists as Grotius and Selden were not aware of the problem of reconciling 'historical law' and 'ideal law'. They were most certainly aware of a gap between the

---

2. A. Funkenstein, 'Natural Science and Social Theory: Hobbes, Spinoza and Vico', p. 207.
3. This is to state very baldly a highly complex problem. By this time a great deal of historical criticism had been applied to Justinian's 'ideal model', so that theoretical historians of law such as Grotius were fully aware of the problems presented by the *Corpus Iuris Civilis*.

two in practice. A great mass of critical textual scholarship surrounding the *Corpus Iuris Civilis*, from at least the fifteenth century onwards, had indeed clearly served to highlight its substantial legal as well as textual imperfections. A parallel problem was also increasingly recognized by these scholars in connection with the 'ius gentium', a term used to describe the unwritten laws, customs or precepts which were thought to be common to all nations. Indeed some jurists identified the term with what would now be called international law. One important difference between the 'ius gentium' and the 'lex naturalis' (natural law), however, was that whereas the latter was said to embody principles or precepts self-evident to right reason and not necessarily expressed in tangible form, the former was held to describe existing and empirically observable practices and customs. Now while the relationship between the two had been subject to much debate amongst legal thinkers, it was generally accepted as axiomatic that the 'ius gentium' could not or at least should not contravene the principles of 'natural law'. Nevertheless it was becoming increasingly difficult to accept the assumed harmony between the two.

What we find, therefore, in Vico's day, is a situation in which a number of traditional assumptions in the field of jurisprudence had for some time ceased to satisfy the most acutely critical minds. Vico's interest in the history of law, not only in the *Diritto universale* but also in the *Scienza nuova*, reflects his interest in these problems. As Pasini has observed,[4] the first step in his reformulation of the issues involved was to highlight the conflict between the development of Roman law and 'natural law'. It is this conflict which is at the root of the 'vero' and 'certo' (the 'true' and the 'certain') dichotomy which the *Scienza nuova* claims to reconcile. Viewed from this particular stand-point the 'certo' refers to the empirical problems associated with establishing the historical facts of Roman law, while the 'vero' refers to the theories or ideals of law, such as 'natural law', the traditional domain of the philosopher. In this sense, the *Scienza nuova* proposes a reconciliation of the 'certo' associated with factual research and the 'vero' invoking theoretical ordering and systemization.

Yet another aspect of the conflict highlighted by Vico is the impact it has on any normative consideration of legal institutions. If, in other words, the study of the history of Roman jurisprudence were to reveal grave deficiencies in particular laws or institutions when judged by the supposedly universally valid principles of the

4. See D. Pasini, *Diritto, società e stato in Vico*, pp. 88ff.

'lex naturalis', this would raise the question of the status of such deficient laws. In the case of ancient laws demanding cruel punishments, even human sacrifices, the conflict with universal principles of justice embodied in 'natural law' was at its sharpest. Since it is a self-evident principle of 'natural law' that there can be no obligation to obey unjust laws, what authority could be claimed for legal systems incorporating such laws?

As we can see, a series of problematic questions is raised in relation to the very notion of the rule of law. In the absence of a clear correspondence between a given legal system and an immutable 'natural law', it seemed impossible to justify the claim of the former to the allegiance of its subjects. Vico believed, of course, that no such correspondence between the two could ever be provided. The continual process of historical change which operated in real legal systems constituted a permanent denial of any such possibility.

Law as Social Contract or Law as Rule of Force

Vico's solution to the above problems was not thought up in abstraction from the major debates surrounding him. To simplify matters, there were then two basic approaches to the problem of justifying the rule of law. One of these was to appeal to some kind of 'social contract' theory such as that put forward by Hobbes.[5] Vico rejected this because of his hostility to theories which implied rational capabilities in early man. There were indeed some thinkers, like Hobbes himself, who, while not claiming that such a contract had a basis in real historical facts or events, argued, nevertheless, that it was necessary to proceed as if such an agreement existed in order to provide a rationale for the rule of law. Otherwise men would destroy society in pursuit of totally selfish objectives. Vico refused to construct a theory on the basis of a fiction of this kind, no matter how well-intentioned its originators might have been. His sense of adherence to the truth of history impelled him to search for a solution which did not require falsifications of the ways in which legal systems actually arise.

A rival explanation to the social contract theory was the argument that the rule of law was, in the final analysis, an expression of the rule of force. According to this theory, no ideal constructs, such as the notions of 'natural law' or 'social contract', accounted either

5. See especially Part I, chapters 14 and 15 of Thomas Hobbes, *Leviathan*.

for the genesis of real laws or for the reasons why they were more or less effective in preserving the social order. The real explanation lay in the coercive power of rulers. Moreover, laws in all epochs have been framed by those in power. But many saw such ideas as morally base, and as legitimizing violence and tyranny. It was indeed frequently the unacceptability of the idea of 'force' or 'violence' as explanatory principles of social existence which led some thinkers to espouse the idea of a social contract, even when the latter was seen as a historical fiction. Later in the eighteenth century, Pietro Verri would do this quite explicitly, while simultaneously recognizing the role of force in the reality of the development of social institutions.[6]

Vico was not able to make such a theoretical compromise. What is more, as I shall attempt to illustrate, he actually espoused a 'rule of force' theory, but one substantially modified and integrated into a coherent prescriptive theory which did not simply justify the rule of the strong. He accepted, in other words, the historical reality of force or the exercise of domination as necessary and essential components of the social order. However, the role of such coercive mechanisms is subordinated, in Vico's theory, to more determining laws of social evolution.

As we shall see below, 'oppression' and 'dominance' are woven into the fabric of a universal pattern of development in such a way as to lead to their extinction.[7] Thus, in the *Scienza nuova*, the coercive power of the strong is not described as the reprehensible pursuit of the arbitrary desires of rulers. It is, rather, part of a social process describing the development of the 'senso comune' or universal pattern of thoughts and feelings shared by all nations. Ultimately, the 'senso comune' becomes the basis of what Vico calls the 'authority of the human race', and thus carries the weight of responsibility for creating systems of law. It also explains why systems of law, judged as primitive and barbaric in the light of later developments, are more or less adequate for their times.

---

6. In his *Discorso sulla felicità*, Verri first of all accepts an important role for the powerful in his description of how society had developed up till then. Such individuals would frequently bring great benefits to society, but in order to do so would have to 'subjugate the people' by force. Nevertheless, Verri could not accept that the notion of 'force' could play any positive part in our thinking about social development. He is thus forced to utilize the fiction of a social contract: 'the purpose therefore of the *imaginary* social pact is the well-being of all those making up society', because otherwise 'if force alone granted rights, the absurd conclusion would follow that resistance alone could take them away. In this way *the social order would not be based on justice but on mere usurpation and violence.*' (P. Verri, *Del piacere e del dolore ed altri scritti*, p. 100. Italics mine.)

7. See *SN* 1086–7.

Now if we return, for the moment, to the earlier period during which Vico was still struggling to formulate such a theory, we can see it beginning to take shape in the *Diritto universale*. In the introductory synopsis of this work on jurisprudence, he makes one of his many difficult and cryptic comments, which in this case (granted its crucial importance) warrants a certain amount of exposition and analysis. He writes (of himself as author):

> Having established the one principle of both laws and of jurisprudence – i.e. reason – he moves on to the other which is authority. He demonstrates that authority is a form of the 'certo' just as reason is a form of the 'vero'; so that authority is a part of reason, just as the 'certo' is of the 'vero'. From this it follows that tyrants must be tolerated, for they are there by God's ordinance, for through them we have the 'certo'. . . .[8]

The interpretative key to this passage is to be found in the conclusion that 'tyrants must be tolerated . . .'. The passage demonstrates, in other words, how the 'force' represented by these tyrants is to be incorporated into Vico's prescriptive account of legal development. The 'certo' refers to the real facts of history, while the 'vero' denotes the theoretical constructs of the philosopher.

As Vico states in the passage in question, reason relates to the 'vero' of the philosopher in the same way as authority relates to the 'certo' of the historian. Reason ('ragione') should, moreover, be understood, not in the sense of 'pure reason', but as closer to the Italian 'motivo' or, more exactly in this passage, to the English 'rationale'. Thus the philosopher does not simply theorize in an a-historical void, but provides a rationale for a series of facts or events ('certo'). Authority refers to both the actual force and the authority to be found in the 'certo' of historical facts. In other words, what Vico means when he says that 'authority is a form of the "certo"' is that the authority of laws must be found in the *reality* of history and not in fictional propositions.

We are now in a position to reconstruct the flow of the argument and understand why, as Vico says, 'tyrants must be tolerated'. In the first place, as he explains, 'through them we have the "certo"', that is, they are an undisputed fact of history. But the 'certo' is part of the 'vero', that is, any theory of law must take into account the role of such tyrants. Vico goes much further than this: The authority of law must be found in the 'reality' of historical events. Thus the philosopher, in constructing a general theory of

8. *Opere giuridiche*, p. 6.

jurisprudence, should take into account how laws have been formed in the real world (i.e. including their imposition by tyrants), and find within the real world the basis or foundation for the authority of these laws. This is precisely what he means when he says that 'authority is a part of reason': the philosopher, in providing a rationale for legislation, must include in his theory an account or justification for the authority of law. So within this prescriptive theory a role must even be found for tyrants.

So far Vico has outlined the task, but does not actually provide the solution. It is one thing to assert that apparently contingent and historical factors (such as the role of tyrants and despotic rulers) must be incorporated into a satisfactory normative philosophy of law, but quite another to achieve that objective. Vico does not do so until, in the *Scienza nuova*, the role of the ruling classes is incorporated into a universal pattern of development. It is at this point that the interplay and struggles between contending classes are related to a 'senso comune' which is the basis of law.

Throughout this work Vico restates the important principles that 'the "certo" is part of the "vero"' and 'authority is part of reason (rationale)'.[9] He never loses sight of the important epistemological principle that all adequate theories must both take into account, and at the same time explain, the rationale behind events. Also, in the field of law, theory must demonstrate the basis of authority for legal systems. This he achieves gradually, through a number of intermediate stages.

First, Vico asserts, 'civil reason is part of natural reason. And since this civil reason expresses public utility, for this very reason it is part of natural reason.'[10] At this point, the precepts of civil life are infused with the self-evident principles of 'natural reason' because they express 'public utility'. 'Natural reason', therefore, is inherent in 'public utility'. The passage continues, however: 'But it cannot totally conform to reason, because, even in wanting to extend equity to all, at times there results injustice to some.'[11] For the moment, Vico is still attempting to utilize the notion of 'natural reason', the rationality at the root of 'natural law'. And he sees, of course, that the conception of equity which derives from it is, in practice, imperfect. Hence, for the time being, the rule of the strong, to which history conforms only too well, prevents a theoretical reconciliation between real socio-legal relations and ideal ones. In the words of Guido Fassò, a leading student of Vico's

9. Ibid., p. 101.
10. Ibid.
11. 'Ibid.

juridical thought, the problem remains one of finding a new system of universal law in which 'historical law could find a rational explanation and in which its logical necessity could be demonstrated; in which it would no longer be counterposed to natural law as an imperfect imitation or arbitrary modification of it, but rather be understood as its concrete realization'.[12]

Towards A Naturalistic/Historicist Solution

We find in Vico's treatment of 'natural law' in the *Diritto universale* important indications of the strong 'naturalistic' element which will be incorporated into the historicism of the *Scienza nuova*. It is this naturalistic perspective that he employs to bring about a reconciliation between 'positive' and 'natural' law. A step in that direction is taken when he embarks upon a discussion of the 'primi diritti naturali' (primary natural rights) which man shares with other animals. In this discussion Vico is drawing on a particular intellectual current in the 'natural law' tradition which can be traced back to the jurist Ulpian, whom he readily acknowledges as a source:[13]

> Man's life in common with animals. In that part which refers to man's being are contained those rights which the Stoics called the primal rights of nature, which concern human life in those things which it has in common with other animals; and those philosophers define them thus: powers by which God, in creating man, entrusts to him his own protection, by which means he protects his own being.[14]

It is not surprising that Vico should revive, utilize and modify for his own ends this aspect of 'natural law'. He was heir, it must be remembered, to the discussions which had taken place, in Naples, among the members of the Accademia degli Investiganti. In their

12. G. Fassò, *Vico e Grozio*, p. 88.
13. See *Opere giuridiche*, p. 93, 2. It should be pointed out that mainstream thinking on 'natural law' ignored this aspect of the question, that is, the community of actions and instincts common to both men and animals. Nevertheless even Justinian in the *Institutes* (Bk I, ch. 2, sect. 1) borrows a passage from Ulpian to define 'natural law' as that law which nature implants in all animals. Many commentators, however, would argue that such a borrowing was uncharacteristic and misleading. Thomas Collett Sandars, for instance, argues: 'If *ius* is that which nature commands, nature may be said to command the propagation of the species in animals as much as in man, and thus there would be a *ius* common to animals and to men. A jurist to whom the theory of the *lex naturae* was familiar, might easily pursue the subject to a point in which men and animals seem to meet. But the main theory had nothing to do with animals, as it looked only to the reason inherent in the universe and in man', (*The Institutes of Justinian*, Commentary to Bk I, ch. 2, sect. 1, p. 7.)
14. *Opere giuridiche*, p. 93.

writings and debates, these philosophers had repeatedly returned to the question of in-built self-preservation mechanisms in the animal world. Such predispositions towards self-conservation of the species were thought to be inscribed in nature. Shortly after the above passage – and in the context of law – we find Vico extending his 'naturalistic' self-preservation mechanism to man himself: 'And when, since he is mortal, man is unable to continue in his species, he is impelled, like other living things, by nature itself to preserve his being in the genus.'[15]

Before analysing so important a passage, we must make one or two preliminary observations. First, it undoubtedly illustrates the 'naturalistic' thrust of Vico's thinking, highlighting as it does the importance of the principle of 'conservation' or 'self-preservation' under the control of nature. Badaloni has already shown that, in the 1725 edition of the *Scienza nuova*, the idea of 'conservation' was strongly connected with the role of 'providence'.[16] Here, we can see the appearance of the notion even earlier, in the *Diritto universale*. 'Providence', in the *Scienza nuova*, undoubtedly possesses the naturalistic conservationist role suggested by Badaloni. Moreover, the latter links the 'providence'–'natura' –'conservation' connection with the notion of cyclic returns which we find in Vico. Badaloni argues that such a notion of historical returns

> is justified by that law of self-preservation of our species, which Vico has indicated with the name of *providence* (corresponding in many ways to the instinctive wisdom theorized by Leonardo di Capua as part of the animal world), which obliges men, even against their intentions, to act in a way which guarantees their own preservation and that of their descendants.[17]

The notion of 'providence' in the *Scienza nuova* is associated with ideas of 'conservation' and 'nature'; it embodies, that is, the idea of forces or instincts which tend towards the self-preservation of the species.

Now if we return to the last important passage we quoted from the *Diritto universale* (above) we are ready to pursue our analysis. Although we can see that the passage contains the *general* concepts of conservation and nature, if we examine it more closely we find a more detailed indication of how and when such forces are to function. In particular, Vico makes a distinction between 'species' and 'genus'. Nature impels man to survive through the 'genus', we

15. Ibid.
16. Badaloni, *Introduzione a G. B. Vico*, pp. 355ff.
17. Ibid., p. 374.

are told, when he can no longer endure as a 'species'. At first sight this seems a rather perplexing statement, suggesting that nature engineers a reversal to some form of 'animal' existence when man cannot continue his life in 'human' form. The passage occurs, however, precisely in the general context of a discussion of what man has in common with other animals. So there seems little doubt that the contrast between 'species' and 'genus' highlights a difference between man considered in certain specific aspects of his nature, on the one hand, and as a reflection of more general characteristics held in common with the other animals of the 'genus', on the other. Even so, the precise meaning of the contrast has not yet been made clear.

Vico concludes the passage with certain important definitions. Animals or 'brutes', he tells us, do not possess 'conatus' or 'liberum arbitrium' (free-choice).[18] When he comes to define the characteristics most proper to man – those which reveal more specifically the nature of the human 'species' – he writes that within such essential characteristics 'are truly contained those things suitable to or consistent with nature, which pertain to the true life of man; and in describing them one would call them: those things which man does congenial to nature, or *conforming to social life, by which man's true humanity is preserved*'.[19] As we can see from this passage, therefore, the true 'species' existence of man is only preserved as long as his actions are an expression of his fundamental *social* nature.

We are now in a position to define our terms more precisely. In the passage in question, 'species' refers to mankind with specific reference to those social behaviour patterns characteristic of human civilization. 'Genus', on the other hand, refers to the more physical and brutish characteristics which man has in common with other animals. From here the argument can be taken one step further. Vico asserts that when humanity ceases to live or persevere in its truly social or civilized function, nature engineers a return to brutish existence. This is done in order to 'preserve his being' and save it from extinction. In the *Scienza nuova*, we can see exactly how flesh and blood are added to such a notion.

In his mature work, as we know, Vico argues that at a certain stage in human development the whole social texture of human existence is threatened by man's corruption. Then, in order to preserve humanity which would otherwise destroy itself, providence ordains a dissolution of society and a return to a form of

18. *Opere giuridiche*, p. 95.
19. Ibid.

primitive barbarity or bestial existence which then enables the whole process of civil development to begin anew:

> But if the peoples are rotting in that ultimate civil disease . . . then providence for their extreme ill has its extreme remedy at hand. For such peoples, like so many beasts, have fallen into the custom of each man thinking only of his own private interests . . . they live like wild beasts in a deep solitude of spirit and will, scarcely any two being able to agree since each follows his own pleasure or caprice. By reason of all this, providence decrees that . . . they shall turn their cities into forests and the forests into dens and lairs of men. In this way, through long centuries of barbarism, rust will consume the misbegotten subtleties of malicious wits that have turned them into beasts made more inhuman by the barbarism of reflection than the first men had been made by the barbarism of sense.[20]

The transition from the original formulation of this idea to its restatement in the *Scienza nuova* is made possible by Vico's introduction of the process of 'ricorsi' or 'cycles' into history. Whether the 'nature' of the earlier passage can be fully identified with the 'providence' of the later one is a problem upon which we cannot dwell at the moment. However, we can make good sense of the earlier passage if we immerse its concepts in Vico's later historical scheme. When man's 'species' existence is threatened with extinction, that is, when corruption threatens the social fabric of human society, there is a return to animality. And if we consider precisely how this return to primitive existence brings about a regeneration of man's social instincts, we also see how Vico had by this time greatly transformed the notion of 'public utility'.

In the *Diritto universale* the idea of public utility was basic to the laws which govern human society. It was still somewhat abstract and ill-defined, however, and had not helped Vico to bridge the theoretical gulf between the ideals of law and the historical realities of legal systems. In the *Scienza nuova*, his historicism is fully developed, and his characterization of early man is such as to preclude any possibility of the latter possessing a complex rational capacity. The idea of public utility, therefore, as a set of rationally agreed principles, clearly could not retain any function as a motivating factor in constructing norms of conduct and legal sanctions within a primitive social organization. Moreover, since in his bestial state man remains wholly lacking in the *social* dimension of his later existence, the very concept of *public* utility is anachronistic and inappropriate. The concept of 'utility' is not totally abandoned,

20. *SN* 1106.

however. Instead, stripped of its *social* connotations and of its reference to a set of *rational* principles, it remains as a residual determining factor even in primitive existence. So to return to the passage from the *Scienza nuova* quoted above (*SN* 1106), through the effects of 'providence' men, having been reduced to a state of primitive existence, 'are thereby stunned and brutalized, are sensible no longer of comforts, delicacies, pleasures, and pomp, but only of the *necessary utilities* of life. And the few survivors in the midst of an abundance of the things necessary for life *naturally* become sociable.'[21]*

The 'public utility' of Vico's earlier legal discourse is thus transformed here into a more basic and naturalistic component of the frequently mentioned necessity and utility, which are the foundations of early man's social legal development. These instincts subsequently become the basis of the authority of early man's legal customs because they are a structurally essential part of the 'senso comune'; they form, that is, part of that uniform pattern of instinctual behaviour and development common to all nations. The laws and customs which thereby arise are just as much inscribed in man's nature as the natural law of the philosophers was allegedly inscribed in the nature of rational man.

Vico has in this way solved the problem of a dichotomy between real laws and the ideal law based on self-evident principles of natural reason. In other words, the latter express, at the very most, a point towards which legal systems always tend as man himself becomes increasingly rational. Real legal systems have authority, therefore, because they correspond, not to some fictitious natural law derived from an equally unreal rational humanity, but rather to man's nature at any given point on the evolutionary scale. Natural law is thereby dissociated from the world of ideal essences; there are no *eternally* valid principles governing human behaviour because *human nature itself is subject to change.*[22]

Vico's solution to the long-standing problem of the dichotomy between real and ideal law resulted, of course, in his use of a revised terminology. We have seen that 'lex naturalis' expressed what philosophers considered to be eternal principles of natural justice. 'Ius gentium', on the other hand, referred to those unwritten principles and practices *actually found* among existing peoples. These should have expressed the principles of 'natural law', but in

21. Ibid. Italics mine.
22. Even in the *Diritto universale* Vico describes 'natural law' as something towards which the real laws and customs of antiquity were tending. See *Opere giuridiche*, pp. 677–9.

practice students of jurisprudence had already noted considerable difficulties in reconciling the two. Yet, for Vico, there was no longer any conflict, since historically the 'ius gentium' always described laws and practices adequate to the stage of human development which produced them. There was, in other words, no separate and ideal 'natural law' standing above history. The two laws are instead brought together to form Vico's single 'diritto naturale delle genti' (natural law of the gentes). The historicization of natural law thus grants prescriptive status to the 'ius gentium', thereby completing the Vichian revolution in the sphere of jurisprudence.

The problem which we described at the beginning of this chapter was one of reconciling real legal systems and ancient customs and codes with the eternal principles of natural law. While this theoretical dichotomy persisted, there remained, on the one hand, a rationale and justification for laws which lacked any basis in the real world and, on the other, real, historical legal systems and codes with apparently no normative foundation. Such was the gulf which separated positive law and for some theorists also the 'ius gentium' from the 'lex naturalis'.

Vico's 'natural law of the gentes' incorporates what is essential to both dimensions, but unifies them into a single concept. The unifying power behind this solution is, of course, provided by his growing historicism. His conception of human development is such that the 'natural law of the gentes' expresses real laws, *as they evolve*. Law so historicized is adequate for its times. Since, moreover, it expresses the universal characteristics or patterns of development which all nations traverse, its prescriptive sanction or authority is to be found in the 'senso comune'. It thus encapsulates both the historical reality and the rationale behind legal systems; that is to say, it unifies the 'certo' and 'vero' which were formerly divided.

The 'natural law of the gentes' enables Vico to incorporate the role of 'force' into the history of legal development. As we shall examine in detail below, the struggle between social groups for property and other rights and privileges forms part of a process of development whereby the rule of the strong is progressively relaxed in favour of the weaker strata in society. The interchange of 'power' involved in such a process is naturally reflected in legal development, and quite properly so. The law, in short, reflects the real (but changing) power relations in society, and not ideals of 'natural equity' thought up by philosophers. It is a form of moral posturing, therefore, to condemn ancient legal systems for not expressing such ideals. But these anachronistic readings of the past arise precisely from an acceptance of the prescriptive role of the static 'natural law' of the philosophers. Even Grotius is accused of this failing:

> If the most distinguished Hugo Grotius had perceived that difference between the natural law of the gentes and the natural law of the philosophers, on which we have said many things in our first book, he would not have been so critical, so frequently, towards the teaching of Roman jurists on these matters. . . .[23]

For Vico, the concepts of dominance expressed in Roman law mirrored the power relations existing in Roman society. Both form part of the changing pattern of the 'ideal eternal history' which ensures a gradual historical awakening to a need for 'natural equity'. As Pasini has noted, under Vico's argument 'law finally emerges from its a-historical, a-temporal, and therefore a-social Limbo, in order to become immersed in history and acquire a socio-historical dimension'.[24]

The general features of Vico's later historicism thus evolved from a quite specific problem he faced initially in the field of jurisprudence. His attempt to bridge the gap between the real and the ideal in law later becomes an attempt to provide a prescriptive rationale for society. The 'natural law of the gentes' which resulted expressed a mature historicism, but one which contained strong 'naturalistic' currents. It also embraced the concept of 'force', but without surrendering to a theory of society which simply justified the continuous rule of the strong.

Notions such as 'natural law' and 'public utility' which had remained abstract in traditional discourse were, in consequence, fused with others formerly of a predominantly empirical nature, such as 'positive' law or 'ius gentium'. The idea of legal systems developing in conformity with changes in human nature seemed to offer good prospects for a theoretical solution. Not surprisingly, however, in his attempt to transform traditional concepts of jurisprudence Vico was to be confronted from another direction with the problem of orthodoxy.

---

23. Ibid., p. 679.
24. Pasini, *Diritto, società e stato*, pp. 85–6.

10
Law and the Catholic Tradition

The General Context

In the *Autobiography*, Vico gives the impression that he had read Grotius reluctantly and that he had tried to press the ideas of the Protestant author into the service of Catholicism.[1] His remarks to this effect have been accepted without question by most commentators, even though they are highly misleading if used to interpret his thought on legal matters. Thus his attack on Grotius has been seen as a defence of the Catholic position on Original Sin. The excessive rationality which Grotius attributes to early man, so the argument goes, takes no account of his corrupt nature. According to Enrico Nuzzo, Grotius took his starting point from 'dangerously optimistic' theological premises and 'played down the consequences which derived from man's fall and corruption'.[2] Nuzzo then proceeds to argue that according to Vico man's reason had ceased to rule his will with the fall of Adam. The seeds of the 'eterno vero' nevertheless remained implanted within 'corrupt' humanity, and the gradual emergence of his rationality at the third stage of development was intended to represent a kind of restoration or salvation from his fallen state. This is the sense we are to give to occasional theological remarks in the *Scienza nuova*, such as 'man is not unjust by nature in the absolute sense, but by nature fallen and weak'.[3] I shall argue below that Vico has a somewhat different purpose in mind when making such statements in the contexts of his discussions on law.

We have already seen reasons to suggest why there should have been a sudden infusion of apparently orthodox positions into Vico's writings from the time of the composition of the *Autobiography* (1725), together with an attempt to re-orientate the past course and chronology of his intellectual itinerary, in the sombre reminders of the temporal power of the Church and of its capacity for

1. See *Autobiography*, p. 155.
2. E. Nuzzo, *Vico*, p. 77.
3. *SN* 310.

retribution.[4] In the *Autobiography*, Vico claimed that he had begun to read the Dutch jurist for the first time in 1713. Having been asked in 1712 by the Duke of Traetto to write a life of his uncle, the soldier Antonio Carafa, he '*found himself obliged* to read Hugo Grotius' *On the Law of War and Peace*'.[5] Since Carafa was a military man, it was quite appropriate that Vico should acquaint himself with Grotius' famous discussion of the just war in relation to natural law in the *De Iure Belli et Pacis*. Even so, it seems curious that as a student of law he should have needed to justify his reading of such a major authority.

We know from his legal writings and also from the *Scienza nuova* that Vico's interest in Grotius went well beyond questions of war and government. This is why he felt it necessary later to go into even greater detail about his reasons for his interest in Grotius' work: 'And Vico had occasion to penetrate much more deeply into this work of Grotius when he was asked to write some notes for a new edition of it'.[6] But he finally abandoned the task, he tells us, since 'it was not fitting for a man of Catholic faith to adorn with notes the work of a heretical author'.[7]

Nevertheless, in spite of this alleged refusal to annotate the work of a 'heretical' author, he tells us that Grotius became one of his 'four authors', all of whom turn out to be either pagan or 'heretical', a state of affairs Vico justifies through his constant reminders that he approaches such authors with a desire to turn them 'to the use of the Catholic religion'.[8]

There is thus a considerable degree of prevarication in Vico's account of his interest in Grotius. His claim not to have read Grotius until 1713 becomes less and less credible the more we reflect on it. He informs us in the *Autobiography* that his meditations on a revised 'natural law of the nations' and on problems relating to Roman and Gentile civil law began during the nine years of his Vatolla studies (1686–95).[9] It seems scarcely believable that during this prolonged period of intense study, so serious and diligent a scholar and student of jurisprudence as Vico should not have read the work of one of the major authorities on these issues. It is obvious that Vico was attempting to distance himself from the views of the 'giusnaturalisti',[10] with whom, in the Valletta house-

---

4. See B. Croce, *Storia*, pp. 158ff.
5. *Autobiography*, pp. 154. Italics mine.
6. Ibid., p. 155.
7. Ibid.
8. Ibid.
9. See ibid., p. 119.
10. These were a group of lawyers and students of law whose general orientation

hold, he would certainly have participated in discussions of their favourite authors, including Grotius. We must remember, of course, that the 'giusnaturalisti' were part and parcel of the Demo-critan–Epicurean–Gassendian current with which Vico was simul-taneously attempting to sever his past links through his feigned repudiation of Lucretius. But Grotius was also at the centre of yet another debate which brought the Valletta circle into open conflict with the Church.

The Church in Naples had for some time been preoccupied with what it saw as an offensive launched against its temporal powers and possessions by this dangerous group of free-thinking lawyers. Badaloni's study of the debates of the late seventeenth- and early eighteenth-century Naples first drew attention to an important current of juridical thinking which used Grotius to support its attempt to undermine theocratically orientated conceptions of pol-itical power and legal rights. Vico's friend Giuseppe Valletta was the major figure at the centre of the controversy.

Subsequent research has tended to reinforce the general thrust of Badaloni's argument. It has also brought to light interesting infor-mation on the circulation of anti-Inquisitorial writings and the publication of other important works such as Leonardo di Capua's *Parere* which was placed on the *Index* in 1693.[11]

Valletta himself produced a number of works in which he attempted to undermine the very legitimacy of Inquisitorial pro-ceedings. A first step was to distinguish between different kinds of law to which the sovereign was or was not subject. There was, in Valletta's view, a civil law over which a sovereign could exercise control, but there was also a higher 'law of the gentes' over which he could not,

> because if we are not to reject what St Thomas says, there is a greater difference between the right of civil law and that of the Gentes, because while civil law is derived from natural reason in relation to contingent matters so that each legislator can fashion it as he pleases, no legislator can alter the fact that the law of the Gentes is natural . . .[12]

Valletta strengthens his argument against the Neapolitan Church by enlisting its most prestigious theologian, Aquinas, as a propo-nent of natural law as a defence against tyranny in the legislative

---

was to argue for legislation limiting the powers of rulers, both temporal and ecclesiastical.

11. See M. Rak, 'Una teoria dell' incertezza. Note sulla cultura napoletana del secolo XVIII'.

12. Valletta, *Opere filosofiche*, pp. 18–19.

sphere. He goes further, referring to the rights enjoyed by 'the people' who 'although subject to a king, nevertheless maintain the right and the law of the Gentes with which they elect the Prince, the observation of which right cannot be dissolved or reformed by the Prince'.[13]

The reference in this passage to the prince as the choice of 'the people' derives from another aspect of the cultural struggle then taking place, that is, the 'defence of public right in support of the officialdom of the Viceregency, in opposition to the private right of the baronial and ecclesiastical orders'.[14] Valletta's 'law of the gentes' was designed to subject the prince or the viceregency to some form of public control or accountability to the 'popolo', which was in fact largely dominated at the time by the 'ceto civile' of lawyers, academics and other elements of the middle strata of which Valletta, Vico and others felt themselves a part. It was also designed to bring the force of 'natural law' behind a theoretical strategy to subject the feudal aristocracy and the Church to greater control by the viceregency in local matters. The net result would have been to reduce the degree of control which the Church, and specifically the Inquisition, would have been able to exercise over the intellectual and cultural activities of the 'popolo' or 'ceto civile'.

In *Del Santo Officio*, Valletta cites Grotius' appeal to divine, natural and rational law in support of his argument for the abolition of the Inquisition. He argues that when, in a public assembly and with the approval of the sovereign, the abolition of the Court of the Inquisition meets with 'the express approval and universal assent of the whole city and of the noble and popular strata and indeed of the whole kingdom',[15] then such a demand can hardly be resisted. For indeed the initial act of founding the institution was itself a denial of natural law, 'which cannot be renounced or revoked by an act, by consent or agreement, by any Pope or law'[16], and this in full accord with Grotius' argument that no custom 'can prevail over divine, natural or rational law.[17]

Such a use of Grotius and the natural law tradition to attack the Inquisition was part of an overall strategy in which Valletta attempted to demonstrate that the whole ideological orientation of the Church's theology had been perverted by its adoption of the Aristotelian tradition as its theoretical bedrock. This is why, in his

13. Ibid., p. 19.
14. Ibid.
15. *Del Santo Officio*, cited in *Opere giuridiche*, p. xx.
16. Ibid.
17. Ibid.

works *Difesa della moderna filosofia* and *Istoria filosofica*, Valletta offers,

> in opposition to the Aristotelian an alternative Atomist/Platonist/ Cartesian tradition . . . as being more consistent with Catholic teaching. And in order to win support for this tradition (in reality a quite dubious reconstruction of his own), he proceeds to demonstrate, through the skilful and highly tendentious manipulation of innumerable quotations from the Church Fathers and the Greek and Roman Classics, the virtues of the one tradition as opposed to the unmitigated blackness of the Peripatetic heritage.[18]

As Badaloni has observed, Valletta's cultural battle against the Aristotelian tradition is a 'deliberate continuation of the polemic against the Holy Office', and is intended to associate unjust Inquisitorial persecution with an inherently pernicious current of thought 'which goes back to Aristotle and which has triumphed within the church itself'.[19]

Of course, Valletta never did manage to win greater respectability for his group and their ideas. After its defeat, to have been associated with the Valletta circle and with its favourite authors was certainly to court the Church's displeasure. It is not surprising, consequently, that in the *Autobiography* Vico should have underplayed or made excuses for his interest in such authors. So, we are told, he read the *Parere* of di Capua for its good Tuscan prose, just as Cornelio was read for his elegant Latin.[20] It is within this context that Vico felt constrained to justify his reading of Grotius.

The ideological and cultural battles fought by the 'giusnaturalisti' were later taken up by the 'giurisdizionalisti', whose number included the condemned Giannone.[21] Apart from denouncing ecclesiastical abuses and privileges, these thinkers wished to see the power of the Church contained within strict bounds. Criticism of the Inquisition and of Church censorship naturally followed, drawing the swift and vigorous response described earlier. The problem did not disappear, moreover, with Giannone's banishment from Naples. The 'giurisdizionalisti' continued to oppose

18. G. L. C. Bedani, review of G. Valletta, *Opere filosofiche*, *The Modern Language Review*, July (1976), 697–8.
19. N. Badaloni, 'Sul vichiano diritto naturale delle genti', Introduction to *Opere giuridiche*, pp. 133.
20. See *Autobiography*, pp. 133.
21. Franco Valsecchi has observed: 'During the first decades of the century, it is "the bold anti-Vatican army" of the "giurisdizionalisti", led by Giannone and Gaetano Argento, which takes the field to denounce the usurpations and "the attacks by the church on the rights of princes".' (F. Valsecchi, *L' Italia nel Settecento, dal 1714 al 1788*, p. 616.)

what they saw as unwarranted and arrogant ecclesiastical interference in temporal affairs. Such battles were still in progress when Vico was revising his intermediate 1730 edition of the *Scienza nuova*.[22] In a letter, written in 1734, from Cardinal Luis Belluga, a powerful member of the Roman Curia, to the minister Santisteban we can see what kind of pressure existed to compel writers and intellectuals to assume an orthodox stance. Belluga indicated the idea of 'freedom of conscience' as the pernicious source of Neapolitan ideological malaise.[23] It is this, he claimed, that permits the capital to corrupt its youth, 'enabling them to see forbidden and condemned books . . . full of impiety and new and pernicious doctrines which are erroneous, even heretical, on religious matters'.[24] Grimaldi and Giannone, leading 'giurisdizionalisti', were singled out as having sown particularly poisonous seeds. To these individuals and their like, in Naples, was attributed the blame for having spread countless errors 'to the point of making large numbers fall into atheism, and many others into heresy'.[25]

Belluga, as the same letter makes clear, considered it necessary to purge Naples of Giannone's followers and all like-minded groups of lawyers. To this end he advocated the formal re-introduction of the Holy Office of the Roman Inquisition,[26] the confiscation of forbidden and heretical works, the public burning of pernicious writings, and the ban on their importation into the kingdom.[27] As Melpignano has noted, censorship was then tightened even further, so that in 1736 'there appeared an ordinance which punished the acceptance through the customs and the printing of foreign books in the territory of the State'.[28]

But quite apart from the dangerous ideas with which his name was linked in Naples, Grotius represented, in his own right, a disturbing trend in jurisprudence. There was a widespread opinion amongst scholars that his work constituted a break with the tradition in which natural law was firmly located within a theologi-

22. An important study of the problem is contained in Melpignano, *L' Anticurialismo napoletano*.
23. The letter is contained in D. Carpanetto, *L' Italia nel Settecento*, pp. 112–17.
24. Ibid., p. 113.
25. Ibid., p. 114.
26. The Vatican had never accepted that Inquisitorial proceedings should be controlled locally in Naples, and official delegates of the Roman Inquisition remained in the city despite Charles V's decree, in 1709, handing over control to diocesan ordinaries. The state of uncertainty regarding jurisdictional boundaries often worked in favour of suspect authors, and Belluga clearly felt that there were too few condemnations.
27. See Carpanetto, *L' Italia nel Settecento*, pp. 115–17.
28. Melpignano, *L' Anticurialismo napoletano*, p. 79.

cal perspective. Enzo Paci has argued, for instance,[29] that it was precisely the idea of discovering a 'natural', as opposed to a 'supernatural', principle within man by which he could regulate his conduct and laws that first interested Vico in Grotius' work. Some scholars have interpreted Grotius as attempting to create a natural law system which would be independent of theological argument. According to Passerin D'Entreves, 'he proved that it was possible to build up a theory of laws independent of theological presuppositions. His successors completed the task. The natural law which they elaborated was entirely 'secular'. They sharply divided what the Schoolmen had taken great pains to reconcile.'[30] The natural law developed by such thinkers was 'a purely rational construction, though it does not refuse to pay homage to some remote notion of God'.[31] So in addition to representing a link with successive generations of intellectuals hostile in one way or another to the Church, the name of Grotius tended to associate Vico with 'the founder of the modern theory of natural law',[32] and the proponents of dangerous new ideas.

Doctrinal Problems: Catholic Authorities on 'Natural Law'

One of the most surprising features of Vico's discussions of law (both in the *Diritto universale* and the *Scienza nuova*) is the total absence of any reference to the two most important Catholic thinkers on natural law: St Thomas Aquinas and Francisco Suárez. Equally surprising is the lack of attention this extraordinary fact has received. The only comment on their omission that I have come across remains that of Guido Fassò who remarks, with reference to Vico's neglect of the writings of the Dominican and Jesuit theologians, that 'they were not useful to him, and for this reason he never mentions them'.[33] Given his claim to be contributing to Catholic thinking on the subject, such an explanation seems a little casual.

29. See E. Paci, *Ingens Sylva. Saggio sulla filosofia di G. B. Vico*, 110–13. Though written forty years ago this study remains one of the most penetrating surveys of Vico's thought.

30. A. Passerin D'Entreves, *Natural Law*, p. 55. As we can see from *SN1a* 16, Vico was well aware of this view of Grotius' works.

31. Passerin D'Entreves, *Natural Law*, p. 55. It should be pointed out that some scholars, whilst accepting that Grotius may well have been understood as departing radically from the Scholastic tradition, deny that he actually did so. For a discussion and refutation of this view cf. E. B. F. Midgley, *The Natural Law Tradition and the Theory of International Relations*, especially pp. 137–66.

32. Passerin D' Entreves, *Natural Law*, p. 71.

33. Fassò, *Vico e Grocio, p. 88*.

Apart from this omission, their neglect seems highly conspicuous on some quite specific counts as well. We recall that Vico states in the *Autobiography* that his reason for reading Grotius, whom he intends to deploy for the greater glory of Catholicism, was his commission to write the life of Antonio Carafa. Grotius's work *De Iure Belli et Pacis* discusses, amongst other things, the whole question of the practice and morality of war in relation to 'lex naturalis' and the 'ius gentium'. It would seem curious for someone professing devotion to the Catholic Faith to ignore the major Catholic authority on precisely this topic. It seems doubly improbable, moreover, when we consider that the author he did choose to read in this area 'was himself seriously indebted to Suárez'.[34] And while all authorities are agreed on the importance of Suárez in discussions of natural law, as a founder of modern international law, and on Grotius' indebtedness to him, it must be remembered in turn that 'Suárez's philosophy of law was based on that of St Thomas Aquinas'.[35]

As we have already seen, Vico tells us that he had ceased writing on Grotius' work because it was not fitting for a Catholic to write a commentary on a heretical author. Yet, on matters concerning the morality of war and international justice he prefers to study the heretical writer rather than the major authorities of his own faith. It is highly unlikely, to put it mildly, that a scholar of Vico's calibre would not have been familiar with the views of such authorities. His own elaboration of the idea of a 'natural law of the gentes' was a fusion and historicization of the notions of 'lex naturalis' and 'ius gentium'. Both Aquinas and Suárez had given particular attention to such notions, Aquinas to the former and Suárez to both. Grotius and Suárez, moreover, had in common a particular interest in the 'ius gentium'. Yet in his revision of such ideas Vico criticizes Grotius alone for his excessively 'rationalistic' and anachronistic assumptions concerning early man and his laws. But as Frederick Vaughan has demonstrated in one of his earlier writings,[36] all the arguments Vico mustered for his attacks on the natural law of heretical theorists like Grotius, Selden and Pufendorf, were equally valid against the natural law of Aquinas and the authority of Catholic teaching.

All these authors, whether Protestant or Catholic, nevertheless shared deep-rooted 'rationalist' and 'contractualist' assumptions. Vico's 'natural law of the gentes', by contrast, is based on a 'senso

34. F. Copleston, *A History of Philosophy*, Vol. iii, Pt 2, p. 203.
35. Ibid.
36. See F. Vaughan, 'La Scienza Nuova: Orthodoxy and the Art of Writing'.

comune' which, from its origins, has followed a pattern far removed both from the reasoned conclusions of 'homo rationalis' and from any idea of pacts or agreements: 'The natural law of the gentes has arisen with the customs of the nations, conforming one with another in virtue of a human 'senso comune', without any reflection and without one nation following the example of another.[37]*

Consequently, Vico's theory of man's early development brought him into conflict with the teaching of the whole Catholic tradition on the question of the rational soul. There were long periods of human history, according to his theory, in which men were lacking a faculty considered essential to humanity by any definition of Catholic teaching. We can see strong reasons, therefore, why Vico should have avoided any mention of such authors as Aquinas. There could be scarcely a sentence of the *Summa Theologica* which he could have cited with approval. It was one thing, consequently, for Vico to refute a Protestant. However, it was quite another to draw attention to his rejection of fundamental notions in the work of the Church's major theologian.

The case was similar, of course, in regard to Francisco Suárez since Vico's critique of Grotius was implicitly a refutation of the Spanish theologian as well. But there was a difference. A direct refutation of Suárez would have drawn even more attention to certain specific theological questions. For not only does the Spaniard share Grotius' rationalist presuppositions concerning man's essential nature, but, as distinct from the Dutch jurist, he makes the self-evident rational principles of natural law explicitly dependent on a 'lex aeterna divina' (divine eternal law). There is no way, therefore, in which the historicist and evolutionist perspective of the *Scienza nuova* could have avoided direct conflict with the idea of a 'divine eternal law' as the foundation of those immutable and eternal principles of 'right reason' directly implanted into human nature by God.[38] Hence it is hardly surprising that Vico should have chosen to avoid any such confrontation.[39]

The notion of immutable principles of natural justice was not the only idea, however, which came into conflict with Vico's 'natural law of the gentes'. An equally problematic doctrinal concept was

---

37. *SN* 311.

38. See Francisco Suárez, *Tractatus de Legibus ac Deo Legislatore*, Bk II, ch. 4, pars. 8–10. For detailed expositions of the thought of Suárez see Copleston, *A History of Philosophy*, Vol. iii, Pt 2, pp. 202–28, and Midgley, *Natural Law Tradition*, pp. 71–93.

39. The absence of a 'lex aeterna' in Grotius is a further indication in support of the view that his legal thought amounted to a secularization of the notion of 'natural law'. See Fassò, *Vico e Grozio*, p. 23 and Midgley, *Natural Law Tradition*, pp. 141–3.

that of 'free-will', an idea we shall also find him struggling to reaffirm in relation to other aspects of his theory. Before turning directly to this question, however, we must examine another aspect of his theory of law.

Pagan Sympathies Disguised

Among the most apparently gratuitous of Vico's statements on religious matters are his claims that what he is arguing supports the Catholic doctrine of 'grace' and 'free-will'. He repeatedly makes such a claim in connection with his ideas on law. On closer inspection, however, we find that such seemingly casual assertions are preceded by passages which reveal a quite specific purpose. We shall first attempt to outline this purpose before proceeding to discuss briefly the claim itself in the next chapter.

We have seen that Grotius presented something of a problem for Vico, particularly in the Naples of the mid-1720s, and that there were highly contingent, local cultural and historical factors playing their part in this. On a more general level, although Grotius still represented, to the Catholic world, an unwelcome secularizing trend within the natural law tradition, he was nevertheless an important ally in common opposition to a more fundamental and pernicious set of opponents in an ideological battle of greater universal significance than the local problems mentioned earlier.

In *SN* 135 Vico refers to the dispute on 'natural law' between Christian philosophers (including Grotius) and moral theologians, on the one hand, and the pagans Carneades and Epicurus, on the other. He claims to have found a solution to 'the great dispute still waged by the best philosophers and moral theologians against Carneades the Skeptic and Epicurus – a dispute which not even Grotius could set at rest – namely, whether law exists by nature, or whether man is naturally sociable, which comes to the same thing.[40] Vico's suggestion that such conflicting positions really amount to the same thing could hardly be more misleading. His interest in attenuating the real conflict was to conceal the strong affinity between his own theory and the pagan thinkers, in opposition to the highly rationalistic and 'moral' theories of Grotius and the Catholic theologians.[41]

40. See also *SN* 309.
41. There were numerous issues, particularly in relation to 'naturalistic' currents of pagan origin, in which Protestant and Catholic thinkers were united against a common foe.

The true position is, in fact, very different from that presented by Vico. In the opening paragraphs of his *De Iure Belli et Pacis*, Grotius attacks Carneades for undermining the very basis of natural law and justice. The pagan thinker, writes Grotius, had argued that 'men had established rights *prompted by utility* and according to their diverse customs; and even in the same society these often changed with the times. There is therefore no natural law, for all men and all other animals *are impelled by nature to pursue their own utilities.*'[42] Grotius continues his attack on this pagan 'naturalistic' doctrine of naked self-interest, according to which man's behaviour is governed by utility and the natural gratification of his desires, by arguing that the real basis of natural law is some kind of social consensus around agreed values to which all rational men can assent. It is also 'natural', he asserts, to live according to such social conventions – and not simply to yield to utility and self-interest – since human nature is inherently social:

> And therefore what not only Carneades but also others have said, namely, *Utility is the mother of justice and equity*, if we are speaking accurately is not true; for the mother of natural law is human nature herself, which would, even if we needed it for nothing else, still lead us to desire mutual society.[43]

Then, to emphasize the pernicious thrust of Carneades's ideas, Grotius draws attention to St Augustine's condemnation of the pagan doctrine of 'utility' in the *De Doctrina Christiana*, Bk III, Ch. xiv.

The real conflict, as seen by Grotius and the Scholastics, was thus between their own doctrine of natural law which relied heavily on 'homo rationalis' and on the idea of social consensus around certain basic values, on the one hand, and a quite pernicious and unchristian doctrine which legitimized the pagan notion of 'utility' and the 'natural' pursuit of one's desires, on the other. The latter doctrine was associated, moreover, with the Epicurean–Democritan–Lucretian tradition which was automatically suspect to the Church. Its supporters were to be the natural enemies of the idea of free-will and the proponents of a moral agnosticism which denied any value to the doctrines of sin, of good and evil, and of divine grace. Given the striking resemblance of the ideas attacked by Grotius and by the Catholic tradition to those held by Vico himself, we begin to appreciate why his statements concerning his defence of free-will

---

42. Grotius, *De Iure Belli et Pacis*, Vol. i Prolegomena, par. 5. Italics mine.
43. Ibid., Vol. i, Prolegomena, par. 16.

and grace could be so important – and why they occur in the context of his discussions of law.

Utility and self-interest are crucial to Vico's idea of human development. And while at first sight he may seem to agree with Grotius that human nature is essentially social, Vico in reality arrives at his own conception of man's social nature by repudiating the rationalism at the heart of Grotius' arguments and instead infusing it with the very pagan 'naturalism' rejected by the Dutch jurist. If we examine these points in greater detail we shall see exactly how close Vico was to the positions which Grotius and the Catholic tradition attacked in Carneades and others.

We have seen numerous examples of Vico's use of the notion of 'utility' (along with 'necessity') as a driving force in early man's development. He reinforces the naturalism of this perspective with the idea that the pursuit of self-interest is an irresistible drive, since men 'are under the tyranny of self-love, *which compels them to make private utility their chief guide*. Seeking everything useful for themselves and nothing for their companions, they cannot bring their passions under control ['conato'] to direct them toward justice.'[44] Vico calls the force which prevents these socially disruptive passions from destroying humanity 'providence'. It is a 'divine legislative mind', which oversees the process of lawmaking in such a way that otherwise destructive human passions are steered towards social ends, because from

> ferocity, avarice, and ambition, the three vices which run throughout the human race, it creates the military, merchant, and governing classes, and thus the strength, riches, and wisdom of commonwealths. Out of these three great vices, which could certainly destroy all mankind on the face of the earth, it makes civil happiness.[45]

In the subsequent paragraph Vico drives his point home when he states that his argument

> proves that there is divine providence and further that it is a divine legislative mind. For out of the passions of men *all bent on their private utilities*, for the sake of which they would live like wild beasts in the wilderness, it has made the civil institutions by which they may live in society.[46]

The concept of 'providence' as a force overriding not only the passions but also the intentions of men finds frequent expression in

[handwritten marginal note: no – he wants to show how works despite utility]

44. *SN* 341.
45. *SN* 132.
46. *SN* 133.

the *Scienza nuova*. It is the cohesive element within Vico's natural-ism – a naturalism in which utility and necessity are 'the two perennial springs of the natural law of the gentes'.[47] It also raises, as we shall see, some fundamental questions about Vico's notion of 'free-will'.

47. *SN* 347. See also *SN* 141.

11
Law and the Question of Grace and Free Will

Although Vico's conception of human choice and freedom of action will be dealt with more fully at a later stage and in a different context, some discussion of the traditional Catholic doctrine of 'free will' is necessary at this stage. Vico was sufficiently concerned about the relationship of his legal writings to this important area of Catholic teaching to make specific reference to it in the *Autobiography*. Moreover, his name was occasionally linked with Jansenist and neo-Augustinian tendencies in Naples. In order to make sense of Vico's remarks, therefore, and to make some assessment of his real position, it will first be necessary to look briefly at the background and debates surrounding the doctrine of free will.

The problem of grace and free will was the single most important and controversial doctrinal debate within Catholic theology in the century and a half leading up to Vico's time.[1] There were two major phases in this lengthy controversy. During the first of these the initial antagonists were Jesuit and Dominican theologians who divided along partisan lines. This bitter debate took off in dramatic fashion with the publication in Lisbon, in 1589, of a treatise on the reconciliation of free will and grace (*Concordia Liberi Arbitrii Cum Gratiae Donis*) by the Jesuit theologian Luis de Molina. The work was immediately attacked by the Dominican theologian Dominic Báñez and his followers who accused Molina of understating the role of grace in his anxiety to preserve the freedom of the will. In the ensuing struggle the difference which emerged was broadly the following. The Molinists seemed to be suggesting that in respect of all activity conducive to salvation (good works) grace acts not *upon* but *with* the will, whereas the Dominicans appeared to argue that in order to be in any meaningful sense effective, grace must act *upon* human volition in a way which enables it to achieve what it would otherwise find at least more difficult to achieve. In other words, the

---

1. Useful discussions of some of the points raised here can be found in J. Delumeau, *Catholicism Between Luther and Voltaire: A New View of the Counter-Reformation*, and in Justo L. González, *A History of Christian Thought*, Vol. iii.

two sides expressed the classical division of 'optimists' and 'pessimists' regarding human nature: the Jesuits tending to emphasize the human will's own capacity for good, while the Dominicans stressing the role of grace in remedying the will's deficiency in this respect. Vico's remarks on the question in the *Scienza nuova* would undoubtedly seem to range him alongside the 'pessimistic' theologians.

In their more hostile exchanges the Dominicans accused their opponents of Pelagianism[2] and of ignoring important teachings of St Augustine concerning the real operation of grace upon the will. Jesuits, in their turn, responded with accusations of Calvinism[3] against the Dominicans. Both sides, however, were simultaneously claiming to be the correct interpreters of St Thomas Aquinas. After nine years of deliberation, in 1606 a papal commission eventually declared that both views were permissible within the framework of the teachings established by the Council of Trent, and both sides were ordered to refrain from mutual accusations of heresy. Although the Dominicans were thus cleared of Calvinism and the Jesuits of Pelagianism, the rift between the two major theological battalions of the Church was so deep-rooted and traumatic that successive papal decrees were issued (1611, 1625 and 1641) ordering that all works on the subject were to be submitted to the Holy Office for assessment.

The net result of this phase of the controversy was to reinforce the two essential components of the Church's teaching, that is, the efficacy of grace and the real freedom of the will. The Jesuits and Dominicans continued to emphasize the different aspects in their prolonged dispute which became, however, increasingly domestic and technical. But the event which pushed this first phase of the dispute into the background and shattered the orthodox boundaries within which the Church had fought to contain it was the publication in Louvain, in 1640, of the *Augustinus*, the major work of the Dutch theologian Cornelis Jansen.

As I have indicated, the Dominicans had highlighted St Augustine's somewhat sombre view of human nature and its weakness as a corrective to the Molinism of the Jesuits. They did not, however, deny the human will's own capacity for good. But the Augustinianism of Jansen and his followers contained a gloom of an

---

2. The heretical British monk Pelagius (c. 355–c. 425) took what the Church considered to be an excessively optimistic view of man's natural inclination towards good, thus denying the need for grace.

3. Calvinism was generally understood in Catholic circles as denying any meaningful role for the human will, salvation being totally dependent on election.

altogether different order. The idea that human nature was so corrupted after the fall of Adam that it could not even desire the good without first being moved by grace had already been condemned by Pius V as early as 1567 in the work of Jansen's lesser-known fellow Dutchman Michael Baius. But it took the former to revive such ideas, to break with the gentle pessimism of the entire Catholic tradition from medieval times onwards, and gain a following, particularly in France, which threatened to lead large numbers out of the Church.

In the *Augustinus*, Jansen stretches to its limits Augustine's idea that the freedom of the human will has been impaired by the Fall. According to Jansen, our condition is now such that we can love only ourselves and are incapable of altruistic activity. The human will, in other words, in order to perform good works, needs a form of grace which takes it over and wholly determines its course. Nevertheless, once bestowed, its force of attraction is so irresistible that the will is unconscious of being led. To these ideas we must add Jansen's acceptance of a vigorous predestination according to which the human will can do nothing to alter the eternal decree by which God has decided between the elect and the damned. The *Augustinus* was declared prohibited reading in 1641, and a further condemnation followed two years later in Urban VIII's papal bull, *In Eminenti*. In 1653, Pope Innocent X once again condemned specific propositions in Jansen's work, and in 1656 Antoine Arnauld, one of Jansen's leading supporters, was expelled from his post at the Sorbonne. Jansenism had clearly violated the Tridentine definitions which laid down that human volition must remain free, effective and capable of accepting or rejecting grace when it is offered.[4]

Although it undoubtedly had its adherents in Vico's Naples, it is doubtful whether Jansenism can be spoken of as a 'movement' there. Matters were made more difficult for prospective followers by its renewed condemnation in Clement XI's papal bulls of 1705 and 1713, *Vineam Domini* and *Unigenitus*. And although the movement was able to defend itself tolerably well in France, and even win support among the clergy, this was not the case in Naples. Among the accusations levelled at the condemned Grimaldi was that of Jansenist sympathies, a charge seemingly not lacking in some degree of plausibility.[5]

What of Vico's attitude to the doctrines of grace and free will?

---

4. For the details of this definition see H. Denzinger, *Enchiridion Symbolorum*, pp. 792ff.
5. See Grimaldi, *Memorie di un anticurialista*, p. 44, f 1.

His comments in the *Scienza nuova* are not the first indications of a connection in his mind between his legal theories and the question. We find this link expressed in the clearest and most explicit terms in the *Autobiography*:

> So it happened that living in the castle for nine years he made the greatest progress in his studies, digging into laws and canons, as his duties obliged him to. Led on from canon law to the study of dogmatic theology, *he found himself in the very middle of Catholic doctrine in the matter of grace*. This came about particularly through the reading of Richardus, the theologian of the Sorbonne. . . . *Richardus . . . shows that the doctrine of St Augustine is midway between the two extremes of Calvin and Pelagius, and equidistant likewise from the other opinions that approach these two extremes*. This disposition enabled him later to meditate a principle of the natural law of the nations, . . . *and agree with the sound doctrine of grace* in respect of moral philosophy.[6]

This passage raises some intriguing questions. In the first place, the progression from law to dogmatic theology which Vico presents is hardly the spontaneous and natural transition he would have us believe. Dogmatic theology, moreover, covered an extremely wide area, and yet one of the most sensitive theological issues of the time is singled out for mention. He carefully fixes his position on the matter upon an impeccably drawn 'via media', and his closing remarks seek to ensure that the reader fully understands that the *Scienza nuova*, which, in 1725, had shortly before come from the press and was subtitled an 'alternative system of the natural law of the gentes' was based on a sound understanding of the requirements of his faith regarding grace and free will. All in all, the passage gives a quite definite impression of being painstakingly drafted and calculated to produce a specific effect.

If, as I believe was the case, Vico was anxious to avoid suspicion, there were two issues involved. The major issue in theoretical terms related to the 'naturalistic' core of his theory regarding the 'natural law of the gentes', and concerns those passages already mentioned in the *Scienza nuova*. But on closer inspection there seems to be yet another dimension which is specific to this passage – one which suggests a determination to dissociate himself quite categorically from any hint of Jansenism.

We know that Vico's name was occasionally associated with the movement, although no strong links have ever been established. Certainly those passages in the *Scienza nuova* which emphasize

6. *Autobiography*, p. 119. Italics mine.

man's inability to pursue anything other than self-interest could be seen in such a light. So too could his occasional remarks on supernatural grace, in the sense that he makes this force 'take over' a function in which man does not seem to participate through his own volition in any meaningful sense. It seems to me undeniable, however, that such resemblances are superficial and misleading, and that there are fundamental differences between the respective conceptual frameworks of Vico and the Jansenists. Nevertheless, such resemblances, in isolation, could certainly have suggested a connection. Grimaldi, who was in difficulty with the Church when Vico was writing his *Autobiography*, was already widely suspected of Jansenism. Vico, understandably enough, could have been concerned to scotch accusations that were being bandied about at the time.

Unfortunately, however, he had some years before committed to print certain remarks which, if noticed, could have provided ammunition against him. In the *De Antiquissima* of 1710, where, we recall, Vico had not hesitated to acknowledge his association with the condemned de Cristofaro and others, he had had occasion to mention the sensitive question of how God's fore-knowledge of our activities and the irresistible power of His grace could be reconciled with free will. In the short passage in question Vico's proposed solution shows beyond doubt his familiarity with Jansenist arguments. He asks, for instance, how the fact that 'none of us can go to the Father unless the Father draws us to Himself' can fail to destroy man's volition. He resolves the question by referring to St Augustine's assertion that when God draws men to Himself then they are 'not only willing, but also content, even finding pleasure therein'.[7] The problem was that this particular remark had become a favourite quotation used by the Jansenists to defend themselves against the accusation of having destroyed human volition. In other words, Vico could easily be suspected of defending Jansenism in this short section of the *De Antiquissima*.

However that may be, if we return to the passage from the *Autobiography*, we shall see that Vico is not simply establishing his orthodoxy but also quite explicitly distancing himself from Jansenism. The widespread practice of using sources tactically was of special importance on sensitive issues. There is little doubt that Vico's use of a minor theologian such as Richardus to present his case falls into that category; otherwise, it would have been far simpler to endorse the teaching of Aquinas, a byword for ortho-

7. *Opere filosofiche*, p. 111.

But even if V sprouts
Jansenism, is that enough to
convict of unorthodoxy?

doxy in Naples. In addition, Aquinas was accepted unquestioningly by all internal rival factions on the question of grace and free will, and was free of all associations with the polemics and suspect interpretations inspired by even Augustine on the issue. But instead he presents his impeccably sketched 'middle of the road' position in association with a name whose significance would not have escaped the notice of the ecclesiastical authorities of the time.

The Jansenists based their case on a Calvinistic interpretation of Augustine, while at the other extreme we have the Pelagian tendency. In situating St Augustine 'midway between the two extremes of Calvin and Pelagius' Vico was rejecting both heretical tendencies, but by using a ritual statement which had in effect by this time become simply an anti-Jansenist formula.[8] To drive his point home he uses the work of a Jesuit theologian, Richardus, who had made his name and reputation as a virulent opponent of Jansen and defender of the Holy See.[9]

Whatever the ultimate verdict on the question of Vico's attitudes to Jansenism, there seems to me little difficulty in demonstrating a fundamental problem in reconciling his theory of law with the Catholic teaching on grace and free-will, a problem which explains his anxiety to keep stating his orthodoxy. We have seen that Vico's theory is one in which legislation is derived largely from men following their natural, even destructive and anti-social desires. Law originates in men who are 'under the tyranny of self-love', who 'cannot bring their passions under control to direct them to justice' and so 'make private utility their chief guide'. These ideas clearly range Vico alongside the Carneadean, pagan interpretation of the nature of law – a natural enemy of the whole Christian teaching on free-will, good and evil, and divine grace.

Vico attempts to present his system in a more positive and orthodox light by using his concept of 'providence' as a 'divine legislative mind' which, out of men's pursuit of their own selfish interests and in spite of their intentions,[10] itself creates the civil institutions and legal systems we know. He makes the simple assertion, moreover, that such ideas *prove* 'that man has free choice, however weak, to make virtues of his passions; but that he is aided by God, naturally by divine providence and supernaturally by

8. With the demise of the Molinist controversy there was no longer any danger from Pelagian-inspired quarters. In any case, the Jesuits had by this time, via Suárez and others, considerably modified their original Molinism through an increased injection of Thomism into their ideas.

9. Antonius Richardus, pseudonym of Étienne Deschamps, author of *De Haeresi ab Apostolica Sede Proscripta* (1654).

10. See also *SN* 342, 343, 629.

divine grace'.[11] Precisely how Vico's ideas prove such doctrines is left to the ingenuity of the reader. His statement does indeed give the impression of being something of a bluff, for it does not, I think, require great theological expertise to demonstrate that the doctrines in question are placed in serious jeopardy by his overall scheme of things. Let us take the three points he mentions – grace, providence and free will – briefly, one by one.

The Catholic doctrine of grace is straightforward enough. Its essential feature, as far as our discussion is concerned, is that while it is bestowed gratuitously by God to aid man's fallen nature, it cannot assume control of the individual's desires and intentions. The individual will, in other words, may indeed be weak and require assistance in performing a good act or avoiding an evil one. Grace will consequently provide the necessary assistance in either case but only on condition that the individual in question initially intends either to do the good or to avoid the evil for which he is being assisted. But in Vico's theory, legislation, historically, is the work of a 'divine legislative mind' which compensates for men 'all bent on their private utilities, for the sake of which they would live like wild beasts', pursuing what are in themselves, according to Vico, destructive passions. It is thus an 'external' force, operating *in spite of* men's actions, which brings about civil society. But in the Catholic doctrine of grace men must themselves intend and desire the objective for which grace is bestowed as an aid. In other words, *the operation of grace and the intentions of men must be working in the same direction.* By contrast, the whole 'naturalistic' thrust of Vico's discourse reduces all apparent forms of divine assistance to forces which act as remedies for the otherwise destructive effects of men's intentional activities. Even in the most extreme Augustinianism of the Jansenists, the 'taking over' of man's volition leads to an identity of intentions between the divine and human wills. In Vico, the famous 'heterogeneity of ends' leaves a permanent conflict between intentions and results.

Providence is, of course, for students of the *Scienza nuova*, a central problem, for it figures prominently throughout the work. A fuller discussion of the concept will be provided in a separate chapter, but we can even now make a few preliminary observations. Vico introduces the notion of providence into his discussion

11. *SN* 136. It is interesting to note the decidedly Augustinian tone of Vico's presentation of the doctrine. This more 'pessimistic' current within Catholic theology, which emphasized the corruption and weakness of the human will after the fall was undoubtedly more congenial to him, and was an effective camouflage for the essentially heterodox nature of his ideas in this sphere.

of law as the force which steers the blind passions of men into legally and socially useful directions. The classical Thomist discussion of providence[12] is at pains to preserve and attribute full effectiveness, freedom and critical awareness to all occasions of human choice. Aquinas makes it clear that men's actions, including their intentions (since this is where blame or merit is located), must be left intact: 'since rational creatures have control over their actions through free choice, as has been said, they come under divine providence in a special manner; it is evident that since blame or merit is imputed to them, so it is requited with punishment or reward'.[13]

St Thomas is at pains to leave free will intact because man must bear the ultimate responsibility for his actions. It is legitimate, therefore, to conceive of providence as guiding human affairs, but there are certain conditions attached to this. Men, as rational creatures able to discriminate between good and evil, must regulate their activities according to the socially and morally acceptable goals of human society. God, declares St Augustine, 'made man a rational animal, consisting of body and soul, whom he has not permitted should go unpunished when sinning . . .'.[14] Individual men cannot simply abandon themselves to selfish pursuits in the hope that some superior force will compensate for the potentially destructive effects. As in the case of divine grace, therefore, providence also presupposes a basically moral, social direction, at least in intention, on the part of humanity. Without this the whole basis of the Christian notion of individual culpability, of good and evil, is destroyed. But Vico uses providence as an active corrective to the selfish pursuits in which humanity is bound to indulge, and which 'could certainly destroy all mankind'.[15] Such a conception of providence is consequently unacceptable for the very same reasons as those outlined earlier in relation to the doctrine of grace. Moreover, the moral agnosticism of Vico's theory is all the more complete in that he elevates the self-interest and destructive passions pursued by early humanity to the level of organizational cornerstones in his theory of legal and social development. It is important to grasp that in the *Scienza nuova* we are not simply dealing with individual, or even widespread, instances of selfish activity. Vico's theory amounts to a wholesale accommodation of such activity as the norm, and as fundamental to social development.

12. Aquinas, *Summa Theologica*, 1a, q. 22, arts. 1–4.
13. Ibid., a. 2, ad 5um.
14. Augustine, *De Civitate Dei*, Bk V, ch. 11.
15. *SN* 132.

In relation to the problem of free will, we should bear in mind that, for Vico, human choice is 'determined by the "senso comune" of men' and on the basis of 'human necessities or utilities' which are the foundations of the 'natural law of the gentes'.[16] The 'senso comune', moreover, is a naturalistic force wholly immersed in the pursuit of the utilities and necessities of life. As I have argued elsewhere,[17] 'human choice' in early men is, to Vico, significant not in the individual but only within the context of the social choices of whole societies or nations in response to their natural needs or requirements. The determining 'senso comune' which provides the motor force for these choices is a faculty lacking in reflection,[18] and is, therefore, without that basic discriminatory or deliberative capacity which renders 'human choice' subject to moral evaluation. It is, in short, an instinctive drive felt by whole peoples and nations.[19] There can be little doubt, therefore, that Vico's theory undermines the crucial notion of individual culpability based on reflective choice between real alternatives, which is the cornerstone of the Catholic, indeed of the whole Christian, doctrine of free-will. What is more, the naturalism at the root of the 'senso comune' underlies even those aspects of Vico's thought which at first sight might seem far removed from it.

16. See *SN* 141.
17. Bedani, 'The Poetic as an Aesthetic Category', pp. 31ff.
18. See *SN* 142.
19. See ibid.

12
Law and the Struggle for Rights

We will recall, from Chapter 4, that in the context of linguistic development the force of 'natural necessity' was considerably diminished in the final phase of man's evolution. The rational stage, Vico states, is one in which men become 'absolute masters' over their linguistic conventions. Thus, the requirements of 'utility' and 'necessity', the objectives of the instinctive and naturalistic drives so crucial to early man's development, are no longer dominant in the linguistic aspects of the final stage of man's social evolution.

In this chapter, an attempt will be made to show that there is an important area of social change in which Vico's model for language is not followed; namely, the socio-legal sphere. Here, despite initial appearances, his naturalism is kept very much alive even within the third and final phase of human development. This may seem, at first sight, an unwarranted assertion. After all, we know that, when talking of the three phases of natural law in his tripartite scheme, he characterizes the third phase as the 'human law dictated by fully developed human reason'.[1] On the level of government, moreover, 'the third are human governments, in which, in virtue of the equality of the intelligent nature which is the proper nature of man, all are accounted equal under the laws, inasmuch as all are born free in their cities'.[2]

It might seem, therefore, as if there is a strict parallel between the linguistic aspect of social development and the legal and governmental dimensions of man's social evolution. The reader might even be tempted to infer from the above quotations that Vico is implying that in the third epoch men are as much complete masters over these aspects of their social existence as they are over their linguistic patterns of behaviour. If this were so, there would indeed be a corresponding dimunition in the role of 'natural necessity' in the development of laws and governments. But this is not so. However, before dealing directly with this question we must say a

1. *SN* 924.
2. *SN* 927.

little more about the background to Vico's interest in problems of legal development. This will shed light on why he was disposed to retain a strong naturalistic element even in the third and final phase of legal and governmental evolution.

Research into the preoccupations of the circles in which he moved suggests a strong political orientation among Vico's friends and associates.[3] This does not mean, however, that his own writings on law express immediate political concerns or objectives. Rather, many of the debates and problems which engaged his contemporaries and to which they sought immediate solutions became the raw material for his own wider-ranging philosophical reflections. In this sense we can claim that although there is a primarily philosophical aim in the *Scienza nuova*, it does not mean that we have to discount a political dimension in its genesis.

Vico's Naples had certainly inherited some peculiar problems from its own past. After the revolt of Masaniello in 1647 – an unexpected rebellion which surprised and severely shook the Spanish rulers – the vice-regency had pursued a dual policy of appeasing popular and intermediate social groups, on the one hand, and of controlling baronial power, on the other. Representatives of the middle strata were gradually being absorbed into the affairs and management of the growing and complex area of public administration. Thus a 'ceto civile' (civil or administrative class) of administrators and lawyers was forming. This emergent social group proved useful to the Spanish rulers in keeping in check the often troublesome demands and ambitions of the feudal aristocracy.

The new class, however, attracted hostility from two quarters. In the first place, the traditional aristocracy resented the growing interference of these administrators and lawyers in the exercise of its political, fiscal and juridical privileges. But no less ill-disposed towards the newly emergent social group were the ecclesiastical owners of landed property, in many ways even more prone to attack from the 'ceto civile' than the aristocracy.[4] Vico was himself

---

3. Important for a study of this topic are De Giovanni, *Filosofia e diritto in Francesco D'Andrea*; Badaloni, *Introduzione a G. B. Vico*; Mastellone, *Pensiero politico* and his *Francesco D'Andrea politico e giurista (1648–1698). L' Ascesa del ceto civile*; Comparato, *Giuseppe Valetta*.

4. This is understandable if we bear in mind the general ill-feeling, so well described by Franco Valsecchi, resulting from the involvement of the Church in temporal affairs: 'Beside the nobility, as a dominant group, there was the clergy; even more than a privileged class, this was a society in its own right, which, because of its ecclesiastical nature, placed itself outside and above the lay community. Its juridical and fiscal immunities were even greater than those of the nobility'. (*L' Italia nel Settecento*, 422–3.)

part of the 'ceto civile'. Initially, against this background of baronial and ecclesiastical privilege, the major focus of its struggle was the acquisition of more secure civil rights for its own members. But gradually its strategy shifted towards a defence of the pre-eminence of 'public' over 'private' interest. It is at this point that the debate about the relationship between public and private interests begins to appear in a generalized form in Vico's early writings.

In his *Orations* there is a deep concern with the social or communal aspect of civic life. In the first six of these orations, which run from 1699 to 1707, Vico stresses the 'guiding role' in public life of those who undertake serious study. His own 'ceto civile' is, of course, closely associated with such a function. In the fourth *Oration* of 1704, for example, he begins his speech with an exhortation which emphasizes the obligation of the group to employ its erudition for the public good.[5] He is concerned, in this oration, lest 'private advantage' should prove to be the sole motivating force for undertaking study.

While the same theme is a constant one throughout the six early orations, in the far weightier and more substantial seventh – the *De Ratione* – there is an observable shift involving a more elaborate exploration of the problem of public and private interest. Vico seems to have awakened to the danger that his own 'ceto civile', and in particular the more legally expert 'ceto forense', might learn from their feudal and ecclesiastical opponents the art of using the law as a domestic preserve and as an instrument for personal advantage. At this stage he had not yet developed his ideas on primitive society, and he still accepted the idea of an original ideal state within which corruption slowly took root. His argument proceeds in the following manner.

The philosopher–jurists of ancient Rome, Vico declares, 'preserved in its pure form the wisdom of heroic times.'[6] Gradually, however, the patricians began to seek control over all three orders of citizens: plebeians, knights and the senate. To achieve such control they contrived to make the three branches of law (sacred, public and private) their own esoteric preserve, in which 'the patricians alone guarded jurisprudence as consisting of certain mysteries'.[7] In order to secure their secret power over the laws, he continues, the patricians finally bestowed upon them a sacred

5. 'If anyone wishes to obtain from the study of letters the greatest advantage, and to see them always conjoined with uprightness, let him be instructed for the commonweal and for the common good of the citizens.' (*Opere filosofiche*, 747.)
6. Ibid., 823.
7. Ibid., 825.

character, and they made themselves the guardians and interpreters of their meaning.

With the passage of time, Vico further observes, the three branches of law began to move apart. Sacred law became the preserve of the theologians or canon lawyers. There followed the severence of 'private' from 'public' law, 'from which time the philosophy of law began to degenerate'.[8] 'Private' law then increased in importance in the sense that it received far more attention than 'public' law. Since the former offered more tangible rewards, legal scholars tended to concentrate their efforts on the study of natural equity, the basis of private law and private utility. Civil equity, the foundation of public law and common utility, by contrast, suffered relative neglect. This is the situation which, Vico claims, existed in his own day, and he calls for a rethinking of the relationship between the private sphere of natural equity and the broader context of the common weal or civil equity.

The latter stage of the argument in the *De Ratione* marks the origin of important theoretical shifts in Vico's perspective. The reconciliation of private and public interest as expressed in law cannot be left to the 'guiding function' of a wise or learned élite. Such groups, he became increasingly convinced, tend simply to protect their own privileges. But since this is so, there must also be subordinate groups whose own utility or interest is in conflict with that of the ruling class and who are continually pressing for change. Such groups will, of course, seek to redefine and to broaden the terms of natural equity to include themselves. This was in fact an explicit strategy amongst the 'giusnaturalisti' of Vico's day. Thus the idea of a struggle amongst diverse interest groups makes its appearance in Vico's thought.

In the *Diritto universale*, he begins to systematize his reflections on the respective roles of contending interest groups under the law. From being simply a 'danger' to be guarded against, the tendency of the powerful to 'arrange' legal systems to serve their own interests gradually takes on the aspect of a universal principle in all forms of legal development. That is to say, the doctrine is integrated into a greater overall pattern of social relations and thereby absorbed into the overall prescriptive aspect of his theory. He argues, for example, that civil society proper begins when the weak seek the protection of the strong. When this happens we have the seeds of a system of alliances, duties and allegiances which serves as the basis for all subsequent social and legal development. At a

8. Ibid., 829.

certain point 'the clients, finally tired of working the land for others, rose up against the strong, who, in order to resist, united and organized themselves, and the most fierce made himself the leader. In this way, out of the need to defend was born organization (order), which was then called 'civil'.'[9]

Laws follow to appease the lower orders, but all further concessions are firmly rejected. Vico points out a little later that Carneades, along with his followers Epicurus, Machiavelli, Hobbes, Spinoza and Bayle, had all argued that self-interest or utility ('utilità propria') is the real yardstick for law, that justice is therefore variable according to time and place, and that only the weak demand 'natural equity' while the powerful seek to preserve their privileges.[10] But in spite of his ritual condemnation of this school of thinkers we can already see a great measure of sympathy for their ideas as early as the *Diritto universale*.

We now return to our starting point in this chapter concerning the period of rationality, for the demands put forward by the lower orders would seem to be a product of a general growth in mental capacity. In other words, at a certain point men began to measure themselves against their social superiors on equal terms of rationality and demanded equal rights: 'But with the passage of the years and the far greater development of human minds, the plebs of the peoples finally . . . understood themselves to be of equal human nature with the nobles, and therefore insisted that they too should enter into the civil institutions of the cities'.[11] But if we observe carefully, we shall in fact discover that in the later stages of development in the spheres of government and legislation reason by no means replaces 'natural necessity' as the motivating force for change. The specific determinations of this evolved 'natural necessity' are perhaps somewhat different from what they were with primitive man. Nevertheless 'rational' man, as we shall see, does not rise above 'utilità propria' and the pursuit of self-interest to which early man was condemned. On the contrary, his ability to reason becomes an integral part of the mechanism whereby Vico's 'naturalism' unfolds.

The struggles we have pointed to between social groups are 'the most powerful means of making the commonwealths great'.[12] The process is one in which laws are fought for, withheld, manipulated or granted as part of a range of self-interested manoeuvres: 'The

---

9. 'Sinopsis del diritto universale', in *Opere giuridiche*, p. 13.
10. See *Opere giuridiche*, p. 31.
11. See *SN* 1101. See also *SN* 414.
12. *SN* 280.

weak want laws; the powerful withhold them; the ambitious, to win a following, advocate them; princes, to equalize the strong with the weak, protect them.'[13] Such struggles, which Patrick Hutton, amongst others, has analysed as revolving around the acquisition and consolidation of property rights, becomes a universal characteristic of Vico's 'ideal eternal history'.[14] The gradual extension of social status from bonitary tenure (i.e. occupation of land without title) to full citizen rights of ownership is a uniform pattern of development which he detects amongst all nations; and the struggle between plebeians and nobles expresses 'two contrary eternal properties emerging from this nature of human civil institutions which we are here investigating: namely, (1) that the plebeians always want to change the form of government, as in fact it is always they who do change it, and (2) that the nobles always want to keep it as it is.'[15]

From the very beginning Vico makes it clear that utility and self-interest provide the dynamic forces of change in this social interplay. Even with their very first concessions it is 'by a common sense of utility' that the heroes 'were constrained to satisfy the multitude of their rebellious clients . . . .'.[16] Moreover, the tendency of the strong to identify their own private interests with the public good was a necessary part of civil development. For the powerful, 'if they had not had such a great private interest identified with the public interest, could not have been induced to abandon their savage life and cultivate civility'.[17]

In the age of developed reason the popular strata become fully aware of their capabilities and demanded an equal share of power. This, claims Vico, leads to popular commonwealths in which 'the citizens have command of the public good'.*[18] And although it might seem at first sight an ideal state of affairs, he repeatedly tells us that this is not so, for the reason that in popular republics the 'public good' 'is divided among them in as many minute parts as there are citizens making up the people who have command of it'.[19] So a greater rational awareness among the population does not generate any form of social or civic motivation, since 'in the free commonwealths all look out for their own private interests, into

---

13. *SN* 283.
14. See P. H. Hutton, 'Vico's Theory of History and the French Revolutionary Tradition'.
15. *SN* 609.
16. *SN* 597.
17. *SN* 950.
18. *SN* 951.
19. Ibid.

the service of which they press their public arms at the risk of ruin to their nations . . .'[20] Reason, therefore, serves to generate a greater desire and demand for the fulfilment and gratification of individual rights and desires. There is no greater tyranny, argues Vico, than the popular commonwealth: 'witness the anarchies, or unlimited popular commonwealths, than which there is no greater tyranny, for in them there are as many tyrants as there are bold and dissolute men in the cities'.[21] To remedy this situation, in order to preserve the nations from self-destruction, 'a single man must arise, as Augustus did at Rome, and take all public concerns by force of arms into his own hands, leaving his subjects free to look after their private affairs. . . . Hence monarchy is the form of government best adapted to human nature when reason is fully developed.'[22] Only in this way, Vico tells us, 'are the peoples saved when they would otherwise rush to their own destruction'.[23]

As we can see, far from leading to a more enhanced civic consciousness, increased rationality is portrayed here in a negative light as a socially disruptive force.[24] The naturalistic basis of Vico's theory prescribes that in general individuals cannot rise above the pursuit of self-interest. Accordingly, provision for the care of the public good is eventually surrendered to the monarchy.[25] This apparent sentencing of the citizenry to a perpetual pursuit of self-interest is in fact part of Vico's general theoretical framework, so that even in the final phase of human development utility and necessity predominate over reason itself. Consequently, Vico is compelled to resort to a guiding force which he describes as 'a mind often diverse, at times quite contrary, and always superior to the particular ends that men had proposed to themselves; by making such narrow ends into instruments for serving wider purposes, it has always used them to preserve the human race upon this earth'.*[26] So, leaving aside the anomaly we discussed concerning the linguistic aspect of his social existence, the whole arc of man's development is conditioned by a naturalistic pursuit of individual or group interests.

In the passage just quoted, Vico goes on to describe the effects of the superior guiding force which always diverts the potentially destructive impulses and activities of successive epochs of human-

20. *SN* 1008.
21. *SN* 292.
22. *SN* 1008.
23. Ibid.
24. See also *SN* 1102.
25. See also *SN* 1006.
26. *SN* 1108.

ity towards social ends:

> Men mean to gratify their bestial lust and abandon their offspring, and
> they inaugurate the chastity of marriage from which the families arise.
> The fathers mean to exercise without restraint their paternal power over
> their clients, and they subject them to the civil powers from which the
> cities arise. The reigning orders of nobles mean to abuse their lordly
> freedom over the plebeians, and they are obliged to submit to the laws
> which establish popular liberty. The free peoples mean to shake off the
> yoke of their laws, and they become subject to monarchs.[27]

Such a conception of human behaviour, as we have already seen,
cannot be reconciled with the Christian notion of men as rational,
free agents making morally responsible and socially considered
decisions. So, fully aware of having presented a scheme of development in which socially acceptable effects are achieved *in spite of* the
destructive, selfish intentions of men's actions, Vico then attempts
once more to camouflage the unorthodox nature of his argument
by adding, quite blandly at the end of the passage, that what
determined the end result 'was mind, for men did it with intelligence; it was not fate, for they did it by choice'.[28].

Such statements should not mislead us in our analysis. Vico's
conception of legal development relies heavily on the idea of the
pursuit and the defence of self-interest. In this sense he sides, not
with the advocates of 'rationalist' interpretations of 'natural law',
but rather with the advocates of the idea of 'force' as a means of
producing and maintaining legal systems. That is the sense of
Vico's 'utility' in this context. If any doubt remains, the reader
should consult the passage in which he talks of the struggle for
power, stating that:

> in proportion as the optimates lose their grip the strength of the people
> increases until they become free; and in proportion as the free peoples
> relax their hold the kings gain in strength until they become monarchs.
> Wherefore, just as the natural law of the philosophers (or moral theolo-
> gians) is that of reason, so *this natural law of the gentes is that of utility and of
> force*, which, as the juriconsults say, is observed by the nations *usu
> exigente humanisque necessitatibus expostulantibus*, 'as occasion requires and
> human needs demand'.[29]

One could hardly expect a clearer indication that the 'natural law of
the gentes' is a concept which draws heavily on that tradition which

[handwritten marginal note: yes— always a mix]

---

27. Ibid.
28. Ibid.
29. *SN* 1084. Italics in English mine.

favours the 'rule of force' as a starting point for explaining legal systems. The rival 'contractual' and 'rationalist' theories, as we know, Vico found profoundly unacceptable.

We can see, therefore, that Vico's naturalism was not limited to the development of *early* man. In all epochs, utility, self-interest and force are equally important in determining the course of events. The spread of rationality simply brings greater numbers to a realization of their potential for exploiting the opportunities that exist in the struggle for 'natural equity'. In short, the absence of any dynamic force in rationality is fundamental to Vico's naturalism. There is no suggestion in the *Scienza nuova* of an open-ended, unilinear process of development in history such as was fundamental to the Christian eschatological tradition. Accordingly,it is no accident, as we shall see below, that Vico resorts to 'ricorsi' in his scheme of development. These cyclic returns indeed prove to be an essential part of his naturalistic perspective on life and human destiny.

Part V
The Development of Vico's Epistemology and the Science of History

13

The Early Vico and Concepts of Scientificity

The Traditional View

One of the most widely accepted canons of interpretation among students of the *Scienza nuova* is the idea that its main thrust is the application of the 'verum factum' principle to the field of historical enquiry. In other words, this principle, elaborated in the *De Anti-quissima* of 1710, which asserts that we know perfectly only that which we ourselves create, is widely regarded as the guiding principle of the *Scienza nuova*. God, for instance, created nature, therefore only He can have a perfect knowledge of the natural world. Man, by contrast, has created history and can therefore achieve a more complete knowledge in this sphere than he can in the natural sciences, where he attempts to uncover principles and laws which are not of his own making. In this sense, critics argue, we must interpret statements such as the following:

> Whoever reflects on this cannot but marvel that the philosophers should have bent all their energies to the study of the world of nature, which, since God made it, He alone knows; and that they should have neglected the study of the world of nations, or civil world, which, since men had made it, men could come to know.[1]

A whole series of conclusions has subsequently been derived from this interpretation, including Vico's alleged relegation of the natural sciences to a lower order of enquiry and the raising of historical knowledge to the status of what we shall describe in the next chapter as an 'epistemology of privileged insight'.

As shall be discussed below, such an interpretation amounts to a considerable distortion of the *Scienza nuova*. In the first place it will be argued that the 'verum factum' principle was actually of far more limited importance to Vico than is usually supposed. Secondly, it will be shown that it was the more important 'vero'/

1. *SN* 331.

'certo' problem which was at the centre of the *Scienza nuova*.

The passage quoted above in which Vico distinguished between God's knowledge of the world of nature and man's knowledge of the world of nations undoubtedly invokes the 'verum factum' principle. But as with numerous other statements in the *Scienza nuova*, we cannot jump to conclusions as to its theoretical weight. For the principle to be at the centre of the work it has to be shown that it has a real operative function within the theory. We shall see below that this cannot be the case. For the moment, however, we shall simply make a few preliminary comments on the passage in question.

Nicolini's footnote to this passage in his Ricciardi edition of the *Opere*, draws attention to the fact that Vico's distinction is a repetition of the one drawn between 'res divinae' and 'res humanae' by classical Latin authors. But he was also repeating a well-worn theoretical maxim regarding the necessary limits of human understanding of the physical world, as put forward by natural scientists of his own day. Even Galileo had addressed himself to this problem when making his well-known statements on the perfect knowability of mathematics, and on how the latter provided the base-structure of reality. In this way, Galileo was seeking to defend the reliability of empirically acquired knowledge to a theologically hostile and suspicious world of scholars, a problem which also exercised, though in a different way, the minds of Vico and his friends. Vico, it should be remembered, was after all initiating a 'new science', and the contrast he drew above was undoubtedly one way of asserting its legitimacy.

If, however, the distinction between God's knowledge of the natural world and man's knowledge of the civil world was meant to be more than a casual supportive statement we would rightly expect an elaboration of the 'verum factum' doctrine. Yet the passage we have quoted contains by far the clearest reference to this concept we shall find in the *Scienza nuova*; and all the other passages which are commonly referred to as dependent upon it can be interpreted in a different light. Moreover, even *SN* 331 makes no attempt to explain or argue the applicability of the doctrine. *There is in fact no attempt to do so throughout the whole of the work*, which would indeed be strange if it had been meant to occupy the central place attributed to it by many critics. Granted this rather curious state of affairs, we shall now outline briefly the traditional perspective on the work and try to suggest some possible correctives.

As we have already seen, Vico states in the *De Antiquissima* that only God, its creator, can understand with perfect clarity the world of nature and its internal principles of operation. Likewise, man's knowledge of mathematics is absolute since its principles are all creations of the human mind. The truths of mathematics express the necessary modes of operation of human reason and therefore man apprehends them perfectly. Hence, because Vico stated that 'the world of civil society has certainly been made by men',[2] Croce argued in his famous and first major modern study of the *Scienza nuova* that the 'verum factum' principle was being extended to history. Vico's great discovery consisted, in other words, of a 'realisation of a new implication of the theory of knowledge laid down by himself in the former period of his speculations; namely, the criterion of truth consisting in the "convertibility of the true with the created." The reason why man could have perfect knowledge of man's world was simply that he had himself made that world.'[3]

The thesis of Vico's transposition of the 'verum factum' principle to the field of history has since been repeated by nearly all major commentators on his work. One or two further examples will illustrate the point. For instance, Enzo Paci writes: 'The Vichian *New Science* consists precisely of the discovery that within the human mind are present those elements of the truth which, in their construction, involve the same operation, i.e. cognition by causes, according to which man has constructed history'.[4] The basic elements of this interpretation have in fact remained remarkably unchanged ever since that time. Rather more recently, for instance, Isaiah Berlin has again repeated the same notion when observing that the 'truly revolutionary move is the application of the *verum/factum* principle to the study of history'.[5]

Critics have chosen, according to their own interests, to emphasize one or other of the various aspects or implications of the 'verum factum' thesis. As we have already mentioned, one idea which has received much attention is the contention that the science of history contains a higher degree of scientificity than the natural sciences. However, even this idea can be traced back to Croce's study. The 'verum factum', he asserts, in identifying human history as man's creation, 'raised the knowledge of human affairs . . . to the rank of perfect science'.[6] Nearer our own times another critic Luigi Bellofiore has claimed that Vico proposed a revolution of

2. Ibid.
3. Croce, *Philosophy*, p. 23.
4. Paci, *Ingens Sylva*, pp. 103–4.
5. I. Berlin, *Vico and Herder*, p. 26.
6. Croce, *Philosophy*, p. 24.

sorts. According to Bellofiore, Vico argues that the Cartesians are mistaken in thinking of physics as a true science. History, which they have largely held in contempt, is on the other hand a true science. This is because 'the verum factum applies to history, not to physics since man creates history but does not make nature'.[7] As we can see clearly from these, and numerous other commentaries, the contention that Vico 'applies' the 'verum factum' principle in the *Scienza nuova* is used to support the assertion that in this work the author's major proposition is that *man makes history*, and that the science of history enjoys an epistemological superiority over the physical sciences.[8]

So far we have outlined the traditional interpretation in some detail in order to focus upon its major components. We are now in a position to individuate three major propositions arising from this interpretation so that they can be examined separately. It is important to do so because the three elements in question are usually dovetailed into a single interpretative scheme, which is seductive precisely because of its 'unitary' and internally coherent appearance. We shall first identify them and then attempt to demonstrate that none of them can be critically sustained by careful attention to the text.

The idea of a 'special' scientificity for the science of history will be examined in the next chapter. At present we shall confine ourselves to scrutinizing the two other elements of the traditional approach to the *Scienza nuova*. We shall test the validity of the claim that in this work Vico asserts that 'man makes history'. Before doing so, however, we shall need to place the 'verum factum' doctrine within a broader problematic than the one within which it is usually framed. This should demonstrate its true relevance in Vico's thinking and explain the absence of any discussion of it in the text of the *Scienza nuova*. It will also call into question the claim concerning his alleged 'relegation' of the natural sciences to a less epistemologically exalted status than the human sciences.

Before embarking on our analysis proper it is necessary to clarify one or two misconceptions which have found their way into the

7. L. Bellofiore, *La Dottrina della provvidenza in G. B. Vico*, p. 18.
8. Jeffrey Barnouw is at least a partial exception. Although seeming to accept the traditional assumption concerning the 'verum factum' as the basis of the *Scienza nouva*, Barnouw nevertheless argues that 'Vico's development', rightly understood, rather supports the view that the "new science" of the seventeenth century, from Galileo on, provided the crucial inspiration and model for the formation of the human sciences and thus effected a fundamental break with humanistic and pruden-tial orientations. A careful reading of Vico's early works reveals a deep commitment to the continuity of science.' ('Vico and the Continuity of Science: The Relation of his Epistemology to Bacon and Hobbes', p. 609.)

accepted corpus of Vichian criticism. The proponents of the idea that the 'verum factum' principle finds its final application in the *Scienza nuova* point to its author's repeated assertion that man has made the world of civil society as the embodiment of the doctrine in its historicist form. But it is also claimed that it finds its way into the major work after a long period of neglect. It is said that after 1710, following the enunciation of the 'verum factum' principle in the *De Antiquissima*, we do not find it again except in its 'historicist' form in the 1730 edition of the *Scienza nuova*.[9]

The thesis of 'long neglect' is misleading for a number of reasons, and most of all because there is in fact a remarkable continuity in Vico's major epistemological preoccupations, though they lie in quite another direction. This, however, will take time to demonstrate. For the moment, therefore, we shall simply point out that the 'long neglect' argument is factually faulty even on the terms of its own proponents. This is because Vico does in effect make his claim about man creating the world of civil institutions or nations at an earlier stage. He writes, in the *first* edition of his work (1725):

> that the world of Gentile nations has *certainly* ['certamente'] been made by men . . . its principles must be found within the nature of our human minds and in the power of our understanding by elevating the metaphysics of the human mind . . . to contemplate the 'senso comune' of mankind as a *certain* ['certa'] human mind of the nations. . . .[10]

The reader will notice, in this passage, the reference to the concept of the 'certo', something we shall return to later, when we shall argue that it is to this concept, rather than to the 'verum factum' principle that Vico's statement concerning the world of civil society is fundamentally related. And since the problem surrounding the 'certo' (or more properly the 'vero'/'certo' issue) was an abiding one, there is in fact no 'long neglect' to explain.

Interestingly enough, Guido Fassò seems partially to have sensed this problem. In two important studies on the problem of law in the *Scienza nuova* he has called into question the idea that the 'verum factum' principle was the *historically* determining key-concept of the work. Fassò argues that it is the problem of reconciling the 'certo' of existing, historical and ever-changing positive law with

---

9. Pasini, for instance, states that after the 1710 *De Antiquissima*, 'as is well known, Vico does not speak of this principle, even indirectly, until 1730, i.e. until the "second Scienza Nuova". In fact, it is only at this point that he writes: "that the world of civil society has certainly been made by men, and that its principles are therefore to be found within the modifications of our own human mind".' (*Diritto, società e stato*, p. 18.) See also Fassò, *Vico e Grocio*, p. 61 and Verene, *Vico's Science*, p. 58, where the same claim is repeated.

10. *SN1a* 40. Italics mine.

the 'vero' of ideal or natural law which is at the root of the *Scienza nuova*:

> It is clear that Vico considers the essence of his new science to lie in the making certain ['accertamento'] of the 'vero' and the verification ['avveramento'] of the 'certo': that he maintains that the very birth of the *New Science* was due to the discovery of this method, or, if one prefers, to that of the principle of the identity between the 'vero' and the 'certo'; and not, as is commonly held, to the extension of the *verum ipsum-factum* principle from the field of mathematics alone to that of history.[11]

But this priority of the 'vero'/'certo' problem over the 'verum factum' principle applies, apparently, only to the *genesis* of the *Scienza Nuova* and not to its *theoretical substance*, since the 'verum factum', according to Fassò, is the one which functions 'in the depths of Vico's thoughts'.[12] While, therefore, Fassò upholds an alternative problem as occasioning the reflections which lead to the writing of the *Scienza nuova*, this does not really displace the 'verum factum' because 'if it is argued that, in their deepest essential meaning, the two principles coincide . . . I would agree completely and even grant the logical priority enjoyed by the principle of *verum ipsum factum*.'[13] The 'deepest essential meaning' shared by the two principles is never explained. Fassò in effect regresses, after a promising start, to a substantial recapitulation of the traditional thesis, namely, that after a considerable lapse of time the 'verum factum' principle is resurrected and converted from an abstract doctrine to a fundamental element in Vico's historicism.

In fact, Vico's alleged discovery of the applicability of the 'verum factum' principle to the study of history – as seen in his comments about man's creation of civil society – is a repetition of an idea already in circulation. More than half a century before Vico had written the *De Antiquissima* the English philosopher Thomas Hobbes had made, in the most explicit terms, the link between the knowability of mathematics and of civil institutions. First of all he makes exactly the point Vico stresses in his early writings concerning knowledge 'by causes', and then moves on to civil society:

11. Fassò, *Vico e Grozio*, p. 60.
12. Ibid., p. 61.
13. G. Fassò, 'The Problem of Law and the Historical Origin of the *New Science*', p. 8. Verene, in *Vico's Science*, has accepted Fassò's comments on the *historical* priority of the 'vero'/'certo' problem, and also like Fassò seeks an accommodation in which the 'verum/certum relationship can be placed within the *verum-factum* equation' (p. 57), so that it still remains possible to claim that the 'importance of the relationship of *verum* and *certum* for the historical genesis of the *New Science* does not in any way deny the importance of the *verum-factum* principle for the development of Vico's thought . . .' (p. 63).

the science of every subject is derived from a precognition of the causes, generation, and construction of the same; and consequently where the causes are known, there is place for demonstration, but not where the causes are to seek for. Geometry therefore is demonstrable, for the lines and figures from which we reason are drawn and described by ourselves; and civil philosophy is demonstrable, because we make the common-wealths ourselves. But because of natural bodies we know not the construction, but seek it from the effects, there lies no demonstration of what the causes be we seek for, but only of what they may be.[14]

So we find in Hobbes not only the idea of 'applying' the 'verum factum' principle but also the problem of the apparent lesser know-ability of the physical sciences. All these ideas were in circulation, and we know that Hobbes was one of the favourite authors for discussion in the Valletta circle. There is, therefore, more than a slight possibility that a certain amount of ritual repetition was involved when Vico recalled such ideas in the *Scienza nuova*. These factors cast a shadow of even greater implausibility over the idea of a period of 'neglect' followed by a 'discovery' of the applicability of the 'verum factum'. In any case, to examine the problem seriously we must attempt to locate the principle in the wider context of Vico's more lasting preoccupation with problems of scientificity. We hope thereby to illustrate that far from providing simply the initial inspiration of the *Scienza nuova*, the 'vero'/'certo' problem is the true foundation of its epistemological substance, and that the 'verum factum' principle can never be more to Vico than a sup-porting idea of limited and rather ambiguous significance.

The 'Verum Factum' Principle in Vico's Early Works

In Vico's first important work – the *De Ratione* of 1709 – he notes the contrast between positive and ideal law, that is, between the 'certo' of real, historical legal systems and the 'vero' of ideal law based on the universal principles of justice derived from natural law. He also tells us in his autobiography that his desire to discover the universal principles of law was born in him during the Vatolla years from 1686–95, when he first began to read avidly the authori-ties in jurisprudence. There is little doubt that problems of law – the central one being the reconciliation of the 'certo' (real) with the 'vero' (ideal or theoretical) – remained his most important theoret-ical preoccupation, giving rise to the *Scienza nuova*. But the episte-

14. Thomas Hobbes, *The English Works*, Vol. vii, p. 184.

mological question of the relation of the 'certo' to the 'vero' in law was not a problem Vico discovered in the isolation of his own genius. It was part of a much broader debate, one in which he took an enthusiastic part during the period of the Valletta circle discussions. This debate centred around the question of the nature of 'certainty' in both the natural and the human sciences.

In the *De Antiquissima*, Vico elaborates the doctrine of the 'verum factum' principle in some detail. In one very lengthy passage he discusses the nature of cause and effect and how absolute knowledge is possible only for causes and effects of which one is oneself the creator. He continues thus:

> If these things are true, arithmetic and geometry, which in general are not considered to prove 'by causes', in truth really do demonstrate their truths 'by causes'. And they demonstrate 'by causes' because the human mind contains the elements of the truths which it is able to order and arrange; and from such arrangements and compositions results the truth which these [sciences] demonstrate. Thus demonstration is identical with operation, and the truth ['verum'] with the made ['factum']. And for this very reason we are not able to prove physical facts 'by causes', because the constituent elements of natural things are outside us (i.e. our minds).[15]

This doctrine of the 'verum factum', however, must be seen in relation to the attempt Vico was making at this stage to clarify his ideas on the nature, scope and range of scientificity.

His interest in the uncertainty of knowledge in the physical sciences, the absoluteness of our grasp of mathematics, and other connected problems, relates to quite specific debates in which he took an active part. Many of these discussions drew their inspiration from the scientific writings of the members of the Accademia degli Investiganti.[16] One of the major themes raised by these scientific thinkers was the problem of the relationship between the experimentalism of the Galileian tradition and the rationalism of the Cartesian approach. The writings of Descartes had in fact been introduced into Italy by a prominent member of the Accademia, Tommaso Cornelio, and Cartesianism seemed to offer the perfect model for mathematical and deductive reasoning. But the application of such a model to scientific research nevertheless presented certain problems.

In the first place, some enthusiastic disciples tended to blur the

15. *Opere filosofiche*, p. 83.
16. For a more detailed discussion of these scientific thinkers and of possible links with Vico see Badaloni, *Introduzione a G. B. Vico*. Also useful is M. H. Fisch, 'The Academy of the Investigators'.

distinction between the clarity of ideas and deductive processes, on the one hand, and the truth of the propositions revealed by such ideas or processes, on the other. The logical validity and formal correctness of any particular line of argument is no guarantee of the truth of what it asserts. As some of the Investiganti insisted, only experiment can test the *truth*, as opposed to the *structural or procedural correctness*, of scientific assertions. Now the need for experimentation, it must be remembered, was even at that time by no means universally or uniformly accepted or understood. Moreover, those who argued for its absolute necessity identified their opponents as having a tendency to make a priori assertions and then proceed deductively on the basis of such unproved assumptions. Initially, therefore, the new faith in mathematics appeared to many advocates of experimentation as providing the possibility of a renewed attempt from another quarter (i.e. other than from the Aristotelian camp) of imposing a priori assumptions on the investigation of natural phenomena. There existed, in other words, a solid core of thinkers in Naples who argued against the 'mathematization' of natural science. What is more, these staunch defenders of experimentation tended to argue that not even experiments could yield absolute certainty, and that the truths of natural science simply enjoy a greater or lesser degree of 'probability'. It is crucial to realize, therefore, that statements setting out the limits of knowledge in the natural sciences were *not* aimed at reducing their status in relation to other fields of enquiry. As we shall see from the arguments Vico himself used, those who pointed to such limitations in the physical sciences were the strongest defenders of their empirical dimension.

Hypothesis, probability, the absolute validity of mathematical deductions, the 'uncertainty' of scientific knowledge, were thus all part of the theoretical currency existing at the time of Vico's introduction into problems of scientific enquiry and methods of study. As early as his third *Oration* of 1701 we find him pointing out, in relation to falling objects and the law of gravity, that the application of geometrical laws to physical phenomena cannot guarantee the 'certainty' of the conclusions reached. One can never, he argues, hope for such conclusions to be more than 'most probable'.[17] It is in this context, in the *De Ratione*, that the 'verum factum' formula is first introduced:

> For which reason these things which are presented as true in physics by force of the geometric method, are only 'probable', and they receive

17. *Opere filosofiche*, p. 745.

their methodology from geometry, not their proof: we prove geometrical conclusions because we make them; if we were able to prove physical facts we would be their makers.[18]

We begin to see Vico's statement of the 'verum factum' principle in quite a different light. When incorporating the principle in his work, he can be found to be assuming the polemical postures of important members of the Accademia degli Investiganti such as Cornelio and di Capua. In other words, he was indicating, to the over-optimistic advocates of the application of the geometrical method to the natural sciences that mathematics could only provide formal deductive procedures and methods of analysis. The *contents* of the base-propositions in the physical sciences cannot be verified by mathematics, so there is no question of bestowing upon them the absolute certainty of our mathematical truths.

As we examine the matter more closely, we begin to appreciate that he was in reality defending the heuristic powers of scientific enquiry from quite specific antagonists. For instance, we find in the *De Antiquissima* that he was concerned with the protection of the open-endedness of scientific investigation in the face of opposition from the dogmatists, but at the same time that he asserted the *reality* of scientific discoveries against the sceptics who denied the possibility of ultimate knowledge. These then are the two poles of the debate within which we should interpret what Vico writes about the 'verum factum' principle.

In section IV of Chapter I of the *De Antiquissima* – entitled 'Against the Sceptics' ('Adversus Scepticos') – Vico again argues: 'There is clearly no better means by which scepticism can be destroyed than by claiming that the criterion of truth is to have made it.'[19] Against the detractors of those who claim that human knowledge is real and certain, Vico concedes that the ultimate causes of events in the natural world are known with absolute certainty by God alone, its creator. Nevertheless there are other truths which the human mind can grasp with a perfect understanding. He points out that we should take as our model the creative activity of God Himself,

according to whose criterion of truth we must measure human truths. Those are certainly human truths of which we ourselves fashion the elements, which are contained within us, and which by means of postulates we extend *ad infinitum*. And in constructing these postulates, we make those truths which we know in the act of creating them; and

18. Ibid., p. 803.
19. Ibid., p. 75.

for all these reasons we possess the genus or form by which we make them.[20]

In consequence, the 'verum factum' principle is quite clearly an important weapon in Vico's ideological armoury against absolute scepticism. Nevertheless, in the same work he is also engaging with the dogmatists, who would undermine the natural sciences from a different standpoint:

> The dogmatists of our own times hold all truths in doubt except for metaphysics; and not only those truths laid down for conducting practical life, such as moral and mechanical truths, but also physical and mathematical ones. For they argue that there is a single metaphysics which gives us a truth without doubt and that from this, as from an original source, are derived the secondary truths in all other sciences.[21]

Vico's prime target in his attack on the dogmatists is the Aristotelian school. He even chides the master himself 'because he introduced metaphysics directly into physics: so that he discussed matters in physics according to the fashion of metaphysics, in terms of "faculties" and "virtues".'[22] In the case of the Aristotelians, Vico's objection is not simply that they impose a priori propositions on the natural sciences, though this is indeed an important aspect of his opposition to them. He also objects to the categories they employ: 'Now owing to the merits of the best physicists, those modes of discussing according to the attractions and aversions of nature, according to her secret designs which are called "occult qualities" have now, I repeat, been expunged from the school of physics.'[23]

As we may now begin to appreciate, therefore, any interpretation of Vico which represents him as emphasizing the limits set on scientific knowledge, or as attempting to relegate its status in some way puts a very negative construction on his intentions. More than anything else, his overriding concern is to protect the natural sciences from the false assurance implicit in a priori deductive schemes. On this basis he advances a critique of another, more modern group of dogmatists, the followers of Descartes, who delude themselves into supposing that the application of the geometrical method to physics can bestow on it the 'absolute knowledge' which is proper only to the former. In order to dispel this illusion, Vico introduces the 'verum factum' principle again;

20. Ibid.
21. Ibid., p. 71.
22. Ibid., p. 93.
23. Ibid., p. 97.

for, whereas we create the very principles of geometry ourselves, he argues, we do not create the operative principles of the natural world.[24]

Now at this point much Vichian criticism assumes that his use of this principle involves an explicit value-judgement to the detriment of the natural sciences. But that is far from being the case. The stating of the 'verum factum' principle, which does indeed highlight the tentative epistemological foundations of the physical sciences, *is only a first step in the overall argument he is constructing*, and it is quite misleading to stop at this point as if it were the end of Vico's argument. As we shall see, he is at great pains to *protect* physics from the illusion that the geometrical method can be of benefit to it:

> The geometrical method of Descartes corresponds to the sorite logic of the Stoics. . . . But when it is removed from the science of the three dimensions and from the science of numbers and introduced into physics, it is not so useful for discovering new truths as for ordering those already discovered. . . . We conclude, finally, that it is not the geometrical method but direct demonstration which is to be introduced into physics.[25]

The whole burden of Vico's argument is that mathematical knowledge, of which we do indeed possess a perfect mastery, is analytic and not synthetic. It can only help us organize, rearrange or dissect already known facts; it offers nothing by way of a method for discovering new facts. The Cartesian method, moreover, is unsuited to the essentially inductive and experimental character of the natural sciences.[26] In a letter to Padre de Vitry written in 1726 Vico claims that

> the philosophers have weakened our ingenuity with the method of Descartes, through which, content with the clarity and distinctness alone of their perception, they find the whole world of learning open to them without effort or strain in this form. Thus the conclusions of the physical sciences are no longer put to the test, to see if they measure up to experiment.[27].

Rodolfo Mondolfo has argued, in an important study of the

---

24. See ibid., p. 125.
25. Ibid., pp. 123–5.
26. Enrico Nuzzo notes this attitude when he observes that according to Vico 'The Cartesian deductive geometrical method is . . . unsuitable . . . in physical investigations, which, in order to progress, must rely on the inductive and experimental method . . .' (*Vico*, p. 143).
27. 'Lettere', in *Autobiografia*, p. 114. In the same letter Vico complains that the 'sceptics' have gained control of the medical sciences.

'verum factum' before Vico,[28] that by setting up the doctrine as an obstacle to the experimental method Vico displayed an imperfect grasp of the true theoretical and scientific achievements of the Galileian tradition in the natural sciences. Galileo, he points out, had absorbed the mathematical sciences into the language of physics and experimentation in such a way that the scientist could produce, through carefully conducted experiments, an observable 'rehearsal' of 'nature in action'. In this way man's knowledge of such phenomena acquired a significance very close to what Vico described as knowledge by 'making'. In other words, for Galileo, mathematics, which we know from the inside, as it were, provides the base-structure of reality ('ossatura della realtà').[29] This is the significance of the famous anti-Aristotelian polemical statement from the *Saggiatore*, in which Galileo argues that our knowledge of natural phenomena is written in the triangles, circles and other geometrical figures which make up the language of mathematics.[30]

There is no disputing Mondolfo's general point that Vico underestimated the importance of mathematics in the natural sciences and that he had not grasped Galileo's idea of mathematics as the 'ossatura della realtà'. Nevertheless, he in no sense undervalued the importance of experimentation in the sciences. On the contrary, his failure to see the importance of mathematics in the sciences was due to the paradoxical fact that he saw it as a threat to their empirical and most valuable heuristic dimension.

Moreover, it is not strictly correct to say that Vico had no grasp at all of the possible relevance of the 'verum factum' principle to methods in the natural sciences. He certainly did feel that experimentation was in a certain sense *akin* to actually making or causing events in the natural order. The idea is expressed quite clearly in the *De Antiquissima*:

28. R. Mondolfo, *Il "verum-factum" prima di Vico*.
29. I cannot agree with Mondolfo that the 'verum-factum' principle was not clear in Galileo. He gives explicit recognition to this idea when he discusses the difference between our 'intensive' and our 'extensive' knowledge of mathematics. The former, which refers to our manner of understanding mathematics, he claims is absolute and rivals God's own knowledge of such truths, whilst the latter, which refers to the whole corpus of possible mathematical facts, is necessarily limited. Referring to our manner of knowing mathematical truths, he writes, in his *Dialogo sui massimi sistemi*: 'I believe that our knowledge equals divine knowledge in objective certainty, because it succeeds in grasping their necessity, beyond which it seems that there can be no greater certainty.' The 'necessity' Galileo is referring to corresponds precisely to the necessary modes of mental operation in Vico's argument. The passage continues: 'Therefore, to put it more clearly, I would argue that as far as concerns the truth which our knowledge of mathematical proofs gives us, it is the same truth as that which is known by divine wisdom . . .'
(Galileo Galilei, *Opere*, p. 462.)
30. See ibid., p. 121.

in physics those theories are proved in which there is a likeness or correspondence to something we do; and for that reason ideas about natural events are held in the highest esteem and are received with the greatest consensus of all, if we test them with experiments, by means of which we perform something similar to nature.[31]

As we can see, Vico's attitude to the natural sciences amounted to a highly positive appraisal of their necessity and usefulness. The 'verum factum' principle is indeed used by him to point out the limited certitude of scientific conclusions, but it is at the same time part of his overall defence against the dogmatists of the experimental and heuristic foundations of the natural sciences. As we shall shortly attempt to illustrate, induction and validation, processes crucial to the making of new discoveries, are also central to the *Scienza nuova*. This point was appreciated briefly by some late nineteenth-century scholars, but unfortunately clouded and obscured by the powerful arguments of Croce's idealism. Vichian criticism has still not freed itself entirely from the anti-inductivist stamp set on it by the latter, so that the full force of his empirical perspective is rarely perceived. Thus the problem, which Vico sets out quite explicitly, of the reconciliation of the 'vero' and the 'certo', continues to take second place to the 'verum factum'. It is perhaps the rectification of this misconception which requires the most urgent attention with respect to Vico's epistemology.

'Vero', 'Certo' and the Problem of Scientific Knowledge

We have already seen that for Vico the 'uncertainty' of knowledge in the natural sciences is part and parcel of our capacity to make new discoveries. A world of a priori certainties would be irreconcilable with scientific knowledge. Moreover, perfect knowledge belongs to those disciplines capable of restructuring or ordering already discovered facts. We shall now explore a little more fully the concept of 'uncertainty' in science, in order to illustrate how the problem of 'accertamento' or empirical validation was, and remained, at the centre of Vico's epistemological reflections.

In regard to the question of reconciling the 'vero' and the 'certo', the problem to which he gives repeated and explicit recognition in the *Scienza nuova*,[32] it is the 'certo' which provides the real problematic centre. The 'vero' can denote, according to context, either

31. *Opere filosofiche*, p. 69.
32. See, for example, *SN* 138, 140, 163, 325.

the self-evident truths of mathematics or the intrinsic validity of deductive processes. But Vico also uses it to denote the philosophical framework and/or hypotheses which the facts are meant to validate. The discovery of the 'certo' is the process whereby the facts which confirm the theory or hypothesis are actually validated. It is this process of assembling corroborating evidence that ranges his new science alongside the natural sciences in a certain commonality of empirical practice. The problems and ambiguities in the *Scienza nuova* to which this gives rise cannot be used to belie his intentions.

The importance of empirical verification in natural science had been much discussed in Naples before Vico's time by a number of the Investiganti. Some of his later ideas in the *Scienza nuova*, like those on providence as a conservational force, bear more than a passing resemblance to observations of members of this school. Giovanni Borelli, for example, argued in his *De Motu Animalium* of 1680, that careful observation confirmed the idea of an objective and wise guiding-force within nature itself which operated within the animal kingdom. Animals display, he claimed, an instinctive knowledge of poisonous and harmful substances, which suggests an in-built mechanism of self-preservation and/or species conservation.

Nevertheless, man's understanding of this complex world of nature, insisted Borelli and others, cannot be obtained by 'simple' observation alone, by what Aristotelians called 'experience'. For them 'experiment', conducted with the aid of instruments and the control of observed phenomena, was the proper means of scientific validation and would often be found to yield results conflicting with the 'common sense' observations of 'experience'. Nevertheless, even the results of such enquiries could never be more than 'probable' or 'likely'.

The productive 'uncertainty' of scientific enquiry, however, led to 'useful' conclusions, as Vico called them, such as those Borelli reached in his *Delle cagioni delle Febbri Maligne della Sicilia negli anni 1647 e 1648*, in which he concluded that the plague had a chemical origin and that nature ordained a chemical cure, namely sulphur. It is this kind of open-ended enquiry in which fresh conclusions become possible that Vico seeks to protect in his polemics against the dogmatists, and it is the 'usefulness' of such an approach which he continually asserts against the complete relativism of the sceptics. Consequently as early as the third *Oration* we find him repeating the argument of the Investiganti like Borelli and di Capua that only the experimental method can yield positive results in the investigation of natural phenomena.

The 'probabile' (probability) of scientific conclusions was, in other words, an important concept for Vico. The notion was not simply negative – it also had a positive, anti-dogmatic and empirical connotation, and this positive aspect of it was important for his reflections on the nature of science. Central to his problematic, in fact, was the idea that the investigator moves from the 'uncertainty' which accompanies a single instance of a particular set of related events, to the increasing 'certainty' of their necessary relatedness the more often the events are repeated. The transition from numerous repetitions of particulars to universal conclusions or general laws is what Vico understood as the process of 'induction'. To him this process captured the essence of scientific procedure.

The 'probabile' of the Investiganti, therefore, led away from the false certainty of the various schools of dogmatists towards the condition of 'uncertainty' which provides a springboard for the inductive process. As Biagio De Giovanni has observed, for Vico the traditional 'certainty' based on syllogistic logic 'does not advance scientific discourse' whilst, on the contrary, through the pursuit of the less 'certain' but more productive 'probabile', we have a 'natural movement towards the *particular* and the *new*', through which, finally, 'science acquires a more well-founded certainty'.[33] Within the context of the problem of scientific and medical discoveries, Vico writes in the *De Ratione*:

> Indeed, just as he who argues by means of the syllogism grasps nothing new, because the conclusion is contained within its propositions or hypotheses, so he who argues by using the sorite logic does nothing other than unfold a secondary truth which lies implicit in the first. Yet diseases are always new and different, just as are those suffering them.[34]

What is needed, he continues, is a science capable of using the inductive method, of working from the particular to the general: 'For this reason the safest course is for us to pursue particulars, and certainly not use the sorite logic beyond its usefulness in such cases, and to rely for the most part on induction.'[35]

The whole thrust of Vico's thinking on science is well expressed by De Giovanni when he comments on the fact that

> in the face of an arrogant dogmatism and of the danger of a sclerosis in scientific thinking; in an atmosphere which was still largely untouched

33. B. De Giovanni, 'Il "De nostri temporis studiorum ratione" nella cultura napoletana del primo Settecento', p. 169.
34. *Opere filosofiche*, p. 809.
35. Ibid.

by the Newton – Leibniz polemic and ignorant of the new paths opening up to modern mathematical – scientific thought, the reforming purpose of Vico's intentions aims in this latter direction, and revives the use of those very categories which Caramuel, Cornelio and Di Capua had proposed in their critique of Scholastic Aristotelianism.[36]

The 'probabile' of such writers as Caramuel, Cornelio and di Capua, in other words, provides Vico with the foundation on which to build his concept of induction, and for him it becomes a process whereby the hypothesis ('vero') of the investigator is rendered certain ('certo'). The 'vero'/'certo' problem, therefore, which he claims to have resolved in his *Scienza nuova* in so far as it affects the study of history, appears quite early on in his thinking. In the *De Antiquissima* it becomes even more explicit. In a passage in which he discusses the various kinds of philosophies which have existed up to his day,[37] he complains of their inability to analyse and explain natural phenomena. They all fail in one of two respects: either by advancing unwarranted assertions upon insufficient evidence, or by concentrating on particulars without a sufficiently sophisticated framework for their interpretation. It is clear, in other words, that Vico deplores the wide gap between pure philosophy and the crudely empirical pursuits existing in his day.

While it is eventually to the world of human culture, history and institutions that he brings these problems to bear, Vico retained more than a passing interest in the natural sciences. Indeed, it seems that it was perhaps in this area that he took his first serious steps towards the implementation of the inductive method he had so long admired.

It was after the *De Antiquissima*, around 1711, that he wrote his scientific work *De Aequilibrio Corporis Animantis*. He tells us, in the *Autobiography*, that after numerous conversations with the natural scientist Doria on the application of physical laws to medicine, he was persuaded to carry his work further. Since, however, the physical sciences were lacking, according to Vico, in adequate theoretical foundations, he set out to

ground his physics on a suitable metaphysics. . . .he purged Zeno's points of Aristotle's garbled reports, and showed that these points are the only hypothesis for descending from abstract to bodily things, just as geometry is the only way to proceed scientifically from bodily things to the abstract things by which the bodies are constituted.[38]

36. De Giovanni, 'Il "De nostri temporis studiorum ratione"', p. 168.
37. See *Opere filosofiche*, pp. 87–9.
38. *Autobiography*, p. 151.

He goes on to describe how he was led, after his reflections on physics, geometry and their application to medicine, to write his *De Aequilibrio Corporis Animantis* and how, on these matters, he 'had frequent discussions on this subject with Lucantonio Porzio, which won him the latter's high esteem and intimate friendship, maintained until the death of this last Italian philosopher of the school of Galileo'.[39]

Unfortunately, no extant edition of Vico's scientific treatise remains, so we cannot examine how he developed his ideas in relation to particular scientific problems. We have, however, seen a considerable amount of evidence to suggest that the problem of scientific validation was, in one way or another, at the centre of his thinking. While, therefore, Fassò may have good reason for asserting that Vico took his first steps towards his new philosophy when he saw that 'in the sphere of culture there was still no system by which to relate philosophy to philology with any kind of scientific rigor',[40] we should bear in mind that the 'vero'/'certo' problem had already exercised his mind for some considerable time in relation to the natural sciences.

Everything we have said so far, ranging from Vico's polemics against the dogmatists and sceptics to his assertion of the need for an inductive method in the natural sciences, illustrates an important point: namely, that the problem of validation or 'accertamento' was a theoretical preoccupation dating from very early in his academic career. The concrete insertion of the problem into the field of historical research occurred, as we have observed, when Vico began to reflect on the need to reconcile 'ideal' with 'positive' law. The argument about his sudden discovery of the relevance of the 'verum factum' years after his first reflections on it thus tends to muddy the waters, since it obscures the complete continuity of his thought. According to the traditional interpretation, the problem of verification is resolved in the *Scienza nuova* by the 'verum factum' principle, because as a human creation history becomes knowable 'from the inside'. If this had been the case, instead of applying to his new science the 'probabile' and the method of validation which he advocates for the natural sciences, he would have been opting for the dogmatism or a priori approach which he argued was out of place in disciplines which rely on validatory procedures.

The 'verum factum' principle, as we have seen, stresses the

39. Ibid., pp. 152–3.
40. Fassò, 'The problem of Law', p. 7.

importance of the self-evident nature of the knowledge of the things we create. We have tried to put Vico's use of this concept into context and show that it was of limited value to his own ideas on the nature of science. We have stressed, instead, the importance to him of the open-ended pursuit of the uncertain, which can also be seen as a struggle to raise the uncertain to a greater level of certainty as a problem of empirical practice. This, we contend, is the basis of the epistemology of the *Scienza nuova*, where he applies such a process to the study of civil society.

We have a clear indication that Vico was thinking in such terms as early as the *De Ratione*, when he discusses the reasons why, at that time, a science of civil society had not been invented. He writes in this early work:

> But the most serious problem with our method of studies is that whereas we study the natural sciences with great eagerness, we do not do likewise with the study of morals, and especially in that field which relates to the soul's disposition and to its propensities for civil life. . . . And since today the sole object of studies is truth, *we investigate the nature of things because it seems certain; we do not investigate the nature of men because, owing to human choice, it is uncertain.*[41]

Indeed, a science of civil society did not seem possible at this stage, because it lacked the possibility of 'accertamento' or validation which the natural sciences possessed. Put more specifically, the science of civil society, based as this must be on a study of institutions created by human choices, was not possible because, as Vico says, human choice is 'uncertain', not reducible to invariable patterns which can be validated by observation. But such a science *is* possible, as we shall see, by the time he writes the *Scienza nuova*, because *by then he will have discovered that human choice is made certain by the 'senso comune'.*[42] This is the whole point of Vico's statements about 'human choice' and how, in his science, it is 'made certain'. In the next chapter we shall see how traditional tenets of Vichian scholarship have obscured the importance of such passages, and how, by the time of his writing of the *Scienza nuova*, the empirical process of validation (vitiated as this may be by other problems in Vico's epistemology) does seem applicable to the study of civil society. That he should have so vigorously defended the inductive and empirical procedures of the scientific approach was by no means fortuitous or uncharacteristic. For there is a direct and

41. *Opere filosofiche*, pp. 809–11. Italics mine.
42. See *SN* 141 and 390.

unbroken line of continuity between such concerns and his attempt later, in the *Scienza nuova*, to render the study of history more 'certo', and by this means to validate the 'vero' of the theory of development he propounds.

14
'Vero', 'Certo' and the Nature of Historical Knowledge

The Epistemology of Privileged Insight and the Notion of a Special Human Science

In his study of Vico's major work, Leon Pompa has pointed to a circularity in the epistemological position adopted in the *Scienza nuova*:

> The propositions embodied in the 'ideal eternal history' are not epistemologically neutral prior to their empirical confirmation . . . there can be no straightforward appeal to an external historical reality for confirmation, since the epistemological status of the historical world is precisely what requires to be established.[1]

Thus Vico's own comments concerning his proofs 'do not suffice to establish the epistemological status of his Science'.[2] In other words, there is no guarantee that the historical facts and patterns Vico presents in confirmation of his theory have not begged the question by presupposing the validity of the theory itself. His very perceptions of the historical facts and patterns, that is, tend to be predetermined by the hypothesis they are supposed to validate. Pompa argues that we must, therefore, seek in Vico's work 'a further, yet more ultimate, criterion upon which his claims about the epistemological status of Science finally depend'.[3] The highly interesting examination of Vico's epistemology which then follows is, in effect, an attempt to rectify some otherwise substantial lacunae in his empiricism. In the final analysis, Pompa concludes that Vico is putting forward the idea of a special or higher form of intelligibility for the human sciences. But in the process of presenting the arguments for his own case, Pompa also examines in some detail another, related, approach to the problem, which, for reasons that shall become evident later, I shall refer to as the 'epistemology

1. L. Pompa, *Vico: A Study of the 'New Science'*, p. 152.
2. Ibid.
3. Ibid., p. 153.

of privileged insight'. We shall briefly introduce this approach, which has won a certain amount of support in the Anglo-Saxon literature on Vico, before returning to Pompa's views for comment.

The idea of a 'special kind' of knowledge, indeed of a special kind of science, provides a foundation for the arguments of all the proponents of the 'verum factum' theory. A few examples will serve to illustrate how the connection is made between such 'special' knowledge and the 'verum factum' principle. B. Mazlish, for instance, argues that to Vico 'the world of man was by its very essence more susceptible to scientific treatment than the world of nature', and this was because he had 'invoked his basic principle: verum-factum'.[4] Mazlish takes the point a step further when he claims that in the *Scienza nuova* man 'makes, that is, generates or causes his own history. Hence, history is knowable; it is demonstrable; and it is, in consequence, a science'.[5]

According to Donald P. Verene, Vico argues that man has a special awareness or insight into the workings of his own mind by means of a 'recollective fantasia', which is a form of imaginative insight 'upon which humanistic knowledge depends'.[6] Verene's claim goes even further, since according to him Vico postulates a cognitive faculty which 'involves types of knowledge that are substantially unexamined in theory of knowledge'.[7] And it is a similar kind of recollective capacity which Isaiah Berlin has for some time been advancing as the *Scienza nuova*'s major epistemological discovery.

Berlin has given the 'verum factum' principle's application to history a slightly modified form. According to his line of argument, Vico's construction of a special kind of historical understanding undermines the accepted classification of knowledge.

> There exists, for him, yet another type of awareness, unlike *a priori* knowledge in that it is empirical, unlike deduction in that it yields new knowledge of facts, and unlike perception of the external world, in that it informs us not merely of what exists or occurs, and in what spatial or temporal order, but also why what is, or occurs, is as it is, i.e. in some sense *per caussas*.[8]

This allegedly newly discovered form of knowledge would appear

---

4. B. Mazlish, *The Riddle of History. The Great Speculators from Vico to Freud*, p. 19.
5. Ibid., p. 26.
6. D. P. Verene, 'Vico's Philosophy of Imagination', p. 426.
7. Ibid.
8. Berlin, *Vico and Herder*, pp. 21–2.

particularly suited to the construction of a science of history. This is because, according to Berlin, since we are ourselves the creators of history, historical knowledge is a form of 'self-knowledge'. It is, in other words, knowledge of activities in which we continually engage, activities of which we are the authors and *'which we understand, as it were, from inside'*.[9]

Pompa noted the potential of this interpretation, if it were correct, for resolving the problems we mentioned earlier regarding Vico's empiricism. He pointed out that the difficulty of validating his historical scheme would be overcome, in Berlin's account, because Vico clearly regards this special knowledge 'from inside' as 'superior to anything based on mere observation'.[10] It also allegedly produces 'truth of another and superior character which the natural sciences cannot hope to reach'.[11] Thus, argues Pompa, we are presented with the idea of a science in which empirical evidence can be by-passed, because it entails the notion that 'we recognise in certain hypotheses a possible mode of human conduct *independently of any empirical evidence of their factual truth'*.[12]

Pompa himself provides a different interpretation of Vico's references to his science as based on a study of the 'modifications of the human mind'.[13] He argues that Vico's appeal to these modifications of the mind are meant to 'guarantee the truth of his explanations' and that they must constitute 'an appeal to some prior knowledge the historian has of what is historically and socially possible'.[14] This access to an understanding of history (i.e. the prior knowledge just mentioned) is defined by Pompa as a form of self-reflection. He claims that 'the peculiar intelligibility of history rests upon insights into our own nature which are accessible to us by virtue of our capacity to reflect upon ourselves . . .'[15] By means of this self-reflection, which is a rational activity of our developed understanding, we can tap the resources of our own natures and give an added dimension to our understanding of early man. The historian thus acquires 'knowledge of modes of thought more primitive than those which are involved in the practices of his own society'.[16] From these arguments Pompa concludes that: 'History is thus a uniquely human form of knowledge made possible by the exercise

9. Ibid., p. 22.
10. Ibid., p. 24.
11. Ibid., p. 121.
12. Pompa, *Vico*, p. 160. Italics mine.
13. See particularly *SN* 349 and 374.
14. Pompa, *Vico*, p. 161.
15. Ibid., p. 167.
16. Ibid., p. 162.

of self-reflection which is in itself a uniquely human capacity.'[17]

While Pompa parts company, therefore, with the 'epistemology of privileged insight' of Berlin and others he nevertheless insists, in his own account of Vico's epistemology, on a special role for the historian's capacity for self-reflection. Ultimately, it is claimed, this capacity lends a greater intelligibility to history since, 'because it is a human science, it involves an appeal to antecedent, experiential knowledge of what it is to be human, which renders its products *more intelligible than those of any purely natural science*'.[18] The greater intelligibility referred to in Pompa's account can be partially understood by reference to Vico's idea that the development of the individual from infancy to manhood represents a microcosmic parallel to the development of mankind in general. But in the process of self-reflection by which the adult recalls childhood memories, 'it is by virtue of his capacity, in respect of his own childhood, to *reflect* upon his own earlier beliefs and so to have knowledge of its causes, that the adult can have *scienza* where the child can only have coscienza'.[19] Thus Pompa concludes his study of the *Scienza nuova* with the following observations:

> In the end, therefore, Vico's conception of a *human* science, and his claim that this is epistemologically superior to any natural science, rests upon a thesis about the capacity human beings have for reaching self-understanding. The necessity to use this knowledge in constructing history makes demands upon the historian over and above those he already shares with the natural scientist. It also, however, allows him to offer explanations which are ultimately more intelligible than any which are available in the natural sciences.[20]

We have argued in the previous chapter that any serious examination of the 'verum factum' principle in Vico's early work must conclude that attempts to link it with a general downgrading of the experimental sciences is highly misleading. Given the interpretations we have just been discussing, we now have to take up this point in relation also to the *Scienza nuova*.

It is almost universally taken for granted that Vico is advancing the idea that 'man makes history'. For the scholars discussed so far in this chapter, this further entails various claims in the *Scienza nuova* regarding special forms of knowledge or intelligibility based on either 'reconstructive imagination' and 'recollective fantasia' or

17. Ibid., p. 169.
18. L. Pompa, 'Human Nature and the Concept of a Human Science', p. 434. Italics mine.
19. Pompa, *Vico*, p. 165.
20. Ibid., p. 185.

on 'self-reflection', all of which activities afford a special status to the science of history.

Pompa's interpretation of Vico's epistemology is based on a particular understanding of his references to 'the modifications of the human mind' in important passages such as *SN* 349 and 374. In *SN* 349, in respect of his science, Vico states what is to him an indubitable principle 'that this world of nations has certainly been made by men, and its guise must therefore be found within the modifications of the human mind'. Of itself, this passage does not state that the study of the modifications of the human mind is an invitation to 'self-reflection' of the kind suggested by Pompa. The strongest support for his case comes from *SN* 374:

> From these first men, stupid, insensate, and horrible beasts, all the philosophers and philologians should have begun their investigations of the wisdom of the ancient gentiles; . . . And they should have begun with metaphysics, which seeks its proofs not in the external world but within the modifications of the mind of him who meditates it. For since this world of nations has certainly been made by men, it is within these modifications that its principles should have been sought.

We must, however, part company with Pompa at this point, since Vico's reference to 'the modifications of the mind of him who meditates it' does not refer to the mind of the philosopher or historian constructing the science of institutions, but to the primitive mind which meditates the poetic metaphysics to which the whole section is devoted.[21] In the passage, the 'it' refers, therefore, not to the 'science of history' (which is in any case syntactically absent from the passage) but to the 'metaphysics' mentioned earlier in the sentence; furthermore, as the heading of the chapter makes clear, Vico is talking here of the '*Poetic Metaphysics* as the Origin of Poetry, Idolatry, Divination, and Sacrifices'. The 'metaphysics' in question must thus belong to the 'first men, stupid, insensate, and horrible beasts' (who interpret everything subjectively rather than with reference to the external world) with whom the paragraph opens. That the metaphysics in question is that of the primitive mind is made even clearer in the paragraph which immediately follows, *SN* 375, in which Vico states that:

21. The 'him' of the Bergin and Fisch translation fixes too narrowly the Italian 'chi' which, although singular in form, can be translated as 'he who', 'whoever' or even 'those who'. The relevant parts of the Italian passage are: Da si fatti primi uomini, stupidi, insensati ed orribili bestioni, tutti i filosofi e filologi dovevan incominciar a ragionare la sapienza degli antichi gentili . . . E dovevano incominciarla dalla metafisica, siccome quella che va a prendere le sue pruove non già da fuori ma da dentro le modificazioni della propia mente di chi la medita . . . .

poetic wisdom, the first wisdom of the Gentile world, must have begun with a metaphysics not rational and abstract like that of learned men now, but felt and imagined as that of these first men must have been, who, without power of ratiocination, were all robust sense and vigorous imagination.

And, as we shall see shortly, such primitive imaginings are most definitely out of the reach of the imaginative reconstructive capacity of rational man – a point which Pompa has himself argued.

Vico is stating, in other words, that since institutions reflect the 'modifications of the minds' of those who create them, philosophers and historians should have begun with a study of the 'modifications of the human mind' which lie behind 'poetic metaphysics'. In this way those constructing a science of history could have understood the primitive thinking which accompanied the practices and institutions of early man, and they could have avoided the 'conceit of the learned' which is the main vice of modern scholars. There is, therefore, in Vico no appeal or invitation to 'self-reflection' on the part of the historian. And as we examine Vico's epistemology further we shall find more reasons for rejecting claims concerning 'special' kinds of intelligibility or knowledge.

Nevertheless, there are critics, such as Isaiah Berlin, who believe that the *Scienza nuova* propounds the view that the re-creative imagination is able to penetrate to areas of inner truth in a more direct way; that there exists an 'inner' access to the feelings, actions and thought processes of others, including men of distant epochs. According to this 'epistemology of privileged insight' it is not simply direct observation or the piecing together of evidence which enables us to reconstruct the past. The faculties of empathy, intuitive understanding and creative imagination enable us to feel our way into the inner world of primitive perception, cognition and feeling.

Leon Pompa has very convincingly drawn attention to the major conceptual and textual deficiencies associated with this view.[22] There are, nevertheless, some additional arguments to be considered. Now it would not be correct to assume that Vico had failed to give any thought to this question of our capacity to enter into the thoughts and feelings of earlier men. He has certainly done so – but not in a manner which supports the claims of Berlin and others. As early as the 1725 edition of his major work we find him making the following observation about our understanding of early men:

---

22. See L. Pompa, 'Imagination in Vico'.

one can scarcely understand, and not at all imagine, how the first men of the impious races must have thought (their condition being such that they had not up to that time heard a human word) or how awkwardly they formed and how crudely they ordered their thoughts.[23]

The distinction between 'understanding' ('intendere') and 'imagining' ('immaginare') is crucial. While we can just about grasp how primitive man must have thought and felt, we cannot do so through our own imaginations. The imaginative reconstruction 'from inside', as it were, is here definitely excluded by Vico. In the same passage he likewise denies the usefulness of comparisons with mental deficients or existing tribal societies as a mode of entry into the mind of the early primitive being, because, although such contemporary examples of backwardness or primitive thinking may seem to offer useful comparative points of reference, 'these people are nevertheless born amongst languages, however barbarous, and they must have some capacity for reason and calculation'.[24] Vico is thus at pains to emphasize the distance which separates the world of experience of primitive man from anything accessible to men of his own times. It is clear, therefore, that his own use in the *Scienza nuova* of comparisons between the ways of thinking and speaking of children and those of primitives are analogical and illustrative devices. There is no hint that such comparisons should assume any serious theoretical or epistemological function. When they do occur, moreover, they are very much presented as observations of 'external' phenomena. There is no recourse to empathy or self-reflection, or any other privileged form of access to childhood experience. In fact, we do not even find any suggestion that we can recollect or 're-create' our own childhood mentalities, let alone utilize them for an understanding of primitive cognitive processes.

If we might anticipate, for a moment, a matter which will shortly be dealt with more fully, the irony implicit in the 'epistemology of privileged insight' arguments can be made plain. For in effect it is precisely the impossibility of imaginatively re-creating from inside the world of early man which eventually led Vico to develop the principles of his science. Even in the first edition of the *Scienza nuova*, he tells us that he had been seeking a solution to the problem of understanding the primitive mind for many years:

But concerning what we have said from the beginning – *that one can scarcely understand, and not at all imagine, how the man of [i.e. written about*

23. *SN1a* 42. Italics mine.
24. Ibid.

> *by] Grotius, Hobbes and Pufendorf must have thought, let alone have spoken –* after what is now twenty-five years of continuous and arduous reflection, *we have finally discovered what to this Science is the first principle,* just as the alphabet is to grammar and geometrical forms to geometry. . . . thus *we have found the poetic characters to be the elements of language* with which the first gentile nations spoke.[25]

Thus Vico arrives at his idea of the poetic characters of primitive speech – that is, the language of 'true narration' ('vera narratio') – after a long search in which he found that the direct access of imaginative reconstruction was *not* possible. In the final edition of the work, almost twenty years further on, the point is made even more emphatically:

> the first gentile peoples, by a demonstrated necessity of nature, were poets who spoke in poetic characters. This discovery, *which is the master key of this Science,* has cost us the persistent research of almost all our literary life, because with our civilized natures *we [moderns] cannot at all imagine and can understand only by great toil* the poetic nature of these first men.[26]

By means, therefore, of the deciphering of their 'poetic characters' according to the principles of the 'vera narratio' we are able 'by great toil' to achieve an understanding of the 'poetic' nature of early men. It is because 'we cannot at all imagine' how primitive men thought and felt that Vico emphasizes the laborious nature of the research:

> To discover the way in which this first human thinking arose in the gentile world, we encountered exasperating difficulties. . . . [We had] to descend from these human and refined natures of ours to those quite wild and savage natures, which we cannot at all imagine . . .[27]

It is difficult to see how the arguments which attempt to justify the alleged 'application' of the 'verum factum' principle through recourse to notions involving intuitive and imaginative recall, and direct access from inside to special forms of knowledge, can survive these clear denials of any such epistemology.[28] However, lest any

---

25. *SN1a* 261. Italics mine. See also *SN1a* 316.
26. *SN* 34. Italics mine.
27. *SN* 338.
28. Verene, in his *Vico's Science,* wishes to defend what he has for some time argued regarding Vico's claims about 'the power to know from the inside, to grasp the object in its inner nature' (p.101) against such arguments, and does so with recourse to the 'verum factum': 'For the *verum-factum* principle to function in the *New Science* we must be able to make our way back in some way to the origin of human thought and activity and we must be able to do this in such a way as to remake the human world as something true for us' (p.101). Our purpose here is to

lingering doubts remain about Vico's denial that we can reconstruct early man's mental process from inside, we shall allow ourselves the indulgence of one final and explicit statement on the question:

> But the nature of our civilized minds is so detached from the senses, even in the vulgar, by abstractions corresponding to all the abstract terms our languages abound in, . . . that it is naturally beyond our power to form the vast image of this mistress called 'Sympathetic Nature.' . . . It is equally beyond our power to enter into the vast imagination of those first men, whose minds were not in the least abstract, refined, or spiritualized, because they were entirely immersed in the senses, . . .[29]

In a brief survey of certain aspects of Vico's philosophy, Nicola Badaloni claims that in Vico's epistemology no recourse to any philosophy of mind is sufficient for our understanding of history, since 'man possesses no privileged knowledge in the area of self-knowledge'.[30] Having rejected any epistemology of 'privileged access' to knowledge, Badaloni then goes on to state more positively that the *Scienza nuova* does not represent the transfer of any philosophy of mind (such as the 'verum factum' principle) to the field of history, 'but is rather (or is intended to be) the theoretical outcome of an investigation into history'.[31]

As we shall see presently, the 'investigation into history', for which Vico felt he had prepared the ground, was to operate according to an empirical method he believed he had borrowed from Bacon. His raw materials were the early myths and legends of 'poetic man' who produced fables by way of 'natural necessity'. The only 'guarantee' which Vico offered in this investigation lay not with any direct or privileged access to knowledge, but in the 'vera narratio' which ensured that the 'poetic' images were the authentic expression of the primitive mind without the distorting and mediating effects of rational reconstruction. The 'vera narratio', as we have seen in earlier chapters, was intended to provide the 'certo' of historical research. We shall now see how this, in turn, was meant to validate the theory of history through its detection of recurrent historical patterns.

---

argue that Vico does *not* intend us to reconstruct history by means of a special knowledge from the inside (i.e. via the 'verum-factum'), but by means of the 'vero'/'certo' process of validation.

29. *SN* 378. See also *SN* 700.
30. Badaloni, 'Vico nell' ambito della filosofia europea', p. 246.
31. Ibid.

'Vero' and 'Certo' in the *Scienza nuova*

We noted in the previous chapter that for the early Vico 'absolute knowledge' was associated with analytic rather than synthetic orders of enquiry. It was associated, in other words, with mathematics and, by extension, syllogistic processes of deduction, which, in his view, could never of themselves lead to new discoveries. Induction, on the other hand, the practice of formulating general laws or principles on the basis of repeated observations, could do so. This problem of 'accertamento' was closely linked with the problem of the 'vero' and the 'certo', that is, the problem of validating theory by recourse to occurrences in the real world. Hence the two orders of enquiry, represented by the 'verum factum' principle and the 'vero'/'certo' relationship respectively, are not readily reconcilable. Essentially, to the former belong a priori and/or 'immediate' knowledge, whilst the latter denotes the world of empirical enquiry. I do not think, therefore, that one can accept the proposition expressed by Fassò that the 'verum factum' principle has logical priority in the *Scienza nuova* whereas the 'vero'/'certo' problem accounts for the genesis of the work. In fact, we have already gone part of the way towards discrediting the idea that the 'verum factum' principle has any real or meaningful function at all in the work.

It is not intended, in what follows, to deny that the idea of the 'verum factum' makes its appearance in allusive and illustrative form in the work. What will be contested is that it *functions* in any meaningful theoretical sense. And while it will be argued that the 'vero'/'certo' problem is the really functional conceptual focus of Vico's epistemology, this will by no means imply that the latter principle is without its own problems in the *Scienza nuova*.

While it is true to say that no major offensive has up to now been launched against the contention that the 'verum factum' lies at the heart of the *Scienza nuova*, rumblings of doubt and dissatisfaction have nevertheless occurred from time to time. Regrettably, however, their subversive potential has never been systematically explored. Eugenio Garin, for example, has seen Vico's notion of 'providence' as an obstacle to the claim that he successfully appropriates the notion of 'verum factum' into his concept of history. He argues that only in Hobbes is the principle truly applied, 'because in his thought the state is a truly human artefact, and human alone, without providential interventions'.[32] B. Mazlish, who, as we have

32. E. Garin, 'Appunti per una storia della fortuna di Hobbes nel Settecento italiano', p. 518.

seen, accepts the idea that Vico wishes to 'apply' the 'verum factum' principle to history, nevertheless finds the consequences problematic. Mazlish's doubts are worth noting:

> There is one other criticism of Vico, however, which needs to be made at this point. It concerns, specifically, his verum-factum. Even if we grant him his point – and there is much to be said for it – how can we really claim that man consciously 'makes' his history? . . . In paragraph after paragraph . . . Vico brilliantly illustrated how man intends one thing, for example, the satisfaction of his bestial lust, and makes another, the marriage institutions. Can we, then, in all seriousness, say that man 'makes' the unintended consequences . . .[33]

Vico states, of course, that the unintended consequences are the results of a 'providential' engineering, which makes Mazlish's point all the more effective. Now, what is surprising, given the very obvious merit of such critical observations, is the lack of a sustained return to the text to re-examine the original assumptions, and so test whether Vico really did articulate such apparently vulnerable propositions.

The two passages most favourable to the traditional 'verum factum' thesis are *SN* 331 and 349. These are certainly important passages, and it is fitting, therefore, that any serious challenge to the dominant interpretation on this matter should begin with these. The claim that in these passages Vico states his fundamental doctrine that 'man makes history' does not seem to me difficult to refute. It is based on the well-known statement, repeated elsewhere in the work, that 'the world of civil society has certainly been made by men, and that its principles are therefore to be found within the modifications of our own human mind'.[34] If we examine this statement carefully we note that the traditional interpretation is based on a clear conceptual error. Neither here nor in *SN* 349 and 374 (where he substitutes 'this world of nations' for 'the world of civil society') does Vico state that it is *history* which man makes. He certainly must be claiming that man creates *institutions* of which 'the civil world' and/or 'the world of nations' consist – but he *does not claim that man creates the pattern of development of these institutions, which is their history*. This distinction is fundamental to understanding what he does claim. History, for Vico, is the pattern which man, the modifications of his mind, and the institutions which reflect such modifications, unwittingly produce. Man, according to Vico, creates civil institutions, and both man and his creations

---

33. Mazlish, *The Riddle of History*, p. 29.
34. *SN* 331.

evolve according to a common historical pattern which is beyond his control. Indeed, this course of development – the 'ideal eternal history' which is superimposed on both man and the institutions he creates – is in reality the creation of a providential force superior to man. Hence the 'unintended consequences' in human history. The proposition, therefore, that man creates his own history, would have struck Vico as absurd, since man himself, and not the force he described as providence, would have had to design his own mental and social development for this to be the case.

Not only does Vico not claim that 'man makes history', but the problems expressed by Garin and Mazlish in this regard can be seen to derive from a failure to distinguish between civil institutions and the mind which creates them and the common pattern of development or 'ideal eternal history' to which they are both subject. Expressed another way, the activity by which man creates institutions should not be confused with that of creating the broader overall pattern of historical development within which this activity takes place.

While commentators may themselves wish to conflate these two activities, Vico was never tempted to make any such identification. The proposition that 'man makes history' would hardly have been difficult for him to state had he wished to do so. But apart from ignoring the distinction we have just indicated regarding Vico's view of institutions and their pattern of development, this 'humanistic' interpretation of his intentions overlooks many other facets of his historical perspective. If we may briefly mention a point to which we shall return at a later stage, but in a different context, it is clear, for example, that the pattern of the 'ideal eternal history' is what determines the 'modifications of the human mind' and not the reverse. The course of historical development is in no real sense subject to alteration by human volition. Vico insists that his science of civil institutions demonstrates *necessary and invariable* forms of development because,

> since these institutions have been established by divine providence, the course of the institutions of the nations *had to be, must now be, and will have to be* such as our Science demonstrates, *even if infinite worlds were born from time to time through eternity*, . . .[35]

Likewise it is not possible, as some critics have done, simply to dismiss the notion of providence in the *Scienza nuova* as a non-functional accretion. One very clear function it possesses is pre-

---

35. *SN* 348. Italics mine. See also *SN* 1096.

cisely that of highlighting the fact that man does not have control over the course of history. When Vico does speak specifically about history it is clear that its forms of evolution are both decided by a superior force and actually unfold independently of, and frequently contrary to, men's intentions:

> Our new Science must therefore be a demonstration, so to speak, of what providence has wrought in history, for it must be a history of the institutions by which, *without human discernment or counsel, and often against the designs of men, providence has ordered this great city of the human race*. For though this world has been created in time and particular, *the institutions established therein by providence are universal and eternal.*[36]

It thus seems quite clear that in Vico's thought man does not 'make history' in any meaningful sense. There can be no question, therefore, of any 'application' of the 'verum factum' principle to history.

Nevertheless, it could be argued, Vico may still be applying the 'verum factum' principle to our knowledge of institutions, for there can be no denying that the latter are made by men. On the face of it, a more reasonable and limited proposition would thus emerge from this somewhat attenuated assumption: namely, that while we cannot have any 'special' knowledge of the principles of historical development which we do not create, we do have privileged access to an understanding of the civil institutions which we ourselves make. At first sight, this presents itself as a plausible interpretation of *SN* 331 which argues that whoever reflects on the fact that men have made the world of civil society,

> cannot but marvel that the philosophers should have bent all their energies to the study of the world of nature, which, since God made it, He alone knows; and that they should have neglected the study of the world of nations, or civil world, which, since men have made it, men could come to know.

As we noted in the previous chapter, Vico's complaint concerning the lack of attention to the study of civil institutions goes back at least to the *De Ratione*. It is not surprising, moreover, that he should employ the well-known Hobbesian 'civic' version of the 'verum factum' principle to repeat the complaint in the *Scienza nuova*. It must be stressed, however, that this cannot, of itself, be taken as an assertion of the epistemology or method he intends to adopt. If he had intended it to be read in such a light we would rightly have expected some theoretical argument as to the applica-

36. *SN* 342. Italics mine.

bility of the principle to the object of enquiry in the *Scienza nuova*. There is not a word of explanation concerning the nature of the 'direct access' or 'special knowledge' which the principle allegedly affords into civil institutions. In point of fact, the 'verum factum' finds no explicit mention in the work at all.

SN 331, while certainly containing a recall of the principle, is in fact, as we suggested earlier, more in the nature of a strategic than a purely theoretical statement. The 'res divinae'/'res humanae' comparison could, in addition, lend an air of respectability to a proposed new science which, as we shall see, the Church had good reason to suspect.

This strategic or tactical use of the 'verum factum' principle is likewise very much in evidence in the other well-known passage which is used in support of the argument that the 'application' of the principle to the study of history is Vico's great discovery:

> Now, as geometry, when it constructs the world of quantity out of its elements, or contemplates that world, is creating it for itself, just so does our Science [create for itself the world of nations], but with a reality greater by just so much as the institutions having to do with human affairs are more real than points, lines, surfaces, and figures are. And this very fact is an argument, O reader, that these proofs are of a kind divine and should give thee a divine pleasure, since in God knowledge and creation are one and the same thing.[37]

A close reading of this passage reveals that Vico, while using the 'verum factum' allusion in a general, tactical supportive manner, is careful *not* to state that its principles apply to his science. The reason for this will become plain when we examine the more important statement which immediately precedes the passage quoted above.

What Vico is saying in the first part of the above passage is that the science of civil institutions will construct its knowledge of such institutions on the basis of the principles which that science initially lays down, just as geometry is also led to make inferences on the basis of its initial principles or elements. In this sense both disciplines create for themselves their objects of knowledge. There is no recourse, in this part of the argument, to the 'vero' or to 'absolute knowledge'. Even if there were, however, this would make little difference for it would still have to be shown that an appeal to such principles is a *functional* aspect of the work. And when, in the subsequent section of this excerpt, Vico does introduce his allusion to the 'verum factum', it is in a careful and

---

37. *SN* 349.

calculated manner. It is *'in God'* that knowing and making are one and the same, while man's creative activity is 'of *a kind* divine', and such as to give 'a divine pleasure'. The figurative, loose and associative manner in which Vico here compares God's absolute knowledge with man's proofs 'of a kind divine' has little in common with the theoretically explicit, clear and forceful arguments to be found in the *De Antiquissima*, where man's capability of using the 'verum factum' principle was described with care and precision.

Even where he compares his science with the creation of geometrical forms there is no mention of the 'absoluteness' of the knowledge which the latter provides. Instead, he emphasizes the fact that the institutions created by man are more *real* than the 'points, lines, surfaces, and figures' produced by geometrical abstractions.[38] Vico's refusal to be explicit regarding the 'verum factum' formula can hardly be gratuitous. His reason for this, as we shall see, is that his real epistemological concerns lie in a quite different direction. Once we seriously question the self-generating consensus surrounding the question of the 'verum factum' in the *Scienza nuova*, we begin to see how little it really figures in his thinking. To the later Vico it remains a fascinating but unserviceable idea which he occasionally uses as a supportive device. But it never amounts to more than a peripheral, if evocative, piece of speculative ornamentation.

In the previous chapter, when we examined Vico's early thinking on problems of scientificity, we found that there tended to be two epistemological camps in such matters; one being to rely upon a priori forms of knowledge. According to this particular current, as Vico understood it, the certainty of the original starting point was meant to guarantee the conclusions *deduced* from the initial premisses. Thus, he argued, the Cartesians, by applying the mathematical certainties of geometry to physics, felt they had achieved this objective. Vico opposed these dogmatists by stating that the truths of mathematics were analytic and not synthetic, and that they could not of themselves provide new facts but simply dissect evidence once it had been discovered. New discoveries, he argued, belonged to a different order of enquiry and required a synthetic or 'inductive' procedure. This provided the heuristic principle behind the

---

38. Some critics have stressed also this greater 'realism' provided by the alleged 'application' of the 'verum factum' principle to history. Such arguments remain to say the least problematic, since there is no discussion in the *Scienza nuova* relating this 'realism' to more profound or 'special' forms of knowledge. Likewise, there is no explanation of how it might affect the method of enquiry in Vico's new science. Statements about the greater 'reality' of certain sciences vis-à-vis mathematics were quite common in Vico's time. Given the empirical thrust of his epistemology, his reference is most likely to be to this aspect of such statements.

approach he favoured. In other words Vico substituted for the a-
prioristic science of the dogmatists the principle of empirical practice which guaranteed the open-ended nature of intellectual enquiry.

The 'verum factum' principle, as we saw, was used to highlight
this distinction. By means of it Vico was able to show why we have
such an absolute grasp on analytic principles and mathematical
procedures: it is because we create them ourselves. His own preoccupation with the reconciliation of theory ('vero') with the
real world of events ('certo'), which first made a sustained appearance in his *Diritto universale*, had by this time been transformed into
a question of discovering principles whereby historical verification
can be applied to theories of various kinds. This empirical orientation is what Vico carries over into the *Scienza nuova*, and it is this
which provides a fundamental principle of continuity in his
thought. When we look afresh at *SN* 349 we see that it provides the
true theoretical basis of the passage. Moreover, when he does talk
explicitly about his epistemology he tells us he is using Bacon's
inductive method.[39]

It is important to grasp that the traditional attempt to locate the
'verum factum' principle at the centre of the *Scienza nuova* runs
directly counter to such statements, places this work within the a
priori camp, and actually associates it with the dogmatism which
Vico was at pains to combat. The whole purpose of the 'verum
factum' idea is to give a privileged cognitive insight into certain
truths. The less effectively it works in producing such a 'direct'
access to knowledge, the more irrelevant it becomes; and the more
it is effective, the nearer it approaches a priori knowledge and
methods, thus diminishing the need for empirical procedures. For
this reason it is not possible for the 'verum factum' and the
'vero'/'certo' perspectives to co-exist as epistemological foundations
of the same science. *They pull in opposing theoretical and methodological directions.* While the 'vero'/'certo' problem is inherently a
problem of empirical procedures, the 'verum factum' formula
derives its essence from the absoluteness of self-evident truths.

The reader will meanwhile remember that as early as the *De
Ratione* Vico had complained that his contemporaries studied nature 'because it seems certain' whilst ignoring the study of civil
society, since such a study seemed uncertain, 'owing to human
choice'.[40] This important statement illustrates why, at that stage,

39. See *SN* 163, 164, 359.
40. *Opere filosofiche*, p. 811.

he could not conceive of a science of civil institutions. He does not argue that what is lacking is an immediate access to self-evident truths such as those of geometry. It is not direct access to the 'vero' which is the principal problem, but the relative inaccessibility of the 'certo'. Vico is arguing, in other words, that the two areas of the 'natural world' and the 'civil world' offer widely differing possibilities of 'accertamento' or validation. The facts relating to the behaviour of natural phenomena are more stable and, by means of observation and experiment, more easily reducible to the 'certo' of proven data. This is not the case with human institutions and customs because, he argues, human choice on which they are based renders men's actions less stable, predictable, and amenable to processes of inductive enquiry.

Vico's original problem, therefore, in founding a science of history was to detect stable patterns (the 'certo') in human behaviour and development similar to those one could discover in the natural order. Without them there would be a permanent lack of available evidence by which to confirm any theory of historical development: the 'vero', in other words, would remain unconfirmable since the 'certo' would be lacking. This is clearly a problem of *empirical verification*. Indeed we know that this is the problem to which Vico explicitly addresses himself in the *Scienza nuova*, where he talks in a number of different ways of the reconciliation of the 'vero' with the 'certo'.[41] But most important of all, he clearly thinks by this time that he has achieved this reconciliation, that he has found a way of introducing the principles of empirical verification into the study of civil institutions and their historical development. He claims, in fact, that he is adapting the inductive method of Bacon, that is, transposing it from the study of natural phenomena to the world of civil institutions.

Vico makes this claim in the clearest possible terms. In Book 1 of the *Scienza nuova* he outlines the basic principles of the work. In one particular passage he numbers these axioms and divides them clearly into those propositions which outline the universal laws of his theory of history, and certain others which confirm that theory 'in fact'. He writes that those belonging to the first group, namely, axioms v–xv,

> *which give us the foundations of the true*, will serve for considering this world of nations in its eternal idea, by that property of every science, noted by Aristotle, that science has to do with what is universal and

41. See *SN* 138, 140, 163, 325, 359.

eternal [*scientia debet esse de universalibus et aeternis*].[42]

But such universal principles need confirmation, and the remaining axioms, xv–xxii (owing to an oversight Vico puts axiom xv in both groups),

> *will give us the foundations of the certain ('certo').* By their use we shall be able *to see in fact this world of nations which we have studied in idea,* following the best ascertained method of philosophizing, that of Francis Bacon, Lord Verulam, but *carrying it over from the institutions of nature,* on which he composed his book *Cogitata (et) visa, to the civil institutions of mankind.*[43]

Vico clearly believed, at this stage, that it had become possible to transfer the method of induction, as he understood it, from the natural sciences to the study of human institutions. We shall see shortly why it is that human behaviour was no longer invested by him with the inherent instability attributed to it in the *De Ratione*. Our first step, however, must be to emphasize the significance of this shift of perspective.

The science of history became possible when Vico began to believe that there was sufficient validatory evidence available in the study of human institutions to confirm theories of history: in other words, when historical events display the 'certo' which has for so long been available in the natural sciences. Now if we return to the passage in *SN* 349 in which Vico allegedly utilizes the 'verum factum' principle, we shall in fact discover that it is the 'certo' of empirical enquiry which really interests him. First of all he repeats, in slightly modified form, the statement made in *SN* 331 that the world of civil institutions has been made by men and that its changing forms reflect the 'modifications' of the human mind. More significantly, however, he adds the statement which is in reality at the centre of his epistemology, namely, that 'history cannot be more *certain* than *when he who creates the things also narrates them*'.[44] As we can see, history becomes *certain* when the men who create civil institutions also narrate or authentically record historical events. The empirical problem of validation, in other words, is linked with the 'vera narratio'. We shall now attempt to show how clearly, in point of fact, the above statement draws together two crucially related aspects of his epistemology, and how this has resolved his earlier problem relating to the fundamental instability

42. *SN* 163. Italics in English mine.
43. Ibid. Italics in English mine.
44. *SN* 349. Italics mine.

of phenomena based on human volition.

Vico's view of the empirical process requires that if we wish to explain events in terms of particular theories, these events should display sufficiently regular patterns from which to infer or validate the general laws of the theory which covers them. When examining history, therefore, he seeks those facts, events, institutions or practices which display a certain regularity of occurrence. Consequently, if men have over the centuries repeatedly created their institutions according to discernible patterns, general laws governing such patterns can undoubtedly be inferred:

> Now since this world of nations has been made by men, let us see in what institutions all men agree and always have agreed. For these institutions will be able to give us the universal and eternal principles (such as every science must have) on which all nations were founded and still preserve themselves.[45]

This is the real purpose behind his statement that men create institutions. The idea that men create their institutions is explicitly related to the 'certo' or stable and universal pattern which can validate the theory Vico intends to propose.

The crucial factor, of course, which enabled him to move from a position in the *De Ratione* in which he saw human activity as lacking this 'certo' or stable pattern to a position in which he could discern it, was the 'senso comune'. By means of this concept he was able to shift the focus of analytic attention away from the vagaries and chaos of the variables in human behaviour which the doctrine of free-will demanded. In its place, he focused on the common substratum of human activity and experience which exists at a more fundamental level than at that of reflective choice. This, consequently, had to be postulated as existing on a more instinctual and less 'variable' plane. Thus, in the *Scienza nuova*, for analytic and scientific purposes, Vico had to move away from the 'uncertainties' of human choice to the more 'naturalistic' and fundamental level of the 'senso commune' which provides the stability and recurrent patterns of the 'certo'. He could hardly be more explicit than when he states: 'Human choice, by its nature most uncertain, is made certain and determined by the "senso comune" of men',[*46] and we have already seen that 'senso comune' is defined as judgement without reflection, and is experienced by whole peoples, nations or indeed all humanity.[47]

45. *SN* 332.
46. *SN* 141.
47. See *SN* 142.

Thus humanity creates its institutions according to the patterns described in earlier chapters, moving from a rigid natural theogony or collective god-creating process to the increasingly complex institutions of later epochs. Now having conceived of the 'senso comune' as the underlying, stable, instinctive level of empirically observable human evolution, some form of access to the data it provided had to be found. This was precisely the function of the 'vera narratio'. Once the code for interpreting the world of myth had been uncovered, the historian, because he had access to the reliable and 'naturally' expressed mental processes of early man, would be able to relate the 'modifications of the human mind' to the development of institutions which reflect those changes. In *SN* 390 Vico states that his philosophy 'reduces to certainty human choice, which by its nature is most uncertain – which is as much as to say that it reduces philology to the form of a science'. All the elements expressed above come together in this concise formulation.

The 'senso comune', therefore, provides the observable pattern of evolution of structures of thought and feeling on the basis of which humanity creates its institutions. The 'vera narratio' is the guarantee that the evidence provided by early myth is untarnished by rational reconstruction and is thus a reliable record of those primitive structures of thought and feeling. When, in other words, early man both creates his institutions and at the same time – through myth – records or 'narrates' the state of mind which they reflect, the historian has access to the most 'certain' empirical evidence, which is the basis of any science. Thus, if we return to our starting point in *SN* 349, we can see what Vico means by asserting that 'history cannot be more *certain* than when *he who creates the things also narrates them*' (Italics mine). But although Vico's intentions were to provide an empirically based historical science, there was a further dimension to his endeavours which rendered this a problematic objective.

15
Vico's Method in Practice

The 'Certo' and its 'Normative'/'Prescriptive' Dimension

We have seen that Vico's conception of a science of history involves procedures of *empirical* validation. There is, however, another, *extra-empirical* dimension to the new science which cannot be described adequately or fully in a single term or with a single concept. 'Normative', 'prescriptive', even 'apologetic' can all at times be used to characterize the extra-empirical purpose I am referring to. It relates to a desire on Vico's part to provide not simply an open-ended, morally agnostic account of social evolution, but also an argument about what *must* be, about the *necessary* order of things. His almost obsessive concern with the latter has been largely ignored by the literature on the *Scienza nuova*. In this chapter we will see that tensions and contradictions arise out of Vico's attempt to produce a science of history which can deal with both his empirical and his normative/prescriptive aspirations simultaneously.

In its straightforward empirical sense, the 'certo' denotes the facts of history which are meant to confirm Vico's theory of historical development. Within the prescriptive perspective, on the other hand, it utilizes those same facts but this time as indicative of broad principles which 'justify' or 'authorize' particular patterns of development in history. This is why the term 'certo' is so frequently associated with the notion of 'authority' in his writings, particularly in the sphere of law. Our attempt to clarify this difficult and multi-dimensional concept of the 'certo' can thus quite appropriately start with some observations in this area.

We will recall that the initial difficulty, which Vico began to resolve in the *Diritto universale*, lay in justifying the *authority* of changing laws for which it was not possible to find justification in terms of the eternal principles of natural justice. Vico's solution to the problem lay in the concept of an *evolving* 'natural law' (the 'natural law of the gentes') which could accommodate the 'certo' of changing legal systems as adequate prescriptive requirements of the epochs in which they arose. These legal systems, moreover, were the natural expression of the 'senso comune' or structures of thought and feeling from which they derived their authority.

The 'certo', therefore, also points to historical reality in such a way as to highlight its normative or prescriptive dimension. It is for this reason that Vico repeatedly stresses that his science 'comes to be a philosophy of authority, . . .'[1] Within this normative dimension of social and legal development he includes the selfish activity of tyrants, and the struggles for emancipation undertaken by popular strata of society. Thus the 'certo' also denotes those realities of history which the traditional exponents of an eternal and rationalistic natural law found morally repugnant and which they associated with the totally unacceptable 'rule of force'. But since in his view these unpleasant realities (which are included within what Vico describes in the following passage as an 'obscurity of judgement') expressed fundamental laws of human development, they were not simply necessary evils but at certain points in history the very basis of the authority of legal systems. This explains the otherwise puzzling connection he often makes in the *Scienza nuova* between the notions of 'certo' and 'authority': 'The certain ["certo"] in the laws is an obscurity of judgement backed only by authority, so that we find them harsh in application, yet are obliged to apply them just because of what is certain ["certo"] in them'.*[2] Hence even the 'uncivilized' and 'tyrannical' laws of the periods of barbarism possessed the right and proper 'authority' of laws.

A more complete definition of 'certo', then, is one which takes full account not only of its meaning as a principle of empirical validation, but also of its description of certain aspects of human activity which were regarded by many as reprehensible and yet form part of the normal pattern of social development. One of the reasons why Vico is so cryptic in his handling of this aspect of the 'certo' is that it reflects a battle he did not himself dare to make too explicit, namely, the battle he was waging against the traditional control exercised by rationalistic and unhistorical schemes of doctrinal and moral theology over theories of man and society.

Such cautiousness on Vico's part also explains why the normative/prescriptive aspect of the 'certo' (i.e. 'authority') often seems to slip into the text almost gratuitously. So, in an otherwise typical passage in which he equates the 'vero' with philosophy and the 'certo' with philology, we also find him insinuating the idea of

1. *SN* 350. See also *SN* 7, 386 and *SN1a* 90.
2. *SN* 321.

'authority': 'Philosophy contemplates reason, whence comes knowledge of the true ("vero"); philology observes the authority of human choice, whence comes consciousness of the certain ("certo")'.*[3] The reference to the 'authority of human choice', when examined, re-introduces the notion of the 'senso comune' as the source of such authority. Following closely upon the above statement Vico reminds the reader that 'human choice . . . is made certain ("certo") and determined by the "senso comune" of men'.[4] The 'senso comune', viewed as the pattern of instinctual and evolutionary laws, provides not only a solid core of stable empirical evidence by defining the 'certo' and thus enabling us to discern the 'ideal eternal history';[5] it is also the foundation of authority in society, as Vico makes plain when he argues that 'the nations were governed by the certainty of authority . . . namely, the "senso comune" of the human race, on which the consciences of all nations repose'.*[6]

I do not believe that the normative aspect of the *Scienza nuova* has received the attention it merits. It is important, though, to give it due weight since it places Vico's empiricism within a more accurate if problematic historical context. The problem of reconciling the 'vero' of theory with the 'certo' of historical facts (as we see clearly in the case of his preoccupation with law) did not originate as an exclusively epistemological or empirical question. The problem of *justifying* the apparently arbitrary 'authority' of changing legal systems weighed equally on his mind. And while in Vico's day questions relating to empirical practice were still in their infancy, prescriptive attitudes were deeply rooted in a civilization saturated with hundreds of years of Christian morality and theology. Critics who either ignore this fact or else fail to spot the tensions to which it gives rise are prone to exaggerate Vico's 'modernity' and to obscure the very real historical and contingent context of his discourse.

Vico and the Problem of Induction

We have seen that in his new science of history Vico wished to demonstrate that his theory could be validated by historical evidence. This is not, he claimed, the standard practice among histo-

3. *SN* 138.
4. *SN* 141.
5. *SN* 145.
6. *SN* 350.

rians, and he criticized both philosophers, who did not validate their reasoning by appeal to the facts of history, and also historians, who failed to theorize their empirical research. He wished, moreover, to see Bacon's methodology, previously used only in the natural sciences, carried over 'to the civil institutions of mankind'.[7] According to his understanding of this methodology, philosophers would then be able to trace common patterns in the creation of civil institutions because 'these institutions will be able to give us the universal and eternal principles (such as every science must have) on which all nations were founded and still preserve themselves'.[8]

But although Vico claims to be proceeding according to the inductive method of Francis Bacon,[9] we must distinguish between the methodology he claims to be using and the one he actually employs in practice. One of the clearest messages to come from studies in the philosophy of science is that practitioners are notoriously unreliable exponents of their own methodologies. But in addition to this there is the added problem that Vico does not provide us with a detailed account of what he understood by induction.

Nevertheless, we are not totally in the dark on this issue. We see, for example, in the *Scienza nuova*, the same critique of 'unproductive' methods of enquiry as we met in his earlier writings:

> Then came Aristotle and Zeno. The former taught the syllogism, *a method which deduces particulars from their universals rather than uniting particulars to obtain universals*. The latter taught the sorite logic, which, like the method of modern philosophers, makes minds subtle but not sharp. *Neither yielded anything more notable to the advantage of the human race.**[10]

Apart from branding both approaches as unproductive, the passage clearly indicates that one should work from particulars towards universal laws, and not start with the universal and work towards the particular. Moreover, Vico undoubtedly identifies his own view of the proper procedure with the inductive method of Bacon, since the passage continues:

> Hence with great reason Bacon, great alike as philosopher and statesman, proposes, commends, and illustrates the inductive method in his *[Novum] Organum*, and is still followed by the English with great profit

7. *SN* 163.
8. *SN* 332.
9. See *SN* 332.
10. *SN* 499. Italics mine.

in experimental philosophy.[11]

The classical definition of induction as the inferring of a general law from a number of specific instances of its operation by no means describes a straightforward and unproblematic procedure. Broadly speaking, the process can be viewed as being initiated at either extreme of the hypothesis/data polarity. As an instance of the inductive procedure operating in an almost automatic manner from data which force themselves on the observer's attention we have the example of the daily appearance of the sun, which suggests a 'law' of solar (which in the event turns out to be earthly) rotation. Many 'laws' of operation, however, are by no means so amenable to observation. In such cases the investigator takes his point of departure from an initial hypothesis which itself suggests a pattern to be verified. Numerous areas of research, such as medicine, demonstrate how inaccessible many 'laws' remain to observation without recourse to numerous hypotheses.

We simply do not know whether Vico had a comprehensive grasp of such problems. He may have had some awareness of the function of hypotheses or 'things in doubt' requiring confirmation. Referring to the types of procedures used in ancient times, he comments: 'After Aesop came Socrates, who introduced dialectic, employing induction of several certain things related to the doubtful thing in question. Before Socrates, medicine, by induction of observations, had given us Hippocrates'.[12] Elsewhere, however, Vico gives a description which seems close to the classical conception of induction when he claims that 'Socrates began to adumbrate intelligible genera or abstract universals by induction; that is, by collecting uniform particulars which go to make up a genus of that in respect of which the particulars are uniform among themselves'.[13]

But whatever may have been Vico's level of understanding of the problems associated with induction, we can be sure that he understood unequivocally the importance of the general principle of empirical validation. Such a dimension of scientific research is provided, in the case of his own *Scienza nuova*, by his historico-philological research into early 'poetic' institutions. This explains why, in evolving a science of history, 'the first science to be learned should be mythology or the interpretation of fables'.[14] Moreover,

11. Ibid.
12. Ibid.
13. *SN* 1040.
14. *SN* 51. See also *SN* 198.

his repeated assertion of the 'vera narratio', namely, that early men 'are truthful by nature', and that 'the first fables could not feign anything false; they must therefore have been, as they have been defined above, true narration',[15] provides the whole 'naturalistic' armoury ('natural theogony', 'natural necessity', 'senso comune') of stable, detectable patterns of human activity so necessary for empirical observation.

In earlier chapters we expressed certain doubts about the plausibility of the somewhat excessively rigid nature of Vico's 'naturalistic' schemes. We can now see the purpose behind the rather inflexible relations he postulated between early man and the various linguistic and institutional expressions of his nature. His elimination of 'variables', such as the 'uncertainty' of 'human choice', was intended to guarantee the regularity and reliability of observable patterns. But we should now extend our critical evaluation beyond the actual content of these 'naturalistic' principles and assess Vico's claim to have used them inductively – according to Bacon's methodology, as he puts it – to validate his theory of history.

Vico's Empiricism in Practice

W. H. Walsh is convinced that Vico did not, in fact, arrive at his theory of history through a true process of induction at all.[16] Walsh makes no objection to Vico starting out with his 'ideal eternal history', which is in fact a legitimate hypothesis. But he points out that it is not sufficient simply to collate the evidence which confirms it and ignore uncongenial historical data. This simply amounts to selecting the evidence according to the theory itself, and the circularity of such a procedure is only too evident. In his tireless search for evidence which will support his theory, argues Walsh, 'it has to be admitted that he looks all the time for material which will *confirm* his theory', in addition to which 'for all his admiration for Bacon, he does not really know about the negative instance'.[17] It is, of course, always incumbent upon the investigator to attempt to falsify his own theories as a necessary part of adequate testing procedures. This is essential in order to show that alternative hypotheses have been properly eliminated, that the theory one is propounding has greater explanatory power than competing theories, and that it is also capable of accounting for uncongenial

15. *SN* 408.
16. See W. H. Walsh, 'The Logical Status of Vico's Ideal Eternal History'.
17. Ibid., p. 153.

evidence. Judged in the light of such criteria, Vico's science of history will indeed be found wanting.

Nevertheless, while agreeing with Walsh's negative verdict on the question of Vico's use of validatory criteria, I do not think it is entirely true to suggest that he ignored uncongenial evidence. He certainly did refer to such negative data, but it is his manner of treating it which is significant. Max Fisch has pointed out that Vico was, in fact, aware of what appeared to be numerous anomalies in his theory.[18] He admitted that many nations did not appear to follow his tripartite scheme with anything like the degree of precision he had outlined in his model. Yet in that part of the work in which he refers to these exceptions he makes it clear that they cannot call into question the basic pattern of the 'ideal eternal history'.[19] The failure on the part of numerous peoples to pass from aristocracies to free commonwealths and then on to 'perfect monarchies' is accounted for through a variety of special circumstances. Thus in warmer southern climes, 'the Carthaginians were prevented by their native African shrewdness, which was further sharpened by their maritime trade; the Capuans by the mild climate and the fertility of this happy Campania; and the Numantians, finally, in the first flower of their heroism were suppressed by the power of Rome . . . .'[20] Equally, numerous exceptions are to be found in the 'cold climates' of northern Europe. But, Vico argues, in countries like Sweden, Denmark, Poland and England, 'if the natural course of human civil institutions is not impeded in their case *by extraordinary causes*, they will arrive at perfect monarchies'.[21]

Fisch claims, in fact, that the exceptions are more numerous than the rule. He defends Vico by arguing that the burden of his research was focused on the more difficult early period. Beyond that, he argues, 'he has dealt only briefly with the beginnings of the second cycle', and on the whole later period he observes that 'there are only scattered indications'.[22] These remarks, however, suggest that more extensive research would bring to light even further anomalies, and undermine the empirical basis of the 'ideal eternal history' by stressing the paucity of validatory evidence available to support it.

In point of fact Vico seems determined to let neither the numer-

---

18. Introduction to *The New Science of Giambattista Vico*, pp. xxxvii–xxxviii.
19. See *SN* 1088–96.
20. *SN* 1088.
21. *SN* 1092. Italics mine.
22. Introduction to *The New Science of Giambattista Vico*, p. xxxviii.

ous anomalies nor the scantiness of the evidence affect the force with which he asserts his 'ideal eternal history'. Not only does he claim that his scheme accounts for all past ages but adds that it will determine the course of future events. The very section in which he accounts for the 'exceptions' we have just mentioned concludes with the statement that in his new science we find 'the ideal eternal history of the *eternal laws* which are instanced by the deeds of all nations', and that the pattern of this historical unfolding would remain even if 'there were infinite worlds being born from time to time throughout eternity'.[23] In connection, therefore, with the rather restricted evidential support for such a claim, Fisch is correct in stating that 'there is plenty for further workers to do'; but, according to Vico's thinking on the matter, whatever these researchers will uncover, 'the new science will be found to have contained *in principle*'.[24] He has thus produced a theory to account for all past and future historical development which no amount of subsequent evidence, it seems, can invalidate.

We can hardly avoid the conclusion that the actual method employed in the *Scienza nuova* does not measure up to the principles of an open-ended and scientific enquiry such as the method of induction is designed to ensure. If, therefore, Vico was aware of the need for more extensive validatory criteria, and for the use of more rigorous testing procedures, all we can say is that he clearly failed to implement them. In any case, even an imperfect mastery of sound methodological criteria is not, in my view, sufficient to explain the evident force and determination with which Vico asserted his 'ideal eternal history'. We must allow for the possibility of an external factor which compelled him to press his theory at the expense of more objective methodological considerations. And in this regard we must turn to his overriding preoccupation with the non-empirical, prescriptive aspect of his theory. In doing so we also, incidentally, but quite correctly, avoid attributing to Vico a somewhat anarchronistic and unhistorical form of methodological refinement.

We have already noted that a central component of the normative dimension of Vico's philosophy is the 'senso comune', the stable naturalistic substratum of thoughts and feelings which is the ultimate basis for the authority of laws and governments. But at the same time the 'senso comune' is the organizing principle behind the panoply of naturalistic relations (between men and the institutions

---

23. *SN* 1096. Italics mine.
24. Introduction to *The New Science of Giambattista Vico*, p. xxxviii.

they create) which are intended to provide a stable corpus of empirical data. The duality of roles of the 'senso comune', and of the 'certo' which is derived from it, is consequently highly problematic. This is because the theoretical foundations of Vico's validatory or empirical procedures (i.e. 'senso comune', 'vera narratio', 'natural signification', etc.) have their source in a 'naturalistic' philosophy which is part and parcel of the theory of history which the procedures are meant to validate.

In other words, the 'senso comune' and related concepts were central both to the empirical foundations of the enquiry and to the theory of history Vico is expounding. This problem we can leave for the moment. But what we must stress at this point is that the theory of history was an account of a *necessary* pattern of social change which he was prepared to press. The extent, therefore, to which he was determined to insist in advance on this particular theory or pattern of historical change is also the extent to which he must have been prepared to impair the openness of his heuristic procedures.

The coexistence within the same work of a normative intention with the elaboration of an empirical method is necessarily an uneasy one. Yet that is precisely what we find stated explicitly in an important passage in the *Scienza nuova*. In the lengthiest single statement he makes about the purpose of the work, we find a clear and simultaneous formulation of both the normative *and* heuristic principles. In *SN* 7 he states the idea that the traditional disciplines of philosophy ('vero') and philology ('certo') must be reconciled. He then describes the *particular* heuristic techniques he proposes to deploy: the 'vera narratio' and 'natural theogony'. He also introduces the principles of necessity and utility which govern men's actions and thus provide the raw material upon which the historian can base his research. All this, when applied to the study of history, 'reduces it to the form of a science'. But alongside so apparently objective and scientific an enterprise, we are informed that such an approach will uncover 'the design of an ideal eternal history . . .; so that, *on account of this its second principle aspect*, our Science may be considered *a philosophy of authority*'.[25] There is little doubt that the prescriptive aspect of the work is in the forefront of Vico's mind here. And while it is, of course, logically conceivable that he could have arrived at or at least effectively validated his 'philosophy of

---

25. Italics mine. In *SN* 350 Vico stresses again the fact that the 'senso comune' is central to his science, and once more makes plain his 'prescriptive' preoccupation by stating that his science 'comes to be a philosophy of authority, which is the fount of the outer justice of which the moral theologians speak'.

authority' by empirical means, we have many indications in the *Scienza nuova* that this was far from being the case.

In concluding this section, therefore, we can sympathize with attempts to find alternative validatory principles in such concepts as the 'verum factum' and its elaboration into an 'epistemology of privileged insight'. We have found, however, that not only is there insufficient textual evidence to give such an idea a serious methodological or epistemological basis, but also that such a reconstruction creates false oppositions (for instance, Vico's alleged relegation of the natural sciences to a position inferior to that of the human sciences), in addition to being in conflict with what he himself says about his methodology.

From his acquaintance with the natural sciences of his time, Vico undoubtedly gained a genuine appreciation of the value of empirical procedures. Indeed he repeatedly claimed to have based his new science of history on such procedures, even though we may wish to register a different conclusion regarding this claim. There is little doubt that Vico forced the evidence for, and was more than a little enthusiastic in pressing, his theory of history. A possible reason for his doing so has been indicated, namely, his overriding concern to find a necessary pattern in social change which fulfils the prescriptive requirements of his theory. Underlying this necessary pattern there is a 'philosophy of nature' which pervades the historical picture describing his evolutionary scheme. As we turn to consider more directly Vico's conception of historical forces we shall continue to find this naturalism occupying a central place in his scheme of things.

Part VI
Vico's Naturalistic Historicism

16
The Problematicity of Vico's Notion of 'Providence'

Along with the notion of 'cycles' or 'ricorsi', the concept of 'providence' is perhaps the most problematic idea in the *Scienza nuova*. As Isaiah Berlin has remarked, 'Vico's conception of Providence is not among the clearest of his basic notions'.[1] Given its prominence in the work, the idea has received surprisingly limited attention. The reasons for this probably derive from a combination of the author's lack of definitional clarity on the matter and the evident desire of Vichian scholarship to stress his 'relevance' and 'modernity'. Nevertheless, the concept has not been totally ignored and a brief survey of its main interpretations is useful.

Croce reduced providence to a manifestation of the 'unity of the spirit', understood in its Hegelian sense as the unfolding of the universal 'mind'.[2] This particular presentation of Vico's idea has been followed by other, non-idealist but in some ways equally partisan attempts to 'modernize' its conceptual content. Sabarini, for instance, proposed an existentialist version of providence as 'the dynamic structure of human consciousness' which, he argued, '*translated into modern day terminology*, denotes nothing other than being and its temporality'.[3]

Again, some commentators have taken Vico's claims to orthodoxy as interpretative keys to its meaning and have argued accordingly. Franco Amerio is one of the best known in this respect.[4] He bases his interpretation on the claim that the really operative historical division in the *Scienza nuova* is twofold rather than threefold and that such a division expresses the theological dichotomy between a state of original sin and a subsequent state of grace. So, when referring to providence in its relation to the actions of men, Amerio claims that it 'operates naturally through their acts of

---

1. I. Berlin, 'Vico and the Ideal of the Enlightenment'. p. 653.
2. See Croce, *Philosophy*, pp. 126–43.
3. R. Sabarini, *Il tempo in G. B. Vico*, p. 79. Italics mine.
4. F. Amerio, *Introduzione allo studio di G. B. Vico*. Also Amerio, 'Sulla vichiana dialettica della storia'.

knowing and volition'.[5]

We have, however, seen how providence, in the *Scienza nuova*, is described as a force which steers the course of history *in spite of* human volition and intentions, which are normally directed towards the pursuit of private interests. Similarly, more than a little ingenuity would, I fear, be required to justify Amerio's claim that Vico makes original sin and free-will 'two interpretative keys to the unfolding of history'.[6]

Luigi Bellofiore, however, although also giving a clearly Catholic gloss to the *Scienza nuova*, nevertheless avoids the somewhat excessively 'instrumentalizing' tendencies of Amerio. Yet not even his more subtle approach totally dispenses with a proselytizing intent, as we can see from his claim that Vico's providence, is, as he puts it, 'in harmony with the most profound and authentic Christian thinking; *but also acutely modern*'.[7] An accommodation of Vico's views on providence with orthodox Catholicism is achieved by identifying them with a rather vaguely outlined 'spiritualismo cristiano'. Vico thus finds a place within a variegated and all-embracing spiritual movement which is described as a 'varied and multiform tradition which goes from Plato to Augustine – via neoplatonism – to Scotus, Malebranche, Vico, Gioberti, Rosmini and to modern and contemporary representatives of Christian spirituality'.[8] Once again, the tendency to proselytize is accompanied by a strong desire, particularly evident in the preceding quotation, to emphasize Vico's modernity. And in connection with the passage just cited, it should perhaps be noted in passing that two of those mentioned, namely Gioberti and Rosmini, had both raised objections to the *Scienza nuova* on religious grounds,[9] a fact not mentioned by Bellofiore.

Leon Pompa has observed that 'some of Vico's remarks about providence cannot be taken at their face value'.[10] On closer inspection it becomes apparent that this observation is a preamble to a neutralization of the concept. The notion of providence, Pompa suggests, can be identified 'with common sense itself', and indicates 'man's ability to reach social decisions without doing so in a social capacity'.[11] Providence thus becomes a force to be identified with qualities 'immanent' in human activity. The obvious advantage of

5. Amerio, 'Sulla vichiana dialettica della storia', p. 134.
6. Ibid., p. 139
7. Bellofiore, *La dottrina della provvidenza*, p. 189.
8. Ibid., p. 214.
9. See Nicolini, *La religiosità*, pp. 186–95.
10. Pompa, *Vico*, p. 58.
11. Ibid.

such an interpretation is that providence can be accommodated to a more amenable and modern social philosophy. Unfortunately, as a real operative force in history, it then disappears. In fact, Pompa argues that 'the notion of providence is indeed so natural that one cannot detect in what it consists'. More specifically, 'Vico's explanation really amounts to saying that commonwealths arise because when a certain institutional context exists men can see that a certain political structure is best suited to fulfil its needs'.[12] The effect of this line of interpretation is to play down the clearly and repeatedly expressed tension in the *Scienza nuova* between men's selfish pursuits which tend towards self-destruction and the socially beneficial guiding force of providence which acts in direct opposition to such urges. And since Pompa gives the activity of providence a meaning which fits into a perspective whereby men are themselves the directing force in human history, the conclusion of his argument is that nothing 'is added to this already satisfactory explanation by the pronouncement that we thus see providence directing human affairs', a claim which then becomes 'both gratuitous and empty'.[13]

Similarly, the tendency to neutralize the theoretical function of the concept in question is once more admirably expressed by R. Nisbet, who explicitly identifies himself with Pompa by agreeing that providence 'can be eliminated from Vico's work without in any way damaging its principal elements'.[14] Much as I admire the work of scholars like Pompa, I must confess that I regard the 'neutralizing' interpretation as being the most profoundly mistaken of all.

A crucial element which is shared, however, by all the interpretations we have briefly surveyed is a strong preoccupation with Vico's alleged 'relevance'. It is thus not by chance that in their anxiety to bring him into the twentieth century they all tend either to underplay or else totally to obscure what is *specific* and *historical* in Vico's treatment of providence. If we are truly to understand what the use of the term meant to him, as opposed to what it can mean in our utilization of his ideas, a certain amount of historical discussion is necessary.

'Providence' and the Growth of Scientific Thought

A number of critics have heretofore sensed a 'deliberate obscurity'

12. Ibid., p. 60.
13. Ibid.
14. R. Nisbet, 'Vico and the Idea of Progress', p. 636.

in Vico's handling of providence. Frederick Vaughan is convinced that he is intentionally concealing the real meaning of the term and that this explains why such a key concept remains 'the most elusive aspect of the *New Science*'.[15]

Leon Pompa, in discussing Vaughan's view that Vico was presenting a disguised naturalism, wonders whether the elusiveness of his ideas is the result of confusion in Vico's own mind or whether, as had been suggested, it was an attempt to conceal 'what he well knew to be their naturalistic character'.[16] Pompa argues that Vaughan has not produced sufficient evidence to prove his case,[17] and that the text seems too ambiguous 'to decide conclusively' one way or the other. We have argued throughout this study, however, that Vico is far from confused about the 'naturalistic' character of his ideas. He certainly had to be cautious. But although he could not wear his naturalism on his sleeve, there seems to me little doubt that it carries the main burden of his theoretical system. Morover, it is precisely in pursuing in greater detail the obvious textual manoeuvres surrounding his 'naturalism' that we uncover the greater 'specificity' and historical concreteness of providence.

The idea that a providential force was, in some way or other, at work in human history could almost be described as a universal assumption in Christian Europe up to the seventeenth century. It was at that time, however, with the rapid advance of mechanistic and naturalistic theories of the universe that the idea began to come under closer scrutiny and, in some respects, under serious threat. Bacon, Newton, Descartes, to mention just a few of the most famous proponents of the new scientific outlook, were all aware of the dangers such ideas posed for the orthodox belief in a provident Deity. With the passage of time the problems became intensified, but the idea of the existence of a providential force nevertheless displayed remarkable resilience.

One can grasp more easily the cultural climate of the period in which Vico was writing if one considers for a moment that even in the comparatively free and easy religious atmosphere of early eigteenth-century England 'divine Providence occupied an essential position in the literature of natural philosophy'.[18] Instances started to appear, however, in which providence was little more than part

15. Vaughan, *Political Philosophy*, p. 39.
16. Pompa, *Vico*, p. 60.
17. This observation, which could be extended to other aspects of Vaughan's study, is almost inevitable given the brevity of the work. The latter remains, nevertheless, highly valuable for the areas of further investigation it frequently suggests regarding Vico's 'deliberate obscurity'.
18. C. C. Gillispie, *Genesis and Geology*, p. 10.

of the language of convention, and in which, in such cases as Vico's, the term could be suspected of being a disguised reference to forces or processes about which it was dangerous to be explicit.

There were various ways of responding to the growing problematicity of this most important of theological ideas. As early as the seventeenth century, according to P. M. Rattansi, Francis Bacon had noted the undermining effect of the new knowledge and had suggested that the answer lay in demarcating 'as rigid a separation as possible between religious and secular knowledge' in order to avoid 'errors in philosophy and heresies in religion'.[19]

By the end of the seventeenth and in the early eighteenth century debates around such matters grew livelier in European scientific circles and involved major figures such as Leibniz and Newton. Much of the discussion concerning the manner of justifying a role for providence centred upon the question of the nature and extent of natural and physical laws. Other problems debated concerned the character of providential interventions in nature or history, and whether such occurrences implied initial faults in God's creation; whether providential assistance in safeguarding God's design was manifest in 'occasional' and highly notable interventions, or whether God's initial act of creation amounted to the setting in motion of a self-regulating system having all the appearance of self-sufficiency.[20] Amongst believers such debates were charged with a certain urgency, since a demonstration that God's providence could be reconciled with a scientific view of the universe was a counter to more seditious discussions tending to undermine the whole fabric of theological thought. David Kubrin has noted how the central preoccupation surrounding the question of the relation of providence to a mechanical universe arose out of 'a general concern that the banishment of Providence from the present world would lead men to believe that the world had always been without Providence',[21] indeed that the very idea of a Creator could be abandoned.

By the early eighteenth century the notion of providence had become a vital question in theories dealing with the natural or historical unfolding of Creation. One can see immediately, therefore, the relevance of all these discussions about providence to the *Scienza nuova* which Vico was then writing, and to his concept of

19. P. M. Rattansi, 'The Social Interpretation of Science in the Seventeenth Century', p. 15.

20. For a brief outline of some aspects of such debates, see R. Attfield, 'The Assault of Physical Theology' in his *God and the Secular*, pp. 68–98.

21. D. Kubrin, 'Newton and the Cyclical Cosmos: Providence and Mechanical Philosophy', pp. 149–50.

an 'ideal eternal history'. But if the problem of safeguarding the place of a providential order in history was an important issue even in the relatively liberal atmosphere of northern Europe, one can imagine its significance in the tenser religious climate of Vico's Naples.

'Providence', Orthodoxy and Vico's Creation of a 'Rational Civil Theology'

The notion of providence had entered into the scientific discussions of the Neapolitan Investiganti in the latter half of the seventeenth century. It had then frequently been used to describe a 'naturalistic' force underlying the instinctive sagacity and self-preservatory impulses which these thinkers detected in the animal kingdom. By the time of the Valleta circle debates, when attention had turned towards the 'naturalistic' and atomist philosophies of Democritus, Epicurus and Lucretius, the ecclesiastical offensive began to take the form of Inquisitorial proceedings. Some reasons for such proceedings have already been discussed in earlier chapters. We should also note, however, that the Inquisitors were given further cause by the fact that one of the notable features of Epicurean philosophy was precisely its hostile rejection of any notion of providence. The opposition of Democritus and Epicurus to any such notion was well known, and had been transmitted through numerous sources, all of which were familiar to the members of the Valleta circle and to Vico. The *De Rerum Natura* of their Latin counterpart, Lucretius, was also widely read at that time.

St Thomas Aquinas' condemnation of these thinkers on account of their denial of providence was unequivocal. Aquinas had, in point of fact, singled out the Democritan/Epicurean tradition as the school from which the pernicious doctrine of 'chance' had originated.[22] But the idea of providence, he argued, was equally undermined by their notions of fate and material determinism: 'This is the mode of argument of those like Democritus and other natural philosophers of antiquity who withdrew the natural course of things from the protection of divine providence and attributed it to material determinism or necessity'.[23] Perhaps the most important source in this regard was Cicero's *De Natura Deorum*, because

22. 'Some, like Democritus and the Epicureans, have totally rejected providence, claiming that the world was created by chance.' (Aquinas, *Summa Theologica* 1a, q. 22, art. 2, Resp.)
23. Ibid., 1a, q. 22, ad. 3.

contained in his account of the debates and polemics between the schools of ancient philosophy was also the Epicureans' attack on the Stoics and their notion of providence.

One of the unmistakable indications we possess of the delicate nature of the whole question of providence in Naples at that time, is contained in Valletta's defence of modern philosophy. As we know, he sought to defend the new ideas in circulation by a series of highly dubious arguments purporting to show the greater suitability of the modern philosophy as a vehicle of Catholic teaching than the Aristotelian Scholastic tradition. An important element of this strategy was the attempted legitimization of the Democritan and Epicurean schools. Valletta was, of course, perfectly aware of Aquinas' condemnation of these pagan sources. Nevertheless, incredible as it may seem, he argues that these writers actually espoused the notion of providence. The Epicureans, he insists, believed that there is a God who 'sustains and imparts motion to this Universe', and not even the impious Epicureans, Petronius and Lucan, 'denied in any way God's Providence'.[24]

Such spurious and tactical distortions of the true position of these thinkers can be found throughout Valletta's defence.[25] An equally astonishing claim is made by him, at some length, regarding Democritus. In substance, Valletta's argument can be reduced to the following terms: 'I think I can assert without any doubt that when Democritus said that *things happen by chance*, he was referring to *Fate*. And by *Fate* he understood the order of things established by Providence and by the Author of Nature, which he calls *Necessity*'.[26] There is, of course, no contradiction in linking the notions of 'chance' and 'necessity' in Democritus, to whom 'creation is the undesigned result of inevitable natural processes'.[27] The problem is that for all the atomists these ideas were important tools in their attacks on the concept of a provident Deity. Valletta's rather desperate attempt to interpret such ideas as synonymous with the very notion they were meant to attack demonstrates how important the latter had become at the time as a test of orthodoxy.

A wider historical factor which is relevant to Vico's treatment of this problem is that one of the responses of Christianity to the threat from the growth of scientific thinking was the development from the seventeenth century onwards of what came to be known

---

24. Valleta, *Opere filosofiche*, p. 291.
25. See ibid., pp. 235, 236, 241, 242.
26. Ibid., p. 235.
27. For a discussion of the coexistence of these apparently conflicting ideas see C. J. Glacken, *Trace on the Rhodian Shore: Nature and Culture in Western Thought from Ancient Times to Eighteenth Century*, pp. 65ff.

as 'natural theology'.[28] This represented an attempt to demonstrate the rationality of belief in a provident Deity by the use of arguments about the order, beauty, harmony and complexity of the natural world. In this way it was hoped that scientific discoveries would strengthen rather than undermine the belief that such a complex universe pointed to an intelligent creator.

In Catholic Europe, where the Church tended to retain tighter control over all branches of theological teaching and development, 'natural theology' did not develop or flourish in as open and flexible a manner as it did in the less doctrinally centralized centres of the Protestant north. In this context we must bear in mind the increasing stature of Aquinas, from the sixteenth century, when the *Summa Theologica* replaced Peter Lombard's *Sentences* as the major theological teaching text. Thus, typical of the kinds of arguments to be found in Catholic 'natural theology' were Aquinas' famous 'five demonstrations' of the existence of a provident Deity 'by which all things in nature are ordered to their ends'.[29] Yet, while there were significant differences of approach between the more doctrinally controlled natural theology of the Catholics and the relatively more open discussions of the predominantly Protestant thinkers,[30] it is nevertheless true to say that in both cases, 'they claim to take the world as a whole as their datum',[31] thereby attempting to give religious belief a basis in man's *observation* of the world of nature as distinct from its *revelation* by God.

The question of providence, therefore, was a fundamental notion within natural theology.[32] It was also, when we examine its role in the *Scienza nuova*, the force which engineered the eventual beneficent results of the diverse, disparate and self-destructive activities of humanity. The threat to religious orthodoxy, as we have seen, arose in Vico's detailed descriptions of these activities: the creation of language and letters through a process of 'natural signification'; the description of early human activity as lacking in reflection and any capacity for choice; the pursuit of self-interest; the abandonment of the traditional natural law with its eternal principles of natural justice; the surreptitious espousal of the role of 'force' in history, and so on. All these, together with his almost exclusive

---

28. A useful discussion of this can be found in R. Attfield, *God and The Secular*, pp. 150ff.

29. Aquinas, *Summa Theologica*, 1a, q. 2, art. 3, Resp.

30. For a fairly detailed outline of these developments see C. C. J. Webb, *Studies in the History of Natural Theology*, pp. 1–83.

31. J. Richmond, *Theology and Metaphysics*, p. 3.

32. For an authoritative Catholic illustration of this see G. H. Joyce, S J, 'Providence and the Problem of Evil'.

dependence on Protestant, pagan and generally suspect sources, produce an increasingly convincing picture of a fundamental heterodoxy in Vico's system of ideas. We shall now see how his handling of providence strengthens this conviction.

Vico protected himself from suspicion as best he could and with no little skill and ingenuity. We have seen him employ a variety of methods, ranging from what we have described as disengagement and camouflaging techniques to a highly selective use or avoidance of suspect or orthodox sources as the occasion demanded. His difficulty with regard to providence was intensified, however, because, on the one hand, it was an important theological idea very much at the centre of discussions in natural theology, and, on the other, it was, in Vico's system, the naturalistic force guiding the very forms of human activity and development which caused him so many theological problems. It tended to be more troublesome and awkward to handle, therefore, than any other single notion in his work. So, in spite of the fact that the 'immediate and superficial impression is that the divine providence of Vico is the divine providence of the Christian church to which Vico publicly subscribes',[33] his equivocations were risky and potentially far-reaching, and required a correspondingly bolder form of camouflage than any he had employed so far.

Vico knew that to attempt to relate his notion of providence to the traditional teachings on which Catholic natural theology relied would have entailed substantial doctrinal contradictions. In this connection, Vaughan's observation that 'there is not a single reference to Thomas Aquinas or any other Christian theologian who wrote on providence'[34] is highly pertinent. Yet Vico well understood that to ignore such authorities could in itself court suspicion. His response to this problem was to adopt an audacious strategy in which he claimed to be inventing a new, 'civil' theology to cope with developments with which the existing natural theology could not. In this way he could hope to avoid comparison with authoritative Catholic sources on the subject of providence, and possibly throw a smoke-screen over his neglect of their writings. Vico's handling of this complex manoeuvre is another of his masterstrokes which, as far as I am aware, has escaped the attention of commentators. Such an inspired piece of improvization does deserve some detailed attention, if only because of its sheer ingenuity.

Vico makes his point in the second paragraph of the *Scienza*

33. Vaughan, *Political Philosophy*, p. 39.
34. Ibid.

nuova, in order to head off, immediately, any criticism that might arise from his neglect of traditional authorities. He prepares the ground by arguing the case for a fresh approach. In its existing state, natural theology, by drawing its demonstrations entirely from the natural order, was incomplete. Its exponents, therefore, by 'contemplating divine providence only through the natural order, have shown only a part of it'.[35] In other words, these philosophers had not demonstrated providence 'in respect of that part of it which is most proper to men, whose nature has this principal property: that of being social'.[36] He claims to remedy this deficiency by demonstrating that providence is manifest specifically in the affairs of men. He intends, that is, to highlight the role of 'providence in the world of human spirits, which is the civil world or world of nations'.[37] In this sense, he argues, his *Scienza nuova* 'becomes in this aspect a rational *civil theology* of divine providence'.[38]

Later in the work, Vico repeats his point about the inadequacy of existing natural theology, but before doing so – and just in case his criticism might appear somewhat seditious or subversive – he reinforces the impression of orthodoxy by attacking, as he does repeatedly throughout the *Scienza nuova*, the traditional Stoic and Epicurean targets of ecclesiastical invective:

> this Science must therefore be a rational civil theology of divine providence, *which seems hitherto to have been lacking*. For the philosophers have either been altogether ignorant of it, as the Stoics and Epicureans were, the latter asserting that human affairs are agitated by a blind concourse of atoms, the former that they are drawn by a deaf [inexorable] chain of cause and effect; . . .[39]

He then continues with a slightly amplified form of his earlier statement:

> or they have considered it solely in the order of natural things, giving the name of natural theology to the metaphysics in which they contemplate this attribute (i.e. the providence) of God, and in which they confirm it by the physical order observed in the motions of such bodies as the

35. *SN* 2.
36. Ibid.
37. Ibid.
38. Ibid. Italics mine. Vico may have been inspired, in his own adaptation of a 'teologia civile', by a distinction in classical antiquity between 'civil' and 'natural' theology (see *SN* 366), with which he was familiar probably via St Augustine's *City of God*. For a discussion of 'civil' and 'natural' theology in later classical paganism see Webb, *Studies*, pp. 15ff.
39. *SN* 342. Italics mine.

spheres and the elements and in the final cause observed in other and minor natural things.[40]

The traditional arguments, therefore, from cause and effect, from cosmic order and harmony, and from teleology are henceforth to be supplemented by Vico's demonstrations of providence drawn from the historical studies of human institutions and civil society. Thus the traditional distinction between 'natural' and 'revealed' theology is recast and complemented by the addition of a third branch of his own making. In this way, he inserts his new science into the orthodox tradition by redefining 'our Christian theology' as 'a mixture of *civil* and *natural* with the loftiest *revealed* theology; *all three united in the contemplation of divine providence*'.[41] This deft manoeuvre, in which Vico purports to invent a new, third area of theological discourse, is an extraordinary piece of camouflage. It seeks at a stroke to legitimize the whole enterprise by passing it off as a novel theological investigation, while simultaneously using this novelty as an excuse for not discussing his notion of providence with reference to any of the accepted authorities.

Considered as an abstract proposition, and taken at face value, Vico's proposal does not seem in the least implausible to the unsuspecting reader. There is no inherent reason why the traditional boundaries of theistic demonstrations from 'non- revelational' sources should be restricted to arguments from nature, from cosmic order and the like. The proposition becomes all the more seductive if we consider that Vico was, in fact, charting a new course in historiography, and that the rigour and systematicity he himself applied to it highlighted a particular 'pattern' which could be claimed to demonstrate the existence of a provident Deity. But the cumulative evidence we have so far built up during the course of this study clearly indicates the need for scepticism when considering his theological statements. A brief consideration of some of the specific features of Vico's providence will be sufficient at this stage to vindicate the claims made so far concerning his desire to avoid comparison with mainstream orthodox thinking.

Vico's 'Providence' and Catholic Teaching

Eugenio Garin is one student of Italian philosophy who sees a fundamental ambiguity and unorthodoxy in Vico's use of the

---

40. Ibid. See also *SN* 385 and 390.
41. *SN* 366. Italics mine.

concept of providence. He claims that Finetti's criticisms of the *Scienza nuova* were undoubtedly well-founded 'from the point of view of Catholic orthodoxy'.[42] Finetti brushes aside Vico's claim to orthodoxy as ridiculous. Taking Aquinas' treatment of providence as his starting point, he highlights a number of contradictions, focuses on Vico's arguments that providence brings about man's state of bestiality, his lack of rationality, his inability to act other than in the pursuit of selfish objectives, etc., and observes that Vico does not, in effect, present anything that a 'mere naturalist' would not argue.[43] The comparison with Aquinas is worth taking a little further.

We have had numerous occasions to point out that in the *Scienza nuova* providence is a force which directs the outcome of human history 'without human discernment or counsel', and frequently 'against the designs of men',[44] and that in the early stages of human history men lacked the reflective and volitional capacities to make rational, freely deliberated choices. Vico's naturalistic scheme, moreover, excludes such unpredictable variables as those involved in such choices. Yet it is precisely these variables which are essential to the Catholic, indeed the Christian, definition of man as a rational creature always able to choose between good and evil. Consequently, in discussing the concept of providence Aquinas is at pains to protect the volitional, rational and free quality of the human act as essential within the Christian tradition. If we consider St Thomas' claim that, 'since God exercises providence over all things, the operation of secondary causes is not excluded, which really carry out its ordered policy',[45] two crucial doctrinal points must be noted. First, that the notion of 'secondary causes' refers to the activity of human subjects, and is meant to ensure that the workings of providence do not eliminate the real operational effects of such activity. Secondly, and equally important, both the providential and the human processes work towards the same ends. In other words, providence, in the orthodox sense, cannot be a force which frustrates or thwarts the intentions of men since the latter can legitimately be allowed to run whatever amoral or a-social course is dictated by human passions – which is certainly the case in the *Scienza nuova*. There are, of course, important theological reasons for this which, as we shall see, Aquinas was anxious to safeguard in his account of providence.

but man designs are only mistaken conceptions of good

42. Garin, *Storia della filosofia italiana*, Vol. iii, p. 1021.
43. See Finetti, *Difesa dell' autorità della Sacra Scrittura*, pp. 71ff. and 77ff.
44. *SN* 342.
45. Aquinas, *Summa Theologica*, 1a, q. 22, art. 3, ad. 2.

We have already generally remarked upon the moral agnosticism of Vico's scheme in which men follow the blind instincts of passion and the pursuit of self-interest. For a work which makes the numerous theological claims we have noted, there is an astonishing lack of any reference to the principles of Christian morality. In fact, his theory of human development raises to the status of 'norms' baser aspects of human behaviour that Christian morality teaches men to resist and overcome. For Vico, providence acts as a *corrective* to such forms of behaviour. But in the Christian view, as the Jesuit theologian G. H. Joyce points out, 'it is man's great privilege, in virtue of his intelligence, *to exercise forethought* and *to cooperate consciously* in the execution of God's providential plan'.[46] Yet, according to the *Scienza nuova* this is precisely what does not occur in history. Providence acts as both a directing and remedial force overriding the free play of man's pursuit of self-interest.

Given that the activity of God's providence in the eyes of the theologian always aims at morally good and desirable objectives, it is important that these objectives should be shared by men as morally responsible agents. Aquinas is most insistent on this point. To allow the outcome of human actions to be determined, as Vico does, by an *external* force, and not to follow the inner logic of freely willed intentions to their conclusion is to reduce rational creatures to 'physical things', 'which are acted upon so that they are directed towards a goal by something else; they do not act on their own initiative like rational creatures who direct their own actions by free choice, on the basis of which they decide and choose . . .'[47] It is precisely in order to safeguard the crucial ethico-Christian dimension of human activity that Aquinas emphasizes that rational creatures 'come under divine providence in a special manner',[48] because 'some blame or merit is imputed to them, and thus some punishment or reward is demanded'.[49] So, as Joyce has stressed, man falls under God's providence with the voice of reason, through the dictates of conscience, 'and the sanctions of reward and punishment'.[50]

Not only are such requirements totally absent from Vico's discourse, but the *Scienza nuova* clearly violates each one of these doctrinal and moral principles. It is hardly surprising, therefore, that he should not wish to discuss providence with reference to

46. Joyce, *Principles*, pp. 566. Italics mine.
47. Aquinas, *Summa Theologica*, 1a, q. 22, art. 2, ad. 4.
48. Ibid., 1a q. 22, art. 2, ad. 5.
49. Ibid.
50. Joyce, *Principles*, p. 567.

orthodox authorities. It is difficult, moreover, to envisage his
so-called 'civil theology' as anything more than a specious attempt
to justify his evasion of the fundamental requirements of his publicly avowed faith. In fact, he substitutes for a tradition of moral
theology which requires that men should at all times attempt to
direct their actions according to Christian morality, a 'civil theology' in which men, compelled by the destructive pursuit of their
own desires, *'beyond any design of theirs, . . .* were brought together
in a universal civil good called commonwealth'.[51]

Frederick Vaughan was correct, therefore, to point out that Vico's
providence is a force which 'draws public good out of private
vices'.[52] Vico says as much himself:

> It will then be evident that this public virtue was nothing but a good use
> which providence made of such grievous, ugly and cruel private vices,
> in order that the cities might be preserved during a period when the
> minds of men, intent on particulars, could not naturally understand a
> common good.*[53]

While there can be little doubt about the doctrinally suspect nature
of such a use of providence – and Finetti's attack on it was more
than justified from this point of view – there was, nevertheless, an
acceptable theological sense in which providence could be said to
turn to advantage humanity's corrupt practices. Vico attempts to
link his own theory to this venerable tradition by putting forward
the claim that the operation of providence which he has described
provides 'new principles by which to demonstrate the argument of
St Augustine's discussion of the virtue of the Romans . . .'[54] Here
Vico's reference to Augustine's discussion of Roman virtues (*City
of God*, Book V, Chapter 12) is mistaken, for the Church Father's
argument concerning the Creator's ability to bring good out of evil
through providence occurs elsewhere (Book XIV, Chapter 11).
More importantly, however, what Augustine does have to say
about Roman virtue directly contradicts Vico's own line of argument. It is true that Augustine talks of the conflict between public
and private objectives, and that the Romans, in his eyes, had
obtained from God's providence power, honour and glory even
though they did not worship Him. But this was by no means
providence's 'turning to good use' Vico's 'grievous, ugly and cruel
private vices'. On the contrary, Augustine states again and again

---

51. *SN* 629. Italics mine.
52. Vaughan, *Political Philosophy*, p. 41.
53. *SN* 38.
54. Ibid.

that the glory of the Romans was the reward of virtue. The good man, he writes quoting Sallust, 'goes the true way, that is, by virtue leading him directly to his possession of honour, glory, sovereignty. That this was the Romans' course, their temples showed, Virtue's and Honour's being so close together. . . .'[55] The passage continues with a positive appraisal of Roman virtue, which is rewarded by the glory which would otherwise have been denied the Empire. Vico clearly uses Augustine in a manner quite out of keeping with the latter's intention.

Once more, therefore, we find a quite misleading reference to an orthodox source or idea which Vico is claiming to 'demonstrate', at the very point of its subversion. It is consequently very difficult to avoid the impression that there was a deliberate strategy in all this to defend himself. Vico was, of course, more than conscious that his argument differed from that of Augustine – which is why he claimed to be supporting the latter by the use of '*new* principles'.

Vico's discussion, at this point, concerned the way in which providence utilized primitive humanity. But if the reader expects the dawning of rationality to bring with it a sense of the 'common good', such an expectation does not materialize in the *Scienza nuova*. And while men do indeed identify their own interests with those of increasingly large social units, ranging from the family to the entire nation, this development does not take place according to principles which conform to any conceivable scheme of Christian morality. Vico's most perfect stage of government, for example, is the monarchy, and this acts as a restraining force countering the chaotic effects resulting from the pursuit of the conflicting 'private' rights and interests of individuals. In other words, the 'common good' never becomes an operating principle in the conscious activity of men, but at most the objective of an external force which engineers the consequences of men's actions in that direction. Hence the prescriptive demands of Christian morality find no place in Vico's scheme.

Moreover, he nowhere indicates that monarchies can persist indefinitely. They arise, as we said earlier, to keep in check the divisive impulses of the subjects over whom they rule, since in the preceding form of government, that is, 'in the free commonwealths all look out for their own private interests . . .'.[56] Further, when under the monarchies the social strain is too great, because 'such peoples, like so many beasts, have fallen into the custom of each

55. Augustine, *City of God*, Bk V, Ch. 12, p. 159.
56. *SN* 1008.

man thinking only of his own private interests',[57] so that the very human social fabric is threatened, providence prescribes a solution. This is brought about in such a way that:

> through obstinate factions and desperate civil wars, they shall turn their cities into forests and the forests into dens and lairs of men. In this way, through long centuries of barbarism, rust will consume the misbegotten subtleties of malicious wits that have turned them into beasts made more inhuman by the barbarism of reflection than the first men had been made,[58]

whereupon mankind returns to a state of barbarity, to the 'primitive simplicity of the first world of the peoples'.[59]

An important function, therefore, of Vico's providence is that of 'preserving' the human race through a recourse ('ricorso') or cyclical return to barbarity. This concept of historical 'cycles' is as central to his naturalism as it has proved elusive and embarrassing to his critics. It is also, as we shall see, a further source of conflict with Catholic orthodoxy.

57. *SN* 1106.
58. Ibid.
59. Ibid.

17
'Ricorsi'

The Conceptual Necessity of Historical 'Cycles'

The notion of 'ricorsi' or historical 'cycles' has been one of the most elusive concepts in Vichian studies, despite its importance for our understanding of such ideas as providence in the *Scienza nuova*. Even Luigi Bellofiore, in his study of providence, refers to the 'ricorso' as this 'least known' concept,[1] yet surprisingly he pays little attention to it in his work. So while it is universally known that Vico wrote of historical 'cycles', a survey of Vichian scholarship would probably reveal that Book 5 of the *Scienza nuova* ('The Recourse of Human Institutions Which The Nations Take When They Rise Again') is by far the most neglected part of the work.

Its closest rival in this respect is Book 4 ('The Course The Nations Run') which outlines, according to Vico's tripartite scheme, the development of man's social, mental and civic structures: 'three kinds of natures' (916–18), 'three kinds of natural law' (922–4), 'three kinds of governments' (925–7), 'three kinds of languages' (928–31), and so forth. These three evolutionary phases, and their alleged recurrence in history, are understandably somewhat uncongenial and overschematic for modern tastes. And while we can sympathize with the desire to focus on the 'live core' of Vico's writings, we must ask at what expense this is being done. For it is precisely the three epochs and their 'ricorsi' that he claimed to have validated by his newly discovered method. This in itself should suggest that the notion of historical 'cycles' is not so easily detachable from the totality of Vico's theoretical system as has often been supposed – or at least not without considerable damage to its overall coherence.

Attempts have been made to neutralize the theoretical effects of the 'ricorsi' in various ways. Perhaps the most common is to incorporate the cyclic pattern, as Collingwood does, for example, into a 'spiral' of historical development within the overall move-

---

1. Bellofiore, *La dottrina della provvidenza*, p. 26.

ment of an indefinite, progressive advance.[2] Idealists, in the Cro-
cean mould, have, by contrast, interpreted Vico's 'cycles' as recurring periods of renewal in the 'life of the spirit'. Attempts have even
been made to reconcile the 'ricorsi' with a Christian view of
history, so that the Jesuit critic Caponigri has argued that 'ricorsi
must be conceived not as recurrence, but as an advance which is yet
a return upon itself, a movement which is possible only on the
reflective plane of spiritual life'.[3] Such interpretations, however,
must be questioned, for if we examine the *Scienza nuova* more
closely we find that the 'ricorsi' are far from being simple descriptive analogies which lend themselves to such flexible renderings.[4]

Vico did not, in effect, intend to produce mere generalized
resemblances from one historical era to another. The fact that his
attempt to demonstrate the historical repetition of the three epochs
does indeed often appear to regress into rather vague parallels is not
altogether intentional, but more the result of the improbable task
he had set himself. The strain on our credibility produced by Vico's
cycles is, ironically, an indication of his determination to insist on
his point. He would hardly have taken such trouble if the idea were
not central to his scheme. It was clearly not an isolated element in
his theory, or indeed one which he felt free to discard because of the
many difficulties it involved. A writer will frequently defend the
most problematic ideas if they are essential to an overall system he
finds compelling for perhaps other reasons. It is only when we
grasp the totality of Vico's naturalism that we can appreciate the
importance within it of his 'ricorsi'.

One of the major functions of providence, we recall, was to force
a return to barbarity as a means of preserving an otherwise
'doomed' humanity. This protective mechanism actually prompts
Vico's reliance on the notion of cycles. Thus, the rediscovery of
religion in the returned barbarity of the Dark Ages has the same
function in controlling man's otherwise destructive passions as in
the original 'age of the gods':

> But marvelous above all is the recourse taken by human institutions in
> this respect, that in these new divine times there began again the first

2. See R. G. Collingwood, *The Idea of History*, pp. 67–8.
3. A. R. Caponigri, *Time and Idea. The Theory of History in G. B. Vico*, p. 133.
4. The notion of 'ricorsi' is taken also more seriously in Mooney, *Vico*, p. 245–54,
where it is given a more positive if ambiguous value. Papini, *Arbor Humanae Linguae*
(and also in his *Il geroglifico della storia. Significato e funzione della dipintura nella
'Scienza Nouva' di G. B. Vico*) is also an exception to the tendency to play down the
significance of the notion of 'ricorsi' in Vico. Papini, however, sees the notion of
'circularity' as a theme central not only to Vico's conception of the historical process
but also to the internal dynamic of all aspects of his thinking.

asylums of the ancient world . . . .. For everywhere, violence, rapine, and murder were rampant, because of the extreme ferocity and savagery of these most barbarous centuries.[5]

Thus providence ordained a return to the religious practices of the 'latest barbarous times'.[6]

But having postulated one element of the 'ricorso', Vico then feels compelled to continue his account of the return to 'divine' times: 'These divine times were followed by certain heroic times, in consequence of the return of a certain distinction between almost opposite natures, the heroic and the human'.[7] He then undertakes a rather lengthy etymological defence of what he has just asserted.

The need to validate his hypothesis leads him to consider each recurring epoch in turn. Accordingly, in the recurrent 'heroic' period: 'There was a return of the ancient Roman clienteles [fiefs] called commendations'.[8] And in order to build up further the evidence required, there follows a series of historical points of reference: 'There was a return of the kind of census decreed by Servius Tullius, by which the Roman plebeians were for a long time obliged to serve the nobles in war at their own expense'.[9] Also, we find in *SN* 1070, 'There was a return of the *precaria*, which must originally have been lands granted by the lords in response to the entreaties of the poor', and we even find a recurrence of the forms of ownership Vico had traced in earlier epochs: 'There was a return of the two kinds of ownership, direct and useful – *dominium directum* and *dominium utile* – which correspond exactly to the quiritary and bonitary ownership of the ancient Romans. Direct ownership arose first, just as quiritary ownership did among the Romans'.[10] We should notice how, according to Vico, the recurrent forms correspond 'exactly' to their earlier precedents and also in the same order. And finally, 'there was a return of armed courts such as we found above that the heroic assemblies were which were held under arms, and which were called by the Greeks assemblies of Curetes and by the Romans assemblies of Quirites'.[11] As we can see, Vico produces as much evidence as he can to indicate a series of correspondences or returns even within the various stages of each epoch. So if we take the trouble to read carefully Books 4 and 5 of

5. *SN* 1056.
6. *SN* 1055.
7. *SN* 1057.
8. *SN* 1068.
9. *SN* 1069.
10. *SN* 1073.
11. *SN* 1078.

his work we cannot fail to be struck by his determination to establish the 'ricorsi'.

There are, of course, serious incongruities in his scheme, such as when he writes of universities in medieval times, stating that 'finally, with the opening of schools in the universities of Italy . . . minds now more developed and grown more intelligent were dedicated to the cultivation of the jurisprudence of natural equity'.[12] Clearly such a development is inappropriate within a recurrence of the 'heroic' period. Vico makes no attempt to resolve this particular problem, but instead quickly passes on to consider those apparent contradictions in types of government to be found in southern and northern climes – contradictions which, we are assured, do not really impair his scheme. In fact, the universities of the Middle Ages, with their flourishing schools of theological and philosophical learning, were a major source of embarrassment for Vico. Nowhere is this more evident than in his attempts to accommodate Dante within his scheme of historical development.

Within the period of returned barbarity which we nowadays commonly refer to as the Middle Ages, Vico was forced to permit 'survivals' of the older civilization, pockets of Greek and Latin learning kept alive throughout the Dark Ages. This inability to postulate a total return to primitive conditions has been an important factor in inducing critics to interpret Vico's cycle as a spiral, thus reducing the 'barbarization' to a *relative* degeneration which subsequently acts as a springboard for further progress. As such it appears to be a highly plausible assumption at first sight, but seems to me untenable for numerous reasons. Apart from requiring us to isolate the concept of cycles from the remainder of Vico's system, it also presupposes that the idea of indefinite 'progress' into the future is either self-evident or else was a widely accepted concept at the time. Neither of these presuppositions, as we shall see later, can be justified. We must accordingly keep our interpretations within the confines of the historically limited conceptual horizons expressed in the text.

We have already noted, for example, that Vico was unable to think, in constitutional terms, beyond monarchies. There is no evidence whatever that the idea of indefinite historical progression had even occurred to him. If it had, it is simply inconceivable that such a momentous concept would not have been stated in the clearest terms in a work which claims to found a new science of history. So, while there are grounds for asserting that Vico's theory

12. *SN* 1086.

of 'ricorsi' contains contradictions, *there are no grounds for assuming that such contradictions indicate that he meant something else, that is, an idea of indefinite advancement which he did not state.*

If we examine briefly Vico's problem in accommodating Dante to his scheme, we shall see how tenaciously he clung to the idea of historical cycles. The idea of 'ricorsi' was not a concept which was 'added' as an afterthought in the course of his development of a sense of history. Rather, it provided the very framework within which Vico was able to conceptualize his historicism. Even as early as the *Diritto universale* we find a comparison between Homer and Dante within the context of such cycles. In Part II, Chapter 12 of the *De Constantia Iurisprudentis*, Vico discusses the origins of 'poetic' language, and even at that stage Homer's greatness is deemed to derive from the period in which he lived: 'and Homer, endowed with a most fertile talent, at the same time occupied first place among poets, because he was born in an age close to the poetic era, when language was still weak, the senses were all strong, and reason was very weak'.[13] The recurrence of barbarity in Italy likewise later accounts for the greatness of Dante: 'exactly the same fate befell Dante Alighieri who, at the time of the greatest Italian barbarity, without any model or example, became by himself first [among poets], on his own became a supreme poet'.[14] Vico could hardly have been unaware of the highly stylized and convention-ridden traditions of the 'dolce stil novo', from which Dante learnt his craft as a young poet. He puts this aside, however, because he is determined that the greatness of the poetry of both Homer and Dante should conform to the requirements of his naturalistic scheme, according to which the quality of such 'poetic' gifts is directly attributable to 'natural necessity': 'Poetry is born out of natural necessity, whilst up till now all have thought it to be the result of human intention and art'.[15] It is also produced through a process of 'natural signification': 'And in this way the first language of the people was a poetic language, fixed within 'heroic' characters, according to which one could express things by means of natural signs'.[16] We can see, therefore, that Vico's placing of Dante within the framework of a recurrent period of 'heroism' was no mere impressionistic device. It was meant as a *theoretically functional* explanation for his greatness as a poet, which is clear from his recourse to the principles of 'natural necessity' and 'natural signifi-

13. *Opere giuridiche*, p. 471.
14. Ibid.
15. Ibid.
16. Ibid.

cation' which, as we have seen in Part I of this study, are central components of Vico's theory of language, poetry and myth.

That Vico was serious in his application of such norms to Dante's poetry is beyond doubt. In additional notes to the *De Constantia Iurisprudentis*, he develops the idea of the growth of 'poetic' sounds and images from 'ignorance of causes' and 'poverty of language'.[17] Once more, Dante is used alongside Homer to illustrate a simple point: 'regarding this σίζ ["crack"], which Homer used, Dante created a similar word "cric", to express the sound of breaking glass, a word which is now laughed at as puerile'.[18]

About three to four years later, in his first draft of the *Scienza Nuova*, Vico repeats his comparison between the two poets with increasing firmness: 'Hence, just as Greece never gave rise to any greater poet than Homer, so no more sublime poet than Dante was ever born in Italy, because both were fortunate to emerge with incomparable genius towards the end of the poetic era of both nations'.[19] He then goes on to state his theory concerning the inherent epistemological – historical incompatibility between the 'poetic' and 'rational' faculties of the mind: 'Hence the pursuits of metaphysics and of poetry are naturally opposed to each other because the former purges the mind of the imaginings of child-hood, and the latter immerses and steeps it in them . . .'.[20] And to those who would object that Dante in fact displays precisely the kind of learning in metaphysics, philosophy and theology that Vico claims is inimical to great 'poetry', he replies:

> And so that nobody will object to us that Dante was the father and prince of Tuscan poets and, at the same time, most learned in theology, we reply that having come in the era of poetic speech in Italy, which arose in the period of greatest barbarity in the ninth, tenth, eleventh and twelfth centuries (which was not the case with Virgil), *if he had known nothing of Scholasticism or of Latin, he would have been a greater poet*, and perhaps Tuscan speech would have raised him to the level of Homer, which Latin could not.[21]

It is evident, therefore, that those historical factors which prevent a full-scale return to the original conditions of 'heroic' man are seen as limiting factors in this returned barbarity. This is coherent and perfectly in line with the naturalistic concept of creativity we find Vico describing: a concept which requires the exclusion of those

17. See ibid., p. 763.
18. Ibid., p. 765.
19. *SN1a* 312.
20. *SN1a* 314.
21. Ibid. Italics mine.

rational faculties which to him spell the death of all great 'poetry'. Needless to say, this is hardly the view of a philosopher who thinks in terms of an indefinite linear progress or development. Indeed, he makes no attempt to integrate the learning which has been pain-stakingly acquired over the centuries into a broader epistemology of mental operation in which imagination and reason become mutually fulfilling or complementary activities. The rational activ-ity which to us is a fundamental characteristic of the Middle Ages thus remains, in Vico's scheme, nothing more than an anomaly.

This is clear from the manner in which he wished to integrate Dante the poet into the 'senso comune' of his returned 'barbarity'. Between 1728 and 1730 he reinforced his argument about Dante's historical position in a short essay, the title of which is the same as that of Book 3 of the *Scienza nuova* except for the substitution of Dante's name for Homer's: 'Discovery of the True Dante'. Here Vico's intention to see the Florentine poet as the Homer of a returned 'barbarism' is crystal clear. He presents the *Divina comme-dia* in the same terms as he had presented the Greek epic, that is, as 'vera narratio'. Dante's poem must be read, we are told, as a 'history of Italy's barbarian times'.[22] And, in so far as the *Commedia* shares this property of ancient myths and fables, it partakes of the same naturalistic principle of expression

> which is thus disposed and ordained by nature: that, because of a certain uniform course followed by the common mind of nations . . . – which, through natural custom, is open and truthful, *because it lacks reflection*, which when falsely used is the mother of all falsehood – *poets are induced to sing true histories*.[23]

Moreover, he adds that just as

> in the *New science of the nature of nations* we claimed that Homer was the first historian of gentile humanity . . . in the same way the first or one of the first Italian historians was our Dante.[24]

Vico is clearly attempting to invoke, in Dante's case, the full force of his naturalistic scheme, which would, of course, be ne-gated by even a 'spiral' of history which accepts 'homo rationalis' as the proper subject of the historical development of the period. In this sense, the degree of rationality which operates in Dante, the level of discrimination at his disposal and the linguistic and mental artifices he employs, would all deprive Vico's concepts of 'vera

22. *Opere*, ed. Nicolini, p. 950.
23. Ibid. Italics mine.
24. Ibid.

narratio', 'natural signification', and the 'senso comune' of any functional value. So, given his theory of history, the strength of Vico's argument regarding Dante as poet of a renewed 'barbarism' is directly proportional to the thoroughness with which he establishes a return to 'barbarity'. The more critics attempt, therefore, to attenuate the force of the 'ricorsi', the more they oppose Vico's own intentions, and the weaker appears his argument about Dante as the Tuscan Homer.

In Chapter 3 we discussed the logical difficulties involved in Vico's treatment of the Homeric fables as examples of 'vera narratio': namely, that their actual recording could only have taken place at a period when, according to Vico's own theory of human evolution, men had already developed those corrupting linguistic and mental capacities for deception which must substantially have distorted the pristine purity of the original process of 'natural signification'. Now if these difficulties were already considerable in the case of Homer, they were magnified a hundredfold by the time we reach Dante, whose very imagery and symbolism are infused with all the purposive force of his various levels of allegory. One can hardly imagine, in fact, a more consciously structured or philosophically and theologically impregnated work than the *Divina commedia*. It may well be that further reflection on his 'New Principles of Dante Criticism' (the subtitle of the 1728–30 essay) drove home to Vico the enormity of his problem. In any case, while he never abandoned his view of Dante's work as 'naturally truthful', in the final edition of the *Scienza nuova* we find only two fleeting references to this particular function of the 'Tuscan Homer'.[25]

Even so, Vico's decision to compress into a few brief remarks his earlier and lengthier observations on Dante in no way alters his resolve to assert the reality of a recurring 'barbarism'. On the contrary, he is simply side-stepping a major problem-area. His determination not to abandon his theory is effectively demonstrated in assertions such as: 'in the returned barbarian times the nations again became (analphabetical or) mute in vulgar speech. For this reason no notice has come down to us of the Spanish, French, Italian, or other languages of those times'.[26] The 'mute speech' of the original period of barbarity was, of course, literally what the term implied: men communicated through gestures, signs and graphic expressions having a 'natural' relation to the objects sig-

25. See *SN* 786 and 817.
26. *SN* 485.

nified. This was part of a genuinely primitive and brutish incapacity. But although Vico cannot reproduce a total regression to this level in all its details, he does his best to simulate the original conditions. Thus, in the period of recurrent barbarism 'we may assume that in all those unhappy centuries *the nations had reverted to communicating with each other in a mute language*. Because of this paucity of vulgar letters, there must everywhere have been a return to the hieroglyphic writing of family coats of arms'.[27] This passage is followed, moreover, by a further enumeration of 'returns' at other levels: 'divine judgements', 'heroic raids', 'heroic reprisals', and so on, all intended to strengthen the impression of a true 'ricorso'.

The most remarkable feature of Vico's handling of such recurrences is the total absence of any attempt to integrate the obvious anomalies that come to mind into a more plausible portrayal of the periods in question. Such a tendentious reconstruction of the past does, however, make sense within the context of his rigid and inflexible 'ideal eternal history' which forces a return to barbarity after the 'rise, progress, maturity, decadence, and dissolution' of nations, 'even if (as is certainly not the case) there were infinite worlds being born from time to time throughout eternity'.[28] Vico's reference to the idea of 'infinite worlds' is an important indication of the possible origins of his cyclical view of history. This was a frequently stated idea among ancient philosophers and was, of course, frequently condemned by Christian thinkers.[29] We shall discuss this aspect of the problem shortly, but for the present we should note that the concept of 'ricorsi' was attractive to Vico for very good reasons. In the first place, the cyclical conception of continual cosmic birth, corruption, dissolution and regeneration had direct affinities with naturalistic philosophies, a fact which will become more evident as our argument progresses. But, equally important, it provided a workable framework without which it would not have been possible for Vico to have developed his integrated and internally coherent historical scheme. I do not think the importance of this point has in the past been fully understood.

Let us refer back for a moment to the anomalies implicit in his postulated return to 'barbarity'. The reason why we find it so tempting to put forward the idea of a 'spiral' of historical movement as a solution to the problem (thereby incorporating the rationality, for example, of the Middle Ages, into a more acceptable account of

---

27. *SN* 1051. Italics mine.
28. *SN* 1096.
29. Thus the ritual repetition on Vico's part of its falsity.

development) is that *we* are unable to conceive of history except in terms of linear progression. The very idea of spirals is, in effect, a theoretical conversion of cycles into a secondary property of a more fundamental forward linear movement. It is essentially, therefore, a total transformation of the concept, and in terms of textual support quite unwarranted. Isaiah Berlin has noted:

> An identical order of stages is determined by Providence for each 'gentile' society, but no final goal; there is no vision of the march of mankind towards final perfection. . . . Such a conception of progress, whether 'linear' or 'dialectical', would, for Vico, in the first place, be incompatible with his view of the eternal cycles of history[30]

One of the paradoxes of Vichian scholarship is that such fundamental observations can coexist alongside an apparent unawareness of their implications for his overall system of ideas.

We must continually remind ourselves, when reading Vico, that the idea of 'progress' was by no means generally or easily available as a well-defined ideological appurtenance of the time in which he wrote. Baillie's monumental study of the concept illustrates the enormous struggle required, over the centuries, to arrive at a full-fledged conception of historical progress.[31] Baillie shows that such important figures as Bacon and Descartes indeed felt that they were on the threshold of new forms of knowledge. They, like Vico, saw the advancement of science as bringing improvements in material comfort. Vico also appreciated the importance of advances in medical knowledge. Yet, difficult as it is for us to understand, this was still a long way from the notion of an indefinite progressive pattern in the whole social and historical environment. The grasp of the idea of advancement in isolated fields of knowledge or research does not, in other words, amount to a full-scale doctrine of 'progress'. At most, argues Baillie, the thought of those such as Bacon and Descartes 'provides the necessary presuppositions of that doctrine and creates a temper most hospitable to its emergence'.[32]

J. B. Bury, in an important pioneering work, suggested that the idea of 'progress' first emerged in intellectual circles in France as 'an indefinite progress of enlightenment', and was taken up by the Abbé de Saint-Pierre, in whose writings 'we first find the theory widened to embrace progress towards social perfection'.[33] Not even the concept of a general intellectual advancement transfers

---

30. Berlin, 'Vico and the Ideal', pp. 652–3.
31. J. Baillie, *The Belief in Progress.*
32. Ibid., p. 103.
33. J. B. Bury, *The Idea of Progress. An Inquiry into its Origin and Growth*, p. 128.

itself automatically to history as a whole. And even the most partisan of Vico's admirers cannot claim that what he writes about the epoch of rationality and about monarchy as the most perfect form of government can be translated into a teleology of continuous intellectual and social advancement. On the basis of the evidence we possess, his claim to originality lies in the manner in which he perceives the parallel connections and movements on the linguistic, mental and social levels of historical change. That he achieves this remarkable synthesis within the confines of a cyclical scheme is not a fortuitous occurrence. Such a pattern was an integral part of his broader naturalistic philosophy, about which we shall have more to say in the following Chapter.

The Pagan Origins and Doctrinal Implications of the Notion of Historical 'Cycles'

Vico's treatment of the Middle Ages, as we have seen, lacks the moral and theological perspective derived from the Christian eschatological tradition. He sees no moral or theological 'blemishes' in any of the unchristian structural forms of human behaviour which determine the course of history. On the contrary, those epochs of each period which might have been expected to occasion judgement in these terms are treated as the major positive characteristics of the epoch:

> And since the wars of the latest barbarian times, like those of the first, were all wars of religion, there was a return of heroic slavery, which lasted a long time among Christian nations themselves. For because of the practice of duels in those times, the conquerors believed that the conquered had no god, and hence held them no better than beasts. . . . Hence in their wars both sides practice heroic slavery . . .[34]

The moral and theological neutrality of Vico's account is, of course, perfectly in line with a view of history which sees the events described above as expressions of 'necessary' phases of human development.

The reliance of Vico's scheme on the doctrine of 'natural necessity' produces unresolvable tensions with Christian morality. Judged by Christian moral standards, the events described by Vico represent regrettable 'blemishes' within a supposedly Christian society. To the Catholic thinker, the Middle Ages represent an important

---

34. *SN* 1055.

era of rational and theological development within the construction of a Christian civilization. To Vico, however, such elements are an embarrassment and find no positive accommodation in the *Scienza nuova*. His conception of history and that of the believing Christian are, therefore, poles apart: each sees the focal point of the other as the problematic aspect of his own view of history.

But this conflict should not surprise us when we penetrate beneath the surface of the text. For the systematic concealments and silences we have witnessed in connection with other aspects of Vico's thought are also at work here. All the tensions we have noted relate very directly to the cyclical pattern of his 'ideal eternal history' and a Christian tradition which had repeatedly condemned such a cyclical view of history.

The idea of historical cycles was, of course, firmly embedded in the whole motif of birth, death and regeneration so central to the naturalistic thought of classical antiquity. One of the most striking features of the 'ricorsi' in the *Scienza nuova*, however, is the total absence of any reference to such antecedents. Once again, the most likely reason for this is that the idea was already sufficiently suspect without Vico needlessly drawing attention to its pagan origins.

We are repeatedly told in the *Scienza nuova* that its author is utilizing the 'three epochs' of ancient Egyptian origin.[35] What is not mentioned is the fact that in Egyptian thought these epochs were part of an eternal cyclical rebirth of the universe. It is very unlikely that Vico would not have been aware of this connection. For example, he devotes a chapter of Book 4 (*SN* 1009–19) to a refutation of Jean Bodin's conception of the evolution of civil institutions in order to prove the correctness of his own. But Stanley Jaki has drawn attention to Bodin's preference for the Egyptian 48 000-year cosmic cycle as opposed to the Hindu (700 000-year) and Chaldean (470 000-year) as defining units of world history.[36] Therefore, even if we suppose that Vico was unaware of the cyclical implications of his Egyptian borrowings from direct knowledge of the sources, he would have been aware of it through his reading of Bodin.[37]

---

35. See *SN* 173, 399, 432, 737, 915.
36. S. L. Jaki, *Science and Creation: From Eternal Cycles to an Oscillating Universe*, pp. 102–37.
37. In this connection it should be noted that Vico makes no explicit reference to *Methodus*, in which Bodin expounds his cyclical theories. Robert Nisbet is puzzled by this omission, and argues that 'there are too many parallels, too many instances of almost identical thinking on given matters, to suppose anything but belief that Vico was entirely familiar with the *Methodus*'. Nisbet also points out that Vico's

There were other sources with which Vico must have been familiar, and numerous indications that he was steering the reader in the direction of such sources by using a series of indirect pointers. We must remember that he lived in an age when censorship frequently made surreptitious literary techniques necessary, and that the ear of many of his contemporaries would have been attuned to such subterfuges. It is a curious fact that Vico refers the reader to Polybius on a number of occasions, but never mentions him in connection with the cyclical theory of history, where Vico's affinity with him is strongest and quite striking. Polybius was, of course, the first-known pagan historian to have used a coherent cyclical theory. In the course of a comparison between the constitutions of the commonwealths of Greece and Rome,[38] Vico explicitly draws the reader's attention to Book 6, Section 4 (and following sections) of Polybius' celebrated *Histories*. The interesting thing about this reference is that Polybius is doing something far more significant than making the comparisons mentioned – it is from Book 6, Section 4 onwards that he expounds his cyclical theories.

An important and distinctive feature of Vico's conception of historical cycles is that it goes beyond the somewhat *general* naturalistic descriptions of historical recurrence that we find in most classical pagan writings, certainly before Polybius. This is not to deny the existence, in the *Scienza nuova*, of the broader naturalistic foundations of his theory, which we see reflected in the barbaric origins of social, linguistic and cultural developments in human history to which humanity returns for periodic renewal. We find this broader perspective in Polybius also, while he is discussing the origin, growth and destruction of governments. When such events occur:

> as the records tell us has already happened and as reason suggests to us may often happen again, all the traditions and arts will simultaneously perish; but when in the course of time a new population has grown up again from the survivors left by the disaster, as a crop grows up from seed in the ground, a revival of social life will begin. Men will gather together – it is what we should naturally expect of them, as we should of the rest of animal creation – under the impulse of a natural tendency. . . .[39]

---

refutation of Daniel's prophecy concerning the four monarchies 'is virtually Bodin's word for word' (R. Nisbet, *History of the Idea of Progress*, p. 166). The omission is easier to understand once we recognize Vico's problems *vis-à-vis* the Church.

38. See *SN* 285.

39. I have used Ernest Barker's translation of this passage from *The Histories*, in

But Polybius' significance for Vico is more specific. In his important study of cyclical theories of history in western thinking, G. W. Trompf has stressed that Polybius went beyond simple descriptions of the recurrence of 'naturo-historical' events and 'used all his powers of synthesis to demonstrate how mankind's institutions, not just the sweeping changes of nature, conformed to a circling path'.[40] Polybius, in effect, identifies six types of constitution and argues for a fixed sequence. Vico, of course, argues for three, but parallels with Polybius' ideas lie in the rigid order of succession and in the prospect of a final state of anarchy, mob-rule and dissolution of the social order which forces a return to origins. In both cases, moreover, this eventual phase of destruction is preceded by democratic or popular forms of government. As Polybius asserts, 'in due course the licence and lawlessness of this form of government produces mob-rule to complete the series'. The passage then continues with the same emphasis on the naturality of the events as are found in Vico: 'For he alone who has seen how each form *naturally* arises and develops, will be able to see when, how, and where the growth, perfection, change, and end of each are likely to occur again.'[41]

For Vico, the importance of Polybius seems to be that he provides an example of a historian attempting to validate the naturalistic cycle of historical events by reference to specific institutions and forms of government. The examples, mentioned earlier, of Vico's attempts to produce very concrete and literal recurrences fall into this pattern. Indeed the whole of Book 5 of the *Scienza nuova* must be seen in this light. In both writers, in short, we find the details of the eventual dissolution of social existence worked out in such a way as to stress the naturality of their respective schemes; indeed, this is done in both cases by ensuring that there is regression to a form of primitive existence. Consequently, there are numerous passages in Vico which mirror Polybius' description of the final state of corruption among men, where 'they degenerate again into

---

From Alexander to Constantine: Passages and Documents Illustrating the History of Social and Political Ideas, 336 BC–AD 337, p. 108. This brings out slightly better than the standard W. R. Paton translation the affinities with Vico. Cf. also Polybius, *The Histories*, Bk VI, ch. 5, sects 5–8.

40. G. W. Trompf, *The Idea of Historical Recurrence in Western Thought: From Antiquity to the Reformation*, p. 15.

41. Polybius, *The Histories*, Bk VI, ch. 4, sects. 11–12. See also Bk VI, ch. 57, sects. 1–10, where the parallel between historical events and the course of natural decay bears a remarkable resemblance to Vico's description of the process of social degeneration into the anarchy of democratic and popular governments which then forces a cyclical return to primitive origins (cf. *SN* 1102–6).

perfect savages . . . . Such is the cycle of political revolution, the course appointed by nature in which constitutions change, disappear, and finally return to the point from which they started.'[42]

There are some further features of the classical conception of cycles in which Polybius seems to have had little interest but which require some discussion. According to such students of early philosophy as Guthrie, Baillie and Jaki, the concept of historical cycles seems to have dominated, with the exception of Jewish and related cultures, the historical perspectives of the entire ancient world. Baillie has argued, for example, that when Christ lived, the concept of historical change appeared to all non-Jewish civilizations 'as a great *circle* – or wheel'.[43] The direct conflict which such ideas were to generate between Christianity and Hellenistic thought certainly has its roots as far back as the Pre-Socratics.[44] The idea of recurrences originates, in Greek thought, in an attempt to explain the functioning of the universe. Thus, in his search for the primary element, Anaximander asserts that the universe arises, not from any of the so-called elements such as fire, water or air, but from what he calls an 'infinite' nature.[45] This idea of an 'infinite' nature is part of a circular or cyclic, and not a linear, conception of infinity. Anaximander goes on to argue 'that destruction, and much earlier coming-to-be, happen from infinite ages, since they are all occurring in cycles.'[46]

Anaximander is followed by Anaximenes, who stresses one of the critical corollaries of this doctrine of cosmic destruction and regeneration, a corollary which was to be repeatedly condemned by the Church Fathers: the idea of the eternity and indestructibility of the material universe. Throughout Hellenistic culture, as Guthrie has observed, the idea of eternal recurrences in history 'is linked with that of the indestructibility of the world'.[47] That Vico should have been familiar with and have frequently mentioned the idea of 'infinite worlds' is, therefore, in no way surprising.

Guthrie has also pointed out that ideas about the eternity of the universe and about cyclic theories of human affairs are also to be

---

42. Polybius, *The Histories*, Bk VI, ch. 9, sects. 9–10.
43. Baillie, *Belief in Progress*, p. 43. More recently, Robert Nisbet has argued the need for a corrective which makes room in classical antiquity for 'a solid and fertile substance of belief in linear progress' in addition to whatever degree of belief in cyclical ideas may have existed (*History of the Idea of Progress*, p. 32).
44. In addition to the works of Baillie, Guthrie and Jaki, see also Copleston, *A History of Philosophy*, Vol. i, Pt 1, particularly ch. 3, pp. 38–44 and ch. 5, pp. 60ff.
45. See Copleston, *A History of Philosophy*, Vol. i. Pt 1, p. 41. See also Fragment 103B in Kirk and Raven, eds., *The Presocratic Philosophers*, pp. 105–6.
46. Ibid., Fragment 103C, pp. 106–7.
47. W. K. C. Guthrie, *A History of Greek Philosophy*, Vol. i, p. 282.

found in Aristotle and Plato.[48] Now one of the real lacunae in Vico studies is a convincing account of the true meaning of his declared indebtedness to Plato. The Greek thinker, he tells us, is one of his 'four authors'. Yet, judged by traditional interpretations of the *Scienza nuova*, Vico's claim to have based his 'ideal eternal history' on his reading of Plato seems to yield very little in specific terms. Vico's numerous references to the latter in the *Scienza nuova* are diffuse and varied, and often amount to little more than classical scenery. The single most important concept in connection with which Plato is consistently mentioned and praised for defending is providence.[49] But when this is seen in conjunction with what Vico tells us in the *Autobiography*, a clearer picture of Plato's real significance begins to emerge.

We know that in the *Scienza nuova* it is providence which, when necessary for the preservation of the human race, engineers the necessary 'ricorsi' according to the pattern of the 'ideal eternal history'. In the *Autobiography* Vico attributes to Plato the idea of a fixed historical pattern for all nations when he writes of himself that: 'there began to dawn on him, without his being aware of it, the thought of meditating an ideal eternal law that should be observed in a universal city after the idea or design of providence, upon which idea have since been founded all the commonwealths of all times and all nations'.[50]

The interesting question, of course, is whether Vico wishes us to understand, without stating it explicitly, that his indebtedness to Plato extends to the cyclical component in his scheme of an 'ideal eternal history'. Certainly the latter means very little without the 'ricorsi'. Moreover *SN* 1109, in which Plato is praised for demonstrating that providence directs human affairs, follows directly upon one of Vico's descriptions of how the cyclic mechanism is employed to save humanity through a process of decay and regeneration. The linking of Plato with a cycle of cosmic degeneration and renewal, supervised by a greater power for the protection of the world, is in no sense a distortion of Plato's thought.[51] Vico was

---

48. See W. K. C. Guthrie, *In The Beginning*, pp. 65–6 and 68ff.
49. See *SN* 130, 365, 1097, 1109. For an important contribution to our knowledge of how Plato was used and understood in Vico's Naples, see Badaloni, 'Il platonismo moderno' in his *Introduzione a Vico*, pp. 27–38.
50. *Autobiography*, pp. 121–2.
51. Guthrie, for instance, provides the following summary of Plato's *Politicus*, 269c–270a:
   According to the strange myth in which Plato expresses cyclic change in his *Politicus*, the Creator, when he first made the universe, himself imparted its rotation and kept it under his guidance. At the end of an era, however, he released his control, and left to itself it began to revolve in the opposite direction. In this

familiar, moreover, with Polybius' use of Plato in this regard. And whilst this does not enable us to say with certainty that he had the concept of cycles in mind when claiming Plato as one of his chief sources, the idea nevertheless merits further consideration. Plato's alleged support for such ideas as the 'ideal eternal history' and providence indeed remains somewhat vague and problematic without it.

The notion of historical recurrence has frequently been characterized by students of the history of ideas as 'pessimistic', 'particularly the thought of the great conflagration' which marks the end of one cycle while at the same time heralding 'the dawn of the next in the restoration of all bodies to their original position'.[52] This constant return of things to their origins points very sharply to a source of conflict between Vico and the relatively 'hopeful' and forward-looking implications of Christian eschatology and its expectations of a Second Coming. But the contrast is not merely between a secular and a theological view of the universe. The implications of the cosmic pessimism of early Greek thought had further far-reaching consequences in every aspect of secular existence.

We have already encountered the idea that a grasp of the fact that there is a kind of advancement in particular fields of enquiry does not necessarily entail an overall view of progress. Baillie has argued, for instance, that the early Greeks possessed a considerable appreciation of advancement in particular fields, but 'what they knew of the advance of human knowledge and technical skill had little if any qualifying effect upon their general pessimism' because they were not convinced that these advances could bring about any change in 'the essential conditions of human destiny'.[53]

Now if we consider Vico's thinking in its entirety, there is no doubt that he is caught in this 'pessimistic' trap. His preoccupation with the decadence and social dissolution which follow the age of rationality leaves no room for the optimism deriving from Christian eschatology.[54] It also helps to explain how he was able to perceive the benefits of the scientific advances of his own times without being led thereby to a linear view of history. The *Scienza*

---

era, with God's hand removed, everything within it begins to deteriorate, and so continues until God – since its complete destruction is no part of the divine plan – takes control and reverses the direction once more.
(*In the Beginning*, pp. 78–9.)

52. Baillie, *Belief in Progress*, p. 48.

53. Ibid.

54. It is often argued that the idea of progress, and of indefinite social, technical and scientific advancement are derived from this aspect of Christianity.

nuova thus shows all the signs of this cosmic pessimism. We do not find here any sense of man's ability consciously and deliberately to set himself social targets and aspirations beyond the narrow horizons of immediate self-interest.[55] As Isaiah Berlin has rightly noted, there is in Vico no sense of a forward march of humanity towards a distant goal, whether temporal or spiritual. The very texture of his thought can be seen to share the 'pessimism' and unchristian sentiments of the ancient cyclic view of human destiny.[56]

It would be a mistake, however, to think that Christianity was opposed to such a concept purely on the grounds of its general anti-eschatological orientation. The difference in the overall hue and disposition of the two perspectives results from quite specific areas of conflict, and it is in these areas that we find Christian condemnations of the notion of historical recurrence. To return for a moment to its earliest manifestations, the Pre-Socratics' idea of an unbroken chain of eternal motion means that 'the idea of an absolute beginning of this material world does not enter into their heads.'[57] Such an assumption, if taken up, clearly denies the doctrine of God's Creation of the universe and of man. When, therefore, Vico qualifies each mention of the idea of 'infinite worlds' with the phrase 'which is certainly not the case' (*SN* 348), he is pointedly making obeisance to orthodox teaching.[58]

Having read Augustine, Vico knew full well that there was no greater opponent of historical cycles and infinite worlds than the author of the *City of God* . Six chapters of Book 12, along with large portions of others, are devoted to a detailed refutation of such ideas and of their implications. Augustine wished to expunge from

55. Antonio Corsano has observed that Vico's contemporary Pierre Bayle:
firmly shares the anti-Enlightenment and pessimistic convictions of the great libertines, the certainty about the basic immobility of history . . . the lack of belief in the idea that the impressive accumulation of scientific and literary knowledge really leads to a greater rational, moral maturity. In an excellent chapter given to Bayle's philosophy of history Labrousse was right to talk about an anthropology 'à la fois fixiste et déterministe', and has recognized that 'rien ne fait donc obstacle en lui á une vue cyclique de l'histoire' (*Bayle, Leibniz e la storia*, pp. 27–8.).
It is worth noting that Bayle's famous *Dictionnaire* was laden with conceptual tactics and strategies which have given rise to debate about his real intentions *vis-à-vis* religion.
56. In connection with the 'ricorso' and the return of a period of barbarism, Haddock comments on the later edition of *Scienza Nuova* taking a more 'pessimistic' turn. He also notes the author's suggestion regarding a literal return to a primitive state. See *Vico's Political Thought*, pp. 102 and 224 (fn 11).
57. Copleston, *A History of Philosophy*, Vol. i. Pt 1, p. 43.
58. Badaloni has drawn attention to this ritual denial of the doctrine of 'infinite worlds' in relation to what he sees as Vico's acceptance of the doctrine as early as the *De Antiquissima*. See *Opere filosofiche*, pp. 63–5 and Badaloni, *Introduzione a Vico*, pp. 75ff.

Christianity all trace of the 'circular maze of the impious', who, in their enthusiasm for this blasphemous doctrine, found no entrance or exit for the human race, seeing that 'they neither know mankind's origin nor his end'.[59] For this reason it was essential for Augustine to spell out clearly a beginning and an end for humanity.

After destroying his opponents' arguments, Augustine was able to assert: 'These circles now being broken, nothing urges us to think that man had no beginning, . . .'[60] The biblical account of creation and sacred history itself are thus defended, and the linear Christian eschatology can be established, in which 'Christ once died for our sins, and rising again, dies no more . . .: and we (after our resurrection) shall be always with the Lord, . . .'.[61] There is no firmer statement of an eschatological God-centred view of history than Augustine's. Nor do we find a more complete rejection of all those views which seek to explain the movement of history in terms of intrinsic principles, whether they imply self-perpetuating motions of a cyclical nature or self-preserving instincts which cause humanity to revert to its primitive origins and start afresh.

In his attack on the concept of 'infinite worlds' and other associated ideas such as that of an eternal series of cosmic dissolutions and restorations, Augustine defended not simply the general biblical notion of God's temporal Creation of the world. He also defended particular details of the biblical account of that Creation, such as the story of the Flood and the whole chronological development of humanity (as told in the Scriptures) against 'the falseness of that history that says the world has continued many thousand years'.[62] We can thus appreciate the pressure of theological authority on Vico to produce the chronological and biblical accommodations discussed in earlier chapters. Indeed, one of the circle of the 'moderni', Filippo Belli, who must have discussed such ideas with Vico and his friend de Cristofaro, was condemned by the Inquisition for maintaining that the world had existed from infinity.

But the idea of eternal historical cycles contained further doctrinal problems. Apart from the determinism of the celestial revolutions of Babylonian astronomy[63] and the 'Pythagoreans with their disturbing notion of an exact repetition of history',[64] there was the more popularly known Stoic version of cycles with which Vico was undoubtedly familiar, and on which the Church's condemna-

---

59. Augustine, *City of God*, Bk XII, Ch. 14, p. 357 and also ch. 20, p. 364.
60. Ibid., Bk XII, Ch. 20, p. 365.
61. Ibid., Bk XII, Ch. 13, p. 356.
62. Ibid., Bk XII, Ch. 10, p. 353.
63. See Guthrie, *A History of Greek Philosophy*, pp. 351–2.
64. Ibid., p. 458.

tions tended to focus.[65] What was particularly pernicious about the Stoic account was that 'each new world resembles its predecessors in all particulars'.[66] The doctrinal implications of this view amount to a clear denial of human freedom, since to the Stoics liberty 'meant doing consciously, with assent, what one will do in any case'.[67] This fundamental denial of the doctrine of free-will undermines, of course, any meaningful notion of moral responsibility, choice, and thereby salvation. It is the reason for the numerous condemnations, by Christian writers, of the 'chain' or 'reign of necessity the Stoics expressed under the concept of Fate'.[68]

If we turn, at this juncture, to the *Scienza nuova*, some interesting points emerge. Vico also repeatedly attacks the Stoic 'causal chain',[69] thereby distancing himself from the well-known pagan denial of free-will, but he carefully conceals the connection of this idea with the cosmological determinism resulting from an eternal cycle of recurring events – although it is clear, particularly from *SN* 387, that he was aware of such a link. Indeed, given his own cyclical view of history, it is hardly plausible to imagine that a scholar of Vico's stature could have been ignorant of such theories. Thus, his camouflaging technique at this point appears to employ two separate tactical manoeuvres. In the first place, he studiously avoids any reference to pagan thought in support of his notion of 'ricorsi'. In the second, he creates a distance between his cycles and the Stoic 'causal chain' by his ritual condemnation of the latter. If we add to these examples of textual circumspection Vico's carefully repeated reminders that 'infinite worlds' are a speculative and not a real possibility, the impression of a marked strategic undercurrent in his textual handling of the 'ricorsi' is reinforced.

Vico could not, of course, simply ignore the frequent Christian repudiations of cyclical notions. Thus, if he wished to draw attention to supporting authorities or ancient antecedents he could hardly do so openly. In this connection we should perhaps mention what may well be another indirect reference to a pagan source. In *SN* 227, when dealing with the idea of 'natural speech', Vico refers to a point of agreement between the Stoics and the Greek Church Father Origen, in making specific reference to Origen's *Contra*

65. Baillie Comments: 'During the later classical period Stoicism was the most popular of all the philosophies and it was in its very fully elaborated Stoic form that the doctrine of recurrence held the minds of thinking men, as we have observed it holding the mind of Seneca.' (*Belief in Progress*, p. 48.) References to this notion can be found in Seneca, *Naturales Quaestiones*, Bk III, ch. 29, sect. 5 and sects. 7–8.
66. Copleston, *A History of Philosophy*, vol. i. Pt 2, p. 133.
67. Ibid.
68. Ibid., pp. 134–5.
69. See for example *SN* 342, 345, 387.

Celsum, a work in which the latter attacks the notion of historical cycles. What arouses our suspicions is the fact that not far from the two passages in the *Contra Celsum* which mention 'natural speech' we find discussions of Celsus' notions of 'infinite worlds', 'historical cycles', 'determinism', and related ideas. In the first case, a few paragraphs away from the section on 'natural speech', we find Origen condemning Celsus:

> After . . . secretly wishing to attack the Mosaic cosmogony which indicates that the world is not yet ten thousand years old but is much less than this, Celsus agrees with those who say that the world is uncreated, although he hides his real intention. For in saying that *there have been many conflagrations from all eternity* . . . he clearly suggests to those able to understand him that he thinks the world is uncreated.[70]

Regarding the second of these passages, this time in the chapter immediately preceding the section on 'natural speech', we find a lengthy and derisive condemnation of the idea of historical cycles, from which it will be sufficient to select Origen's attack on Celsus himself:

> *it is inevitable that according to the determined cycles the same things always happened, are now happening and will happen.* If this is true, free will is destroyed . . . . If this is admitted, I do not see how free will can be preserved, and how any praise and blame can be reasonable.[71]

This is the classical Christian argument so far. Origen continues:

> Celsus affirms that it is only *the period of mortal life* which *according to the determined cycles* has of necessity always been, and is now, and will be identical. But most of the Stoics say that this is true not only of the period of mortal life, but also of immortal life . . .[72]

The usefulness of such passages to Vico is that they highlight the problem he himself faces with ecclesiastical authorities regarding his 'ricorsi'. They also contain explicit references to 'concealed' intentions and the art of communicating by surreptitious implication. The first passage draws attention once again, very dramatically, to the problematic Mosaic time-scale for the existence of mankind with which Vico had such difficulty.

70. Origen, *Contra Celsum*, Bk I, Ch. 19, p. 20. It is interesting to note, in this passage, the inevitable conflict between the notion of cosmic cycles, which were often conceived of in terms of hundreds of thousands of years, and the restricted time-scale of biblical history. Vico's problems of compression, discussed in Chapter 8, arise from an evolutionary scheme ill-suited to such a limited time-span, and closer to the temporal horizons of cosmic cycles.
71. Ibid., Bk IV, Ch. 67, pp. 237–8.
72. Ibid., Bk IV, Ch. 68, p. 238.

In isolation, of course, the coexistence of such passages with those to which Vico explicitly refers is purely incidental. But skill in concealment consists precisely in engineering such apparently fortuitous and innocent associations. It is inherent in that art to make conclusive proof an impossibility. Relying as we must, therefore, on the sheer cumulative weight of the evidence, it is useful to be able to point to what seems to be yet another illustration of Vico's technique of disguised suggestion.

Leaving aside the fifteen paragraphs which constitute the official 'Conclusion of the Work', in which the author summarizes the grand sweep of his historicism, the *Scienza nuova* ends with Book 5, on 'ricorsi'. With what impression, we may reasonably ask, does Vico wish to leave the reader at the end of this important section? In the closing paragraph he reminds the reader of the pattern of his 'ideal eternal history'. If we look at and compare the histories of ancient and modern nations, he argues, we find a uniform design repeating itself 'by virtue of the identity of the intelligible *substance* in the diversity of their *modes* of development'.[73] The 'eternal laws' inscribed in the 'ideal eternal history' provide, that is, the essential structure of the histories of all nations. Using language which is very reminiscent of pagan descriptions of the eternal cycles in the entire natural order, Vico states that the pattern of the 'ideal eternal history' can be seen in the histories of particular nations 'in their rise, progress, maturity, decadence and dissolution'. He adds that this same pattern would recur 'even if (as is certainly not the case) there were infinite worlds being born from time to time throughout eternity'.[74] The concept of the eternal rebirth of 'infinite worlds' is, as we have seen, pagan through and through, and Vico must, of course, insert his disclaimer. If, as he continually states, it is a pure piece of speculation, why does he insist on repeating it, and thus ensure that the reader never forgets it?

The most interesting part of the closing paragraph, however, is the final sentence, for it is here that Vico states that the essential property of his science is contained in Seneca's statement: 'our universe is a sorry little affair unless it has in it something for every age to investigate.'[75] At first sight this seems a rather puzzling conclusion. But on closer inspection there can be little doubt concerning the purpose of so apparently harmless a piece of rhetoric. It is not simply that Vico chooses to end the whole section of

73. *SN* 1096.
74. Ibid.
75. See *SN* 1096. The original reads: 'Pusilla res hic mundus est, nisi id quod quaerit, omnis mundus habeat'. Seneca, *Naturales Quaestiones*, Bk VII, ch. 30 sect. 5.

the work devoted to the 'ricorsi' with a clear reference to the work of a Stoic philosopher who wrote about the eternal cycles. The passage from the *Naturales Quaestiones* continues: 'Some sacred things are not revealed once and for all. Eleusis keeps in reserve something to show to those who revisit her.'[76] Leaving aside the fact that Eleusis was the centre of the Eleusinian Mysteries – one of the great mystery religions whose teachings were imparted in secret – and that Vico could well have intended this reference to highlight something about the enforced secrecy surrounding some of his own ideas, the crucial point is that the ritual celebrations of this religion honoured the cosmic 'cycle' of birth, death and resurrection. According to its beliefs even human burial, for example, took place in the earth so that men could become part of the cyclical renewal of life. It was a religion whose myths were steeped in the idea that the annual cycle of agronomic renewal was part of a universal cyclical system embracing humanity itself.

Within the confines of the 'deliberate obscurity' employed throughout the *Scienza nuova*, Vico could hardly have made plainer the naturalistic foundations of his 'ricorsi'. His conception of man's return to barbarity and to a beast-like existence also bears a great resemblance to Seneca's belief that 'every living creature will be created anew' and that 'the ancient order of things will be re-established' when 'the destruction of the human race is completed and the wild animals, into whose savagery men will have passed, are equally extinct.'[77] Vico could not, however, openly make use of or adapt such ancient antecedents.

The cyclical view of history is inherently naturalistic. This further explains why Vico's providence, the force which guides the pattern of operations in his 'ideal eternal history', is so far from the Christian conception of providence.[78] Indeed, one of the most eminent Protestant theologians of our times, Rudolf Bultmann, has remarked in passing on the effect of Vico's cycles upon his notion of providence. He illustrates how, through Vico's 'ricorsi', 'divine providence was neutralized, and how he eliminated the idea of the eschatological consummation of history'.[79] Bultmann, in his few

---

76. Ibid., Bk VII, ch. 30, sect. 6.
77. Ibid., Bk III, ch. 30, sects. 7–8.
78. As Vaughan has observed, 'one feature of the orthodox teaching is wholly absent from Vico's conception of providence, namely, the notion of end or *eschaton*. For Augustine and Aquinas, history has meaning of intelligibility only in terms of providence and a final *telos*. The ulimate end, *finis ultimus*, of man is God, i.e. a transcendent end which gives meaning to history. There is no such end in Vico's theory of providential history.' *(Political Philosophy* p. 43.)
79. R. Bultmann, *History and Eschatology*, p. 79.

brief remarks on Vico's philosophy, penetrates to the whole theoretical substance underlying both providence and cycles alike when he states that 'Vico has historicised the concept of nature, but at the same time it must be said that he has naturalised the conception of history'.[80] It is only when we have grasped the full extent of Vico's 'naturalism' that we truly understand the significance of his major concepts.

80. Ibid., pp. 79–80.

18
Vico's Philosophy of Nature

The Extent of Vico's 'Naturalism'

It is now some time since Enzo Paci wrote that the relationship between Vico's 'philosophy of nature' and his historicism was 'clearly decisive for the inner coherence of his thought'.[1] Yet apart from Badaloni's major study on the seventeenth-century Neapolitan background to this aspect of Vico's thought,[2] the overall critical response has not been entirely supportive of Paci's claim. The present work has attempted to redress the balance in favour of Paci's thesis by highlighting the naturalistic content of the major elements of Vico's theory and thus vindicate the claim that the concept of 'nature' in the *Scienza nuova* is a 'functional' notion which establishes the connection between 'the material world and life, between the purely natural world and man'.[3]

The centrality of the concept of 'nature' in Vico's thought determines the semantic value of its linguistic variants. In the *Scienza nuova*, 'natural', 'naturally', 'naturalness' do not have the weak or casual meanings we often give these adjectives, adverbs and nouns in modern speech. Vico writes, for instance: 'our philosophical criticism will give us a *natural* theogony, or generation of the gods, as it took form *naturally* in the minds of the founders of the gentile world, who were *by nature* theological poets.'[4] Hence, as we have already seen, the 'poetic' speech of early man was 'a common *natural* necessity' in all nations.[5] Once our attention is drawn to this aspect of Vico's discourse we begin to notice how much it pervades the fabric of his thought.

Again, when dealing with the origins of the legal system, Vico noted that 'law began *naturally* to be observed, in the manner

---

1. Paci, *Ingens Sylva*, p. 98.
2. Badaloni, *Introduzione a G. B. Vico*. This was the first study to indicate the strong naturalistic connotations of Vico's use of providence as a preservational force.
3. Paci, *Ingens Sylva*, p. 99.
4. *SN* 392. Italics mine.
5. *SN* 435. Italics mine.

examined above, by the founders of the gentes . . .'[6]
In a lengthier passage describing the development from one form of government to another, we can likewise observe how he frequently stresses the 'naturality' of the human activity which promotes the transitions:

> Then came the human governments of aristocratic civil states, and, *naturally*, continuing to practice the religious customs . . . . Afterward, when the time came for popular commonwealths, which are *naturally* open, generous, and magnanimous (being commanded by the multitude, who *naturally* understand natural equity) . . . what had been kept secret was *naturally* made public.*[7]

Thus 'civil equity *naturally* subordinated everything to that law'[8] because 'the heroes . . . *naturally* subordinated their minor private interests. Hence *naturally* as magnanimous men they defended the public good'.[9] This limited selection of passages illustrates how effectively Vico communicates the 'naturality' of human activity and motivation to the attentive reader who might otherwise interpret them according to more traditionally acceptable 'voluntaristic' criteria. We shall return to this particular problem, however, in the second part of this chapter.

It should be noted, moreover, that man's 'naturality' still remains the governing principle even during the final, rational stage of human development. This is so in spite of the numerous passages in the *Scienza nuova* which might appear to point to reason as the single overall determining factor in the third phase of Vico's scheme. While dealing with successive 'natures' of man, for instance, the final stage of humanity is described in the following terms: 'The third was human nature, intelligent and hence modest, benign, and reasonable, recognizing for laws conscience, reason, and duty'.[10] Elsewhere, he speaks in parallel terms of the sciences, that is, 'that they had their beginnings in the public needs or utilities of the peoples and that they were later perfected as acute individuals applied their reflection to them'.[11] Hence, argues Vico, the philosophers may be regarded as the 'old men of the nations' who originally founded the sciences, 'thereby making humanity complete'.[12]

Such passages interpreted in isolation, however, are very mis-

---

6. *SN* 398. Italics mine.
7. *SN* 953. Italics mine.
8. *SN* 950. Italics mine.
9. Ibid. Italics mine.
10. *SN* 918.
11. *SN* 51.
12. *SN* 498.

leading. We saw in Chapter 10 that man's ability to reason leads him to the concept of 'natural equity' in which the seeds of social dissolution are contained, since men pursue their disparate individual rights restrained only by monarchy, which is charged with the public good. This is because even the rational activity of mankind operates within the confines of a greater or stronger naturalistic self-interest. Even those heroes who *naturally* defended the common good, 'if they had not had such a great private interest identified with the public interest, could not have been induced to abandon their savage life and cultivate civility'.[13] Vico's descriptions of the age of reason do not amount, in other words, to an unconditional assertion of the primacy of man's rational faculty. His reflective capacity still operates within the parameters of the overall naturalistic scheme laid down in the *Scienza nuova*.

The primacy of Vico's naturalism is, of course, very much more in evidence when we examine the central principles of his theory. We may recall that one of the main preoccupations of the *Scienza nuova* is to demonstrate the 'authority' of legal systems. It does this by illustrating how laws are generated in social contexts which arise 'in spite of' men's particular intentions, under the wider guidance of providence. This process, in which a predictable chain of social organizations is produced, is the basis of human activity, which leads Vico to claim that his work will demonstrate 'that this is the true civil nature of man, and thus that *law exists in nature*'.[14] For Vico, therefore, law is already inscribed in nature. We had previously arrived at this conclusion, but less directly, in our earlier discussion of law when we saw that the burden of its 'authority' was borne unambiguously by the 'senso comune', defined as the matrix of instinctive judgements 'without reflection',[15] experienced by the whole of humanity in its changing phases of development. But in *SN* 2, as we have just seen, the principle that law derives its 'authority' from 'nature' is stated in a more forthright manner, just as it was in the first edition of the *Scienza nuova* where Vico argued that the study of jurisprudence must reveal the true nature of law, 'uniformly determined for all nations by nature'.[16]

The 'naturality' which pervades the whole of Vico's major work thus dominates his very concept of 'man'. Not even in the age of rationality does humanity free itself from the constraints of the

---

13. *SN* 950.
14. *SN* 2. Italics mine.
15. *SN* 142.
16. *SN1a* 175. See also *SN1a* 198–200 where Vico argues that it is nature and not human design which dictates the course of legal development.

natural order. Both 'law' and man's social capacity are ultimately rooted in 'nature'. This provides an answer to the question which Vico himself poses, 'whether law exists by nature, or whether man is naturally sociable', which, he declares, 'comes to the same thing'.[17]

Vico was very conscious of the fact that he was undermining the traditional view that 'law', and also the social systems which it regulates, are products of man's 'higher' faculties – those which enable him to transcend the purely natural or instinctive order. His whole theory was in fact re-locating man's socio-legal structures at this more 'natural' level of reality. Evidently he had to proceed with caution, but his intent is unmistakable. He asks once again, for example: 'whether law resides in nature or in the opinion of men', and in answer to his own question proceeds to argue that 'the natural law of the gentes was instituted by custom . . . and not by laws. . . . For it began in human customs springing from the common nature of nations . . . and it preserves human society. Moreover, there is nothing more natural . . . than observing natural customs.'[18] The 'common nature of nations' referred to above is determined, in other words, by the 'senso comune'.

The seditious implication of this point, as far as the traditional view is concerned, has been clearly perceived, for example, by Giuseppe Semerari, who notes that Vico, by making law dependent on a naturalistic substratum of behavioural and cognitive patterns, in reality dislodges man's so-called 'higher' faculties as the guiding principles behind his social development. Semerari notes also that the 'senso comune' is indeed 'where the uncertainty of individual choice is overcome', but the consequence, he argues, is that 'for Vico, that truth, which is the truth for man, is not something human'. He then concludes further that because the 'senso comune' is postulated as the basis of social customs and laws, it therefore follows that 'Vico's basic a-historicism is manifest in the principle of the "senso comune".'[19]

This assertion of a fundamental lack of historicism in a thinker generally noted for his historical sense is by no means as rash or audacious as it might appear at first sight. Indeed, it illustrates the point made earlier, for Semerari clearly ranges himself alongside those who believe that history is the product of man's 'higher' volitional and cognitive faculties – precisely those human capacities which Vico had implicitly expunged from amongst the basic deter-

17. *SN* 135.
18. *SN* 309.
19. G. Semerari, 'Intorno all' anticartesianesimo di Vico', pp. 211–12.

minants of historical change. In this sense, Semerari, while he is in my view mistaken in his conclusion about Vico's 'a-historicism', at least shows a coherence which is lacking in many critics who share his historicist assumptions, yet insist on finding these assumptions in the *Scienza nuova*.

What Semerari has observed is that the 'senso comune' represents the 'naturality' which Vico constantly contrasts with human deliberation as the dynamic principle behind historical development. When, therefore, he asserts that 'it was not counsel but nature by which providence was served',[20] we have an unmistakable indication of the naturalistic base on which he considered providence to operate. Hence, as a result of Vico's repeated reminders that his science is a demonstration of what providence has brought about in history 'without human discernment or counsel',[21] we must agree with Badaloni's comment that Vico's discussion of providence 'coincides perfectly with the discourse on naturality'.[22]

When we penetrate further into the semantic range of Vico's naturalism we gain an even more coherent perception of the inner connection between some of the apparently disparate elements of his discourse. We have already indicated, for instance, that providence, in the *Scienza nuova*, has a conservational function. If we pursue the theme a little further we soon discover how central this latter function is to Vico's whole conception of history.

We know that as a young man Vico had pursued the study of medicine under the guidance of Leonardo di Capua. We also know from the detailed studies of Badaloni that one of the central themes which preoccupied the minds of students of medicine at the time was the idea of an in-built 'animal sagacity' which enabled the lower species to avoid 'harmful substances' in the all-important process of self-preservation. We likewise recall from the discussion of law in Chapter 8, that Vico had already absorbed substantial elements of this thinking into his writing in the *Diritto universale*. Man when faced with social dissolution and extinction, was forced to return to the animal level of a 'genus' existence in which the preservational instincts are stronger, in order to maintain the distinctive 'species' characteristics of human society. Thus, even at this early stage, Vico had incorporated into his science of humanity the natural philosophy which inspired many of the debates and discussions in which he took part,[23] and he had begun to transform

20. *SN* 532.
21. *SN* 342.
22. Badaloni, 'Vico nell' ambito della filosofia europea', p. 250.
23. Giuseppe Valletta, for instance, observes that: 'we can perceive in brute beasts

it into a highly organized and coherent system. The natural instincts, for example, that had been observed in the animal kingdom were, in his opinion, shared by man 'because from birth man is taught, by the speedy and indeed immediate warnings of the senses, through pain and pleasure, to pursue those things useful to life and to avoid those harmful ones *in order to preserve his own being*'.[24]

We have already seen quite clearly how Vico proceeds to incorporate the conservational theme into that dimension of his philosophy which deals with the rise and fall of nations. Accordingly, in the first edition of the *Scienza nuova*, providence is explicitly identified with this instinct, so that 'whatever particular individuals or peoples arrange for their own particular ends, which would be the principle cause of their destruction, it, quite independently of and frequently contrary to all their intentions . . . preserves them'.[25] The conservational instinct is, in short, a permanently operating feature in the whole historical process. So Vico describes his science as one which demonstrates how man:

> wants the preservation of his nature. Such a science must demonstrate how, on the changing occasions of human necessity, through a variety of customs, times and states, the mind of solitary man has developed on the basis of its primary objective of preserving its nature: first by preserving the family, then by preserving the cities, then by preserving the nations and finally by preserving the whole of mankind.[26]

Consistent with the thoroughness of Vico's naturalism, therefore, the preservational instinct functions as a lasting component in the overall dynamism of historical change. When he tells us that 'the nations mean to dissolve themselves, and their remnants flee for safety to the wilderness, whence, like the phoenix, they rise again',[27] this is precisely because the third, rational stage of human development results in a corresponding diminution in those instinctive forces necessary for man's preservation. And when men return to primitive barbarity, divine providence is to be admired, because, having given us the senses for the guarding of our bodies, at a time when men had fallen into the state of brutes (in whom the

a certain quality, very different from what we find in man, which serves, however, for their conservation, enabling them to avoid what is harmful and to pursue what is good for them . . . which some people have called natural instinct' (cited in Introduction to *Opere giuridiche*, p. xxvii).

24. *Opere giuridiche*, p. 93. Italics mine.
25. *SN1a* 45. See also *SN1a* 53 and 399.
26. *SN1a* 41.
27. *SN* 1108.

senses are keener than in men), providence saw to it that by their brutish nature itself they should have the keenest senses for their self-preservation.*[28]

We are now in a position to see more clearly the connection between further essential components of Vico's theory. As we noted in Chapter 10, the age of rationality brings with it the threat of social dissolution. In order to avoid the final extinction of humanity, therefore, Vico posits a cyclic return to barbarity as a central feature of his philosophy.[29] We have seen above, in *SN* 532, that 'it was not counsel but nature by which providence was served'. It is stated equally bluntly that the process of social evolution occurs 'without human discernment or counsel' (*SN*342). This 'nature'/'counsel' antithesis is in accord with the whole thrust of his thinking whereby the age of reason entails a threat of social dissolution. So that the *only* way in which humanity can regain the full power of its preservational instincts is through a 'return' to the 'naturality' of its primitive brutish existence.

From the 'genus'/'species' polarity of the *Diritto universale*, to its 'nature'/'counsel' equivalent in the *Scienza nuova*, the idea of a 'ricorso' as a necessary process for the preservation of the human species remains, in other words, an abiding principle of Vico's historicism. The cyclic perspective, therefore, is not simply a convenient framework for the development of this historicism, but *a requirement of the inner logic of his theory*, an inherent consequence of the naturalism underlying his whole conception of human development

Whether the cyclical conception of history was suggested to Vico by his predominantly naturalistic perspective or whether the reverse was the case is really of little consequence, for the two show a high degree of interpenetration, both in his own system and in the history of ideas in general.[30] In fact the intimate connection be-

28. *SN* 707.
29. Nicola Badaloni stresses the functional force of cycles in Vico's theory, and has argued that 'ricorsi' are 'explained by that law of self-conservation of our species which Vico has called *providence* (which corresponds in many ways to the unconscious wisdom which Leonardo Di Capua theorized regarding the animal world). This obliges men, even against their wills, to act in such a way as to guarantee the preservation of themselves and of their descendants.' (*Introduzione a G. B. Vico*, p. 374.)
30. One finds confirmation of this from unexpected quarters. Karl Lowith, for example, has written: 'Compared with Polybius' theory of cycles, Vico's *ricorso* is, however, much more historicized in conformity with his historicized notion of nature. The cyclic recurrence provides for the education and even salvation of mankind by the rebirth of its social nature. It saves man by preserving him. This alone, but not redemption, is the 'primary end' and providential meaning of history. The recurrence of barbarism saves mankind from civilized self-destruction.' (*Meaning in History*, p. 134).

tween the notion of historical cycles and naturalistic philosophy has frequently been stressed in order to emphasize the fundamentally anti-Christian nature of such ideas. Bearing in mind the particular circumstances in which Vico was writing, it cannot be stressed enough that 'the essence of that discovery of history which the Western world owes to the Old Testament really lies in its differentiation of history from nature',[31] because 'in nature the same thing happens over and over again; in history each thing can happen only once. The proper application of the cyclical pattern is thus to the world of nature . . . To make history follow a cyclical pattern is thus to depress history into the realm of nature'.[32]

Vico was, of course, fully aware of this profoundly anti-Christian connection betwen historical cycles and naturalistic thought, and it accounts for many of the tactical manoeuvres and concealments we have described. The prevailing tendency in Vichian scholarship to underplay or ignore the significance of his cyclic view of history is therefore mistaken. Closer attention to the idea of 'ricorsi' and to its essentially 'naturalistic' foundations is, in fact, likely to lead to further fruitful areas of investigation.

It may be possible, for example, to throw fresh light on Vico's problematic references to Plato as one of his major sources. For the idea of cycles, which is mentioned in a number of Plato's dialogues, is specifically related to the same theme of discovering the 'necessities' of life. The speaker in the *Critias* (109d–110a), after one of the periodic catastrophes which destroys human civilization, states that the process of civil construction begins anew. For numerous generations, he argues, the energies of those engaged in this renewal are devoted to obtaining the necessities of life, and the arts which are characteristic of civilized man are slowly and painfully recovered at a later stage in the course of development from such 'renewed barbarism'.[33]

These ideas would undoubtedly have been reinforced by Vico's reading of the *Republic*. We recall, in fact, that in the *Autobiography* he claims to have derived inspiration for his 'ideal eternal history' from Plato's discussion of the ideal republic. While one might not at first sight associate Plato's views in the *Republic* with a naturalistic and cyclical historical pattern, there is in effect a genuine point of contact when he argues that the ebb-and-flow of collective vigour which accompanies the flowering and demise of successive cultures suggests a possible correspondence with the cycle of growth, decay

31. Baillie, *Belief in Progress*, p. 66.
32. Ibid., p. 67.
33. Another passage similar to *Critias*, 109d–110a can be found in *Laws*, 676aff.

and dissolution of states, animals and plants:

> Hard as it may be for a state so framed to be shaken, yet, since all that comes into being must decay, even a fabric like this will not endure for ever, but will suffer dissolution. In this manner: not only for plants that grow in the earth, but also for all creatures that move thereon, there are seasons of fruitfulness and unfruitfulness for soul and body alike, which come whenever a certain cycle is completed, in a period short or long according to the length of life of each species.[34]

In the light of this passage, Vico's remarks in the *Diritto universale* about the dissolution of man's social life and his return to the 'genus' in order to preserve his 'species' existence is particularly interesting. And in relation to the *Scienza nuova*, the above passage occurs, moreover, in the section in which Plato deals with the fall of the ideal commonwealth, a topic which, as we can imagine, would have greatly attracted Vico's attention. There is, therefore, no other single passage in the *Republic* which gives so precise a justification to his claim to have found inspiration in this work.

It becomes increasingly evident, therefore, that the more we examine the naturalistic foundations of the new science, the more its internal unity is revealed. However, not only does this perspective interrelate Vico's major functional principles such as 'ricorsi' and 'providence', but it also permeates, through such concepts as 'natural necessity' and the 'senso comune', all facets of human activity.

We noted in earlier discussions oblique but nonetheless substantial challenges on Vico's part to the doctrine of 'free-will', a sacred principle fundamental to any meaningful notion of Christianity. Since the problem goes to the very heart of his whole philosophy of nature, we must now examine this crucial question in the context of the overall strategy he employed to defend his 'naturalism'.

Vico's 'Naturalism' and the Problem of Freedom of Action

Any such discussion must begin by duly emphasizing that Vico's treatment of free-will is not only highly circumspect but also potentially misleading. For while he frequently claims to be upholding this all-important doctrine, the naturalistic content of his theory in reality casts considerable doubt on such a claim. But we shall not repeat here arguments we have already advanced in earlier

34. Plato, *The Republic*, pp. 262–3.

discussions. Instead let us examine other crucial and more fundamental pointers in this direction.

Referring to Vico's conception of human activity, Badaloni has
pointed out that the pattern of the 'ideal eternal history' means that
'he has reduced to terms of "necessity" that which only in appearance is manifest as "liberty"'.[35] Most commentators, however,
accept at face value Vico's professions of orthodoxy. Luigi Bellofiore, for instance, has argued that even in the first edition of the
Scienza nuova the author was at pains to include an authentic
element of human choice as part of the driving force of all historical
change.[36] The passage in which Vico introduces the notion of
free-will begins: 'The artificer of the world of nations, acting under
this divine plan, is human choice . . .'[37]

It is misleading, however, to ignore the qualifying force of the
context within which this statement is made. For instance, it is
made clear that all human activity takes place within the context of
the 'senso comune', a force which, as we have seen, imposes very
clear limitations on freedom of action. Equally important, however, is Vico's characterization of human choice as being 'by its
very nature extremely uncertain in individual men, but determined, however, by the wisdom of humankind measured against
the human utilities and necessities which are uniformly common to
all the particular natures of men . . .'[38] In the succeeding passage,
moreover, as the text moves further away from his ritual recount-
ing of doctrine, and the implications of its meaning become less
apparent, the qualifications are less circumscribed. Vico argues that
providence engineers the pattern of historical development 'with
the dictates of human necessities and utilities', and that the two
essential features of this pattern are 'one immutability, and two
universality'.[39] Human history can hardly develop freely according
to the free choices of men if it is fixed within an 'immutable'
pattern.

We saw, in Chapter 5, that for Vico an element of human choice
first arose among primitives as a form of restraint. Those early
men began through fear of the gods, 'to hold in *conatus* the impetus
of the bodily motion of lust. Thus they began to use *human
liberty* which consists in holding in check the motions of
concupiscence . . .'[40] and were thus led to form stable family

35. Badaloni, 'Vico nell' ambito della filosofia europea', p. 251.
36. See Bellofiore, *La dottrina della provvidenza*, pp. 26ff.
37. *SN1a* 47.
38. Ibid.
39. *SN1a* 48.
40. *SN* 1098. Italics mine.

relationships. The fact that Vico refers to human choice in terms of 'conatus' is important in regard to his concept of free-will. This should be viewed in conjunction with his radical departure from the traditional conception of human choice as the exercise of the will following rational deliberation. Human liberty, argued Vico, is located within the will, 'the intellect on the other hand being a passive power subject to truth'. Nevertheless 'men began to exercise the freedom of human choice to hold in check the motions of the body . . . (this being the conatus proper to free agents)'.[41] He could hardly argue otherwise, given his repeated emphasis on the lack of any reflective capacity in early man. This apparently ambiguous juxtaposition of confused ideas is nevertheless substantially coherent when seen from the point of view of Vico's fundamental naturalism. The inner logic of his argument, concealed as it is behind what appears to be a deliberate veil of ambiguity, simply requires a certain amount of reconstruction to bring out its hidden implications.

What we have seen so far is that Vico's conception of liberty as 'conatus' is connected with a notion of human choice which is devoid of its traditional 'rational' dimension.[42] This is not surprising, given the dichotomy Vico insists on positing between 'will' and 'intellect'. The fundamental problem which remains is that the exercise of 'liberty' which he sees as originating with the 'first men, stupid, insensate, and horrible beasts . . . without power of ratiocination',[43] can hardly be squared with any traditionally acceptable notion of choice as a process of selection between real and rationally deliberated alternatives. Moreover, whatever Vico meant by human choice, it could not change the pattern of the 'ideal eternal history' 'even if infinite worlds were born from time to time through eternity, . . .'[44]

Constricted on all sides by his overall scheme of 'natural necessity', and deprived of its traditionally essential 'rational' component, it would seem that Vico's notion of 'choice' is considerably impoverished. Indeed, it would appear that he is attempting to safeguard all the force of his naturalistic scheme while at the same time preserving the essential features of an orthodox discourse.

41. *SN* 388.
42. See the earlier discussion in Chapter 6. Papini, *Arbor Humanae Linguae*, pp. 69ff., discusses the notion of 'conatus' in the light of Vico's anti-Lucretian comments in the *Autobiography*, and on the basis of an assumed hostility to the idea as used within the discourse of Hobbes, Spinoza, Leibniz, etc. Papini absorbs the notion into a scientific framework infused with 'a principle of intelligence and finality' (p. 92) imparted by God.
43. *SN* 374–5.
44. *SN* 348.

What we must do for the moment, therefore, is to suspend all presuppositions as to the implications of Vico's conception of 'will' and 'choice' and attempt to uncover its exact meaning as it emerges in specific utterances from the text.

In his attempt to meet both of the above requirements, a crucial role is reserved for the notion of 'conatus', and it is to this concept that he repeatedly relates his concept of free-will and/or human choice: 'From this thought must have sprung the conatus proper to the human will, to hold in check the motions impressed on the mind by the body . . .. This control over the motion of their bodies is certainly an effect of the freedom of human choice, and thus of free will . . .'[45] This makes it clear, however, that any control man exercises over one set of impulses is only possible by granting the absolute determining effects of another set over which he has no control:

> But men, because of their corrupted nature, are under the tyranny of self-love, which compels them to make private utility their chief guide. Seeking everything useful for themselves and nothing for their fellows, they cannot bring their passions under control ['conatus'] to direct them toward justice.[46]

So while providence may well engineer a succession of socially beneficial results, men never rise above the basic passion of self-interest because 'in all these circumstances man desires principally his own utility'.[47]

It seems clear enough, even thus far, that Vico situates human behaviour predominantly within a naturalistic causal framework rather than within the traditional 'voluntarist' perspective of Christian responsibility. Yet when we look a little closer at the notion of 'conatus' we find a further indication of the almost deterministic background within which he had achieved his understanding of it. The passage quoted above (*SN* 340) in which Vico characterizes human liberty as 'conatus' continues thus:

> But to impute conatus to bodies is as much as to impute to them freedom to regulate their motions, whereas all bodies are by nature necessary agents. And what the theorists of mechanics call powers, forces, conatus, are insensible motions of bodies, by which they approach their centers of gravity, as ancient mechanics had it, or depart from their centers of motion, as modern mechanics has it.[48]

45. *SN* 340.
46. *SN* 341.
47. Ibid.
48. *SN* 340.

A brief examination of the function of the term 'conatus' in the thought and writings of one or two thinkers important to Vico may be useful at this point. In much of the scientific and philosophical literature of the seventeenth century, 'conatus' is the term used to describe the link-force or 'virtue' existing between rest and motion – the property, that is, which enables animate objects to translate the apparently immaterial impulses of the world of sense, feeling or thought into activity at the level of the body as physical or mechanical action.[49] The Cartesian dichotomy between immaterial mind and mechanical body was thus resolved by some thinkers in terms of this intermediary force.

Of particular interest in regard to Vico is the fact that apart from appearing in the writings of the Investiganti the notion of 'conatus' was also central to the discussion of human choice in both Hobbes and Spinoza. We have already seen areas of Vico's indebtedness to these two important non-Catholic thinkers, whom he appears ostensibly to repudiate as irreligious while at the same time concealing similarities between elements of their thinking and his own.[50] We shall shortly discover further parallels and additional reasons why he should have tried to obscure such affinities.

The relevance of Hobbes and Spinoza to Vico's 'naturalism' has been noted by Amos Funkenstein who observes that 'Hobbes, Spinoza and Vico tried to define society in terms of nature, and with procedures taken from natural science.'[51] Significantly, Funkenstein notes that Vico saw society as 'a product of a long evolution in which the individual or a group could not, and should not, interfere'.[52] It is within this 'naturalistic'/'deterministic' scheme that human volition and liberty as 'conatus' ('endeavour' in Hobbes's English writings) finds its place. Funkenstein points to the

49. Vico himself discusses 'conatus' in such terms in *De Antiquissima*, Ch. 4, sect. 2. See *Opere filosofiche*, pp. 85ff.

50. The term 'conatus' was used also by philosophers such as Leibniz, for example, in a manner quite different from the way in which it was employed by Hobbes and Spinoza. The special relevance of these two, however, derives from the fact that they were important to Vico, and the concept had a bearing on areas of interest and on ideas which he had in common with them.

51. Funkenstein, 'Natural Science and Social Theory', p. 211.

52. Ibid. There is, however, something of a contradiction in Funkenstein's study. Alongside, or just before, the statement that according to Vico men cannot affect social evolution, we find him arguing that Vico's stress on history as 'spontaneous creativity' allows him 'to challenge the mechanistic – deterministic interpretation of the foundation (and progress) of civil society' (p. 204). He also argues that providence is Vico's attempt to reconcile 'human autonomy' with God's plan (p. 211). This is one further example of the difficulties caused by Vico's declared orthodoxy. Whilst his text presents undeniable evidence of naturalistic and unorthodox thinking, his professions of faith breed a reluctance among critics to break with prevailing voluntaristic interpretations of the *Scienza nuova*.

importance of 'conatus' or 'endeavour' in Hobbes as the concept which is meant to reconcile two apparently conflicting conceptions of human activity. 'On the basis of his theory of *conatus*', he writes, 'Hobbes can hold that an action may be both causally determined throughout *and* voluntary.'[53]

Hobbes' solution to problems concerning the nature and scope of human activity was central to his 'civil philosophy' – in which Vico was greatly interested. Vico's famous remarks about the world of civil society being made by man are almost certainly derived from this source. Hobbes had also argued that monarchy is the best form of government and the most effective institution for securing peace and stability in a society in which men are bound by nature to act out of self-interest. In a manner very similar to Vico, therefore, Hobbes consigns the public conscience to a separate sphere, thus allowing individuals to follow their private pursuits. Enzo Paci has talked about the enthusiasm Vico must have felt on first acquaintance with Hobbes' ideas on early, beast-like humanity, and on the great violence, strength and lack of rationality in those early primitives.[54] The English philosopher, who was accused of atheism, was therefore undoubtedly of greater interest and significance than Vico was prepared to declare.

In his study of Hobbes, J. W. N. Watkins has pointed out that the notion of 'conatus' or 'endeavour' belongs to a fundamentally deterministic view of the universe. It involves the idea that all motion (including ultimately volitional and rational activity) is the effect of the application of an external force on the moving object, and 'conatus' is in effect this external force. Thus man 'is a "conational" system' which shares with other physical systems the characteristic of possessing 'extension and also non extensional properties'.[55]

In animals, whether human or otherwise, there are two kinds of motion, that is, 'vital' and 'voluntary'. As we shall see, the distinction between these two types of motion does not imply that either is less bound than the other to a necessary chain of causal connections. The difference lies simply in the complexity of the connections and in their differing locations within the physiological, nervous and appetite systems of the organism. Vital motion, writes Hobbes,

is the motion of the blood, perpetually circulating (as hath been shown

53. Ibid., p. 193., P
54. See Paci, *Ingens Sylva*, pp. 122ff.
55. J. W. N. Watkins, *Hobbes's System of Ideas*, p. 95.

from many infallible signs and marks by Doctor Harvey, the first observer of it) in the veins and arteries . . . . But if the vital motion be helped by motion made by sense, then the parts of the organ will be disposed to guide the spirits in such manner as conduceth most to the preservation and augmentation of that motion, by the help of the nerves.[56]

The statement that follows this causally conceived description of 'vital' motion is of particular relevance for students of Vico since it illustrates how the notion of 'conatus' or endeavour can be used to produce a particular understanding of 'voluntary' activity: 'And in animal motion *this is the very first endeavour*, and found even in the embryo; which while it is in the womb, moveth its limbs *with voluntary motion.*'[57] Hobbes then proceeds to describe this 'endeavour' or 'voluntary' motion as activity resulting from the conflict between contending 'appetites' and 'aversions'.

Before we venture any further into this area of Hobbes' thinking, it is as well to delineate certain aspects of Vico's own discourse in which we find a similar discussion of 'conatus'. He too describes it as resulting from physiological impulses and activities within the 'nerves', 'blood', 'veins' and the 'animal spirits'. We have seen that in the *Scienza nuova* 'conatus' describes the beginning of 'liberty' in primitive man when, for example, it thundered,

> and Jove thus gave a beginning to the world of men by arousing in them the conatus which is proper to the liberty of the mind, just as from motion, which is proper to bodies as necessary agents, he began the world of nature. For what seems to be conatus in bodies is but insensible motion, . . .[58]

We will also recall that 'conatus' is used to explain the origins of 'moral virtue': 'Moral virtue began, as it must, from conatus. . . . With this conatus the virtue of the spirit began likewise to show itself among them, restraining their bestial lust . . .'[59] When we examine more closely the precise nature of the 'spirit' ('animo') which is the seat of 'virtue', however, we find ourselves within a 'conational' framework very similar to that which we saw earlier in Hobbes. In language which is curiously reminiscent of the English philosopher, Vico tells us that the 'conatus' or 'moral virtue' is administered via the 'animal spirits' working through the nervous system,

56. Hobbes, *English Works*, vol. i, p. 407.
57. Ibid.
58. *SN* 689.
59. *SN* 504.

so that spirit ['animo'] must have its subject in nerves and the neural substance, and soul ['anima'] must have its in the veins and the blood. Thus the vehicle of spirit ['animo'] is the ether and that of soul ['anima'] is the air, as accords with the relative swiftness of animal spirits and slowness of vital spirits. And as soul ['anima'] is the agent of motion, so spirit ['animo'] is the agent and therefore the principle of conatus, . . .[60]

no animus =
mind

While perhaps less clear than that of Hobbes, the physiological framework of Vico's discourse is plain enough.

As stated earlier, the role of the concept of 'motion' is crucial in this type of discourse. It enables Hobbes, for example, to state, in a manner Vico, even had he so wished, would not have dared to use, a highly mechanistic theory of the origin of ideas, since 'conceptions and apparitions are nothing really, but motion in some internal substance of the head'.[61] An equally deterministic description is provided for the human process of deliberation and choice, which Hobbes defines in terms of the passions. He argues, in fact, that the 'whole sum of desires, aversions, hopes and fears continued till the thing be either done, or thought impossible, is that we call deliberation'.[62] That such a process of deliberation is *not* one which raises man above other animals is perfectly clear, as we can see from a series of passages in which Hobbes absorbs traditional notions of will, liberty and freedom of action into the framework of his deterministic scheme: 'This alternate succession of appetites, aversions, hopes and fears, is no less in other living creatures than in man: and therefore beasts also deliberate . .,.. And beasts that have deliberation, must necessarily also have will'.[63] Hobbes is not, lest any doubt should remain on this question, raising beasts to the level of 'responsible' humanity as traditionally understood. Quite the reverse:

Neither is the freedom of willing or not willing, greater in man, than in other living creatures. For where there is appetite, the entire course of appetite hath preceded; and consequently, the act of appetite could not choose but follow, that is, hath of necessity followed. *And therefore such a liberty as is free from necessity, is not to be found in the will either of men or beasts.*[64]

Nothing could be plainer than the deterministic message in this passage. Similarly, while in Vico's scheme the early pursuit of

60. *SN* 696.
61. Hobbes, *English Works*, vol. iv, p. 31.
62. Ibid., vol. iii, p. 48.
63. Ibid.
64. Ibid., vol. i, p. 409. Italics mine.

passion in primitives is transformed through the development of rationality into the pursuit of self-interest, the predetermined nature of such self-centred motivation is not affected. Indeed, this is quite a coherent argument in the context of the 'conational' framework within which Vico's discourse on 'volition' operates. And Hobbes even adds:

> and therefore if a man should talk to me of a *round Quadrangle*; or *accidents of Bread in Cheese*; or *Immateriall Substances*; or of *A free Subject*; *A free will*; or any *Free*, but free from being hindred by opposition, I should not say he were in an Errour; but that his words were without meaning; that is to say, Absurd.[65]

'Choice', 'voluntary action', 'rationality', are consequently misleading terms if we extract them from the deterministic framework within which all actions are causally determined and think of them instead as 'self-originating' forms of activity. We use such terms, according to Hobbes, only *as if* men decide freely on the courses of action they undertake. We need not, therefore, qualify every statement we make about human choice with reminders about the causal determinants of such choices. We also sustain the 'self-originating' illusion concerning human activity because we are usually unable to perceive, calculate or particularize the causal relations involved in the highly complex mechanisms of human behaviour. For Hobbes, therefore, men act freely *only in appearance*. For him, self-determined activity is an impossibility. The advantage of this language of 'appearances' was that writers were able to sustain, in certain sensitive areas, an orthodox discourse while at the same time indicating to the alert reader the sense in which traditional terminology was to be understood.

Although Vico's discourse was naturalistic and at times circumspect, rather than 'mechanistic' and explicit, as in Hobbes, the theoretical problems he faced with regard to determinism and free-will were in effect very similar. Vico points to these problems in various ways. First by characterizing 'rationality' as a purely passive faculty in relation to will, and then by showing quite clearly that even the latter must be understood within a naturalistic and conational framework. There is, therefore, no contradiction between *SN* 340 and *SN* 341. Vico simply moves in these two passages from an assertion of 'freedom of choice' (in which he draws the reader's attention to the conational context of this statement) to the qualifying statement that men are condemned to the

---

65. Hobbes, *Leviathan*, Pt 1, ch. 5, pp. 23–4.

pursuit of their passions.

It is possible to see that Vico's association of human volition with 'conatus' suggests a naturalistic – causal, rather than a 'voluntaristic', context for human choices. This may well be enhanced by a brief consideration of Spinoza as a possible source or influence. Although there are some fundamental differences between the philosophies of Vico and Spinoza there are also some striking similarities. Spinoza had been very explicit about primitive forms of literature. They were, he argued, the expression of minds strong in imagination and weak in reason – and it was a mistake to search them, whether they were the writings of the prophets or of poets like Homer, for concealed wisdom. They were the products of minds steeped in barbaric practices. A corollary of this aspect of Spinoza's epistemology is that to him ideas, in the primitive or 'imaginative' mind, are passive rather than active in nature – an idea we have also found expressed by Vico.

More interesting still for our present discussion is Spinoza's idea that all living things are compelled by nature to strive for self-preservation; and the name he gives to this force is 'conatus'. We saw earlier that, for Vico, man's pursuit of self-interest, even as it becomes increasingly identified with larger social units such as the family and the nation, is basically an instinct for self-preservation. We know also that the basis upon which men exercise their will or choose to pursue such conservatory instincts is 'conatus'. It is hardly coincidental, therefore, that this close connection between 'conatus' and 'self-preservation' should be found in the writings of both authors.[66]

Spinoza makes it abundantly clear, moreover, that in addition to acting as a force for the self-preservation of those beings it inhabits, 'conatus' is also part of a causally determined system of activity:

> From the given essence of any particular thing certain things follow of necessity, nor can things do anything other than what necessarily follows from their determined nature. For which reason, the power or conatus by which any particular thing does, or endeavours to do, anything – either alone or with others – is the same power or conatus by which it endeavours to preserve its own being, and is nothing other than the given or actual essence of that particular thing.[67]

Consistent with his deterministic view of human behaviour and

---

66. Stuart Hampshire, *Spinoza*, has pointed out that 'conatus' represents a 'tendency to self-preservation' (p. 127). He also argues that 'the *conatus* is a necessary feature of everything in Nature, because this tendency to self-maintenance is involved in the definition of what it is to be a distinct and identifiable thing' (p. 122).
67. Spinoza, *Ethica*, p. 278.

motivation, Spinoza argues that our judgements of good and bad are determined by what we desire, and not vice versa:

> By good I understand here any kind of pleasure and anything which in turn leads to it, and particularly that which satisfies our natural desires, whatever they may be; by evil, however, I understand any kind of pain, and especially that which frustrates our natural desires. Indeed we have shown above that we do not desire anything because we think it is good, but on the contrary we designate as good that which we desire and consequently we call evil that which we shun.[68]

The 'conatus', therefore, is part of a causally determined system whereby men — and all other creatures — pursue desires in conformity with their innermost nature for the purpose of their own self-preservation. We are reminded here of Vico's writings on law, in which he argued that men, like animals, are led to pursue pleasant and useful things and avoid harmful ones in order to preserve their being.

Spinoza's theory of 'conatus' is designed, in other words, to accommodate what appear to be freely pursued activities within a causal scheme of human behaviour. Furthermore, he has defined his terms in such a way that it necessarily follows that 'all men pursue their own pleasure in accordance with the necessary laws of Nature', and that the apparent choices of men, arising from the 'conatus', also express the latter's 'tendency to self-maintenance and self-preservation'.[69] There are numerous parallels and echoes of these ideas to be found in Vico's work.[70]

The 'conatus', therefore, belongs within a framework of causal, naturalistic explanations of phenomena which *appear to suggest* but do not actualize the possibility of independent choice and liberty of action in mankind. The concept provides a coherent link between Vico's assertions about human choice, on the one hand, and his claims about the 'necessary' course of human events on the other.[71] It also sheds light on his repeated contention that providence, the force which guides the outcome of history, avails itself of 'nature' and not 'counsel' in furthering its purpose.

Consequently, with the 'conatus' we have another important theoretical component in the *Scienza nuova's* complex system of

---

68. Ibid., p. 299
69. Hampshire, *Spinoza*, p. 133.
70. Badaloni has recently shown that Vico's use of conatus as a concept which enables him to link notions of conservation and liberty within the discourse of a naturalized 'providence' can be traced back to the *De Antiquissima*. See *Introduzione a Vico*, p. 30. See also *Opere fiilosofiche*, p. 97.
71. A succinct but telling account of this connection between 'necessity' and 'choice' in Spinoza can be found in *Ethica*, Pt 1, appendix.

naturalistic relations. Such ideas as the 'natural signification' of language, 'natural necessity', the 'vera narratio' and the 'senso comune' all depend, for their explanatory and operational powers, on the idea of a 'naturally' determined and fixed set of behavioural patterns in human nature. So when we look closely at the naturalism of the *Scienza nuova* we find in it a new and perhaps unexpected level of systematicity. That this is not always expressed as directly as the modern reader might expect is undoubtedly related to those issues of expediency that have frequently been disscussed in this book.

Conclusion

This book has attempted to show that an adequate understanding of the *Scienza nuova* can only be achieved when full weight and recognition is given to the naturalism which underlies Vico's theoretical system as a whole. We have shown that even some of the most cherished and widely accepted interpretations of the work suffer from a somewhat selective analysis of its elements so that the resulting omissions and oversights tend to fracture the essential unity of its perspectives. One factor in particular which has consistently compounded the theoretical ambiguities which are to be found amongst Vico's interpreters is an almost obsessive concern with demonstrating the relevance and modernity of his works.

A deliberate and conscious attempt has been made, therefore, to 'suspend' certain presuppositions which arise almost automatically in the minds of contemporary readers. Instead, the aim has been to focus with greater intensity on what the text itself reveals, and consequently to pay greater attention to Vico's use of deliberate ambiguities and textual strategies as an integral part of the presentation of his thought. An important fact which this study has sought to emphasize is that the reader of the *Scienza nuova* cannot ignore the *strategic* dimension implicit in parts of the work, since this is essential to a fuller understanding of its meaning. One other element in his theory which we have likewise tried to bring into focus is the prescriptive and normative thrust of Vico's account of social change. His naturalism is, in effect, woven into the fabric of a theory possessing a strong sense of purpose, one which aims at finding a justification for successive socio-legal formations which appear to have developed in conflict with the ideal forms of law and social organization thought necessary by the orthodox tradition.

The tenacity and determination with which Vico sets about validating his 'philosophy of authority' nevertheless give rise to a number of problems. For while he evidently seeks to utilize a strong deterministic element in his philosophy and bring the full weight of its naturalism to bear in the demonstration of his scheme, the results are frequently problematic and uneven.

Again, the very temper of contemporary Vico scholarship, quite apart from its desire to demonstrate the modern relevance of his thought, tends to obscure the naturalistic foundations of the *Scienza nuova*. Indeed, most critics, irrespective of their differences, share a broad pattern of modern humanistic assumptions which are only too easily brought to bear on the work's interpretation. It is perhaps for this reason that little serious attention has been given to his concept of the 'vera narratio', to its flaws and limitations and to the theoretical corollaries of this fundamental methodological principle. The naturalistic system of the concepts which Vico constructs around the idea ('natural necessity', 'natural signification', 'natural theogony', the 'senso comune', etc.) is meant to provide an automatic guarantee for the correspondence between every form of primitive expression and its 'natural' signification. Within this scheme, a role of special methodological importance is reserved for the interpretation of myth. In its enthusiastic acclaim for this single element of Vico's overall theory — namely the importance of mythology as a source of historical knowledge — contemporary criticism has on the whole severed this insight from its general naturalistic context. As a consequence, this study has not, on the whole, endorsed the excessive optimism of Vico's methodological aspirations and has passed some critical comments on the inordinate rigidity of his general scheme.

A concomitant weakness of Vico's methodological system is that the 'vera narratio' contains a fatal theoretical flaw: namely, that the original myths offering the sanction for his theory could only conceivably be recorded after a certain stage of human evolution had been reached. By that time, however, men had developed the ability to overlay the original semiotic purity and force of such myths with the deceptive reconstructions of their newly acquired rationality. Vico's system of naturalistic guarantees, therefore, even setting aside the question of their intrinsic plausibility, turns out to be of little practical value.

It is, consequently, not surprising that many of Vico's statements dealing with the details and phases of human development take on the appearance of dogmatic assertions rather than of carefully checked hypotheses. And this brings us perhaps to the most crucial point of conflict between his naturalistic philosophy and the requirements of his method, which claims to employ inductive procedures. In essence the problem lies in his coupling of 'prescriptive' and 'empirical' criteria. This led to his deciding in advance on his particular delineation of the course of the 'ideal eternal history', which he then proceeded to 'validate' by using elements of it as proof. From a purely methodological point of view, therefore, the whole 'naturalistic' apparatus of the *Scienza nuova* (the 'vera narratio', 'natural theogony', 'natural signification', the 'senso comune') turns out to be a *petitio principii*, a manner of pressing the principles of empirical enquiry into the service of a *particular*, pre-ordained philosophy, and thereby of ensuring the desired conclusion.

It is nevertheless when we come to consider the problem of Vico's general position on questions of empirical method and the scientific nature of the *Scienza nuova* that the weaknesses of much contemporary criticism are most in evidence. At this point the distorting effects of the modern humanistic assumptions mentioned earlier are brought to bear on the work. An anthropocentric perspective is placed firmly at the centre of the *Scienza nuova* and Vico is alleged to be claiming that 'man makes history', and that this implies an epistemological priority and special forms of knowledge for the science of history in comparison with the natural sciences.

These fundamentally 'anthropocentric' reconstructions of Vico's thought rely heavily on the idea that the inspiring principle of the *Scienza nuova* is the 'verum factum', and that history is the principle creation of man to which this idea is 'applied'. Such views are, however, fundamentally at variance with the philosophy of nature which really informs Vico's thought. Vico asserts that it is a naturalistic force which guides the course of history, frequently 'in spite of' men's intentions, and according to a pattern which they are neither capable of determining nor diverting. We have seen, moreover, that the 'verum-factum' principle does not occupy the place of central importance in the *Scienza nuova* which has been attributed to it. It is used in Vico's earlier writings to defend the physical sciences against both sceptics and dogmatists, and occupies a peripheral and largely non-functional place in his later work. The idea that it operates as a principle whereby man achieves an understanding of his past 'from the inside', as it were, is explicitly denied in the text.

Such obstinate and systematic misconstructions have a deep-rooted *raison d'être* which is responsible for the unconscious substitution of a fundamentally anthropocentric understanding of history for Vico's own naturalistic and providentially fixed 'ideal eternal history'. So preoccupied has much contemporary criticism become with proselytizing his ideas in this way that it has neglected the overriding conflict between his ideas and the general theological temper of the Naples in which he lived and wrote. Apart, therefore, from a few notable exceptions, most critics have remained, on the whole, unreceptive to the constraints imposed by this intellectual predicament, and thus unattuned to a level of discourse in Vico's work which attempted to cope with the ensuing problems.

In many aspects of his theory Vico found elements which had to be concealed or camouflaged. This is not surprising when we consider that, in Naples especially, the naturalistic philosophy he espoused had close affinities with the growth of scientific thinking in the seventeenth century. He found himself in automatic conflict, in fact, with the general temper and thinking of an orthodox theological and philosophical tradition which was still largely Aristotelian and Scholastic in inspiration. Even the eminent Catholic thinker Étienne Gilson has observed that the build-up in scientific thinking in the seventeenth century arose in opposition to this tradition, and that 'there was scarcely a thinker round about the year 1630 for whom the choice did not seem inevitably to lie between science with its proofs on the one hand, and scholasticism with its uncertainties on the other'.[1] From that point onwards it was increasingly argued in scientific circles that Aristotelian philosophy was unproductive and sterile. It was inevitable, therefore, that Vico, who had shared the interests of the Valletta circle in the Investiganti-inspired developments in the physical sciences, biology and medicine, should find himself at odds with Scholasticism.[2]

Valletta's failure to win respectability in Neapolitan ecclesiastical circles for non-Aristotelian currents of thought, together with the Inquisitorial proceedings directed against other well-known opponents of the peripatetic school, made Vico ultra-cautious in his opposition to the philosophical tradition still embraced by the Church. But his implied opposition is clear enough, and his failure to mention anywhere in the *Scienza nuova* the greatest Catholic Aristotelian thinker of all – Aquinas – speaks eloquently of his sense of distance from such pillars of Catholic orthodoxy.

The neglect of such partly disguised tensions in Vico's work extends also to the more detailed elaboration of his scheme and to the problematic task of containing his concealment within the interstices of traditional beliefs. We have seen, for example, how he attempted to accommodate his linguistic theories to the biblical notion of 'onomathesia'; how he dove-tailed sacred history into his own conception of human evolution; and how he employed a

---

1. É. Gilson, 'Concerning Christian Philosophy. The distinctiveness of the philosophic order', p. 61.
2. 'Peripatetic philosophy which was incapable of producing modern science, fought it out from the day of its birth, combating it in the fields of astronomy, physics, biology and medicine, and meeting with a series of well-deserved defeats from which it has not yet recovered.' (Ibid., pp. 61–2.)

'disengagement' technique whereby sacred and profane history operated according to quite different laws whenever he was unable to effect a reconciliation between them.

The immensity of Vico's problems in this sphere is well illustrated by his abandonment of his early attempt to present Cain, before the universal Flood, as the central character in an antediluvian 'feral wandering'. In the end, he settled for a post-diluvian 'bestialization' which he linked up with the dispersal of nations in Genesis. He did so, moreover, in such a manner as to avoid being associated with the heretical ideas of a number of Protestant writers whom he had read and whose views undermined the orthodox belief that the Hebrews were the first people to populate the earth. To these problems we must add the chronological compressions he was forced to conceive in order to square his theory concerning the first 'beast-men' with the biblical accounts of Gentile history. On all of these matters the mainstream of Vichian scholarship is curiously silent.

There is little doubt that a significant re-orientation of perspectives in Vichian scholarship is long overdue. His unrelenting use of pagan and heretical sources, coupled with his deceptive assertions of orthodox belief, raises the whole question of covert levels of meaning in a particularly pertinent manner. Vico's position *vis-à-vis* the theological, and even the juridical ethos of his age needs to be more subtly delineated in the light of his strategies of concealment and veiled assaults on orthodox positions which were by no means uncommon at the time.[3] In the religious atmosphere of Naples it was hardly surprising that Vico should resort to the use of such devices.

On account of the circles in which he moved, and also because of his unorthodox thinking in the field of law, Vico risked being associated with a 'ceto civile' or social group which sought to undermine traditional areas of ecclesiastical privilege and which was regarded as the source of numerous pernicious ideas. This struggle to establish the values of a lay state free from ecclesiastical domination had increased in intensity in Naples towards the end of the seventeenth and lasted well into the eighteenth century, as did

---

3. Bury, for instance, notes precisely such tactics in the writings of one of Vico's contemporaries, the Abbé de Saint Pierre, whose 'real views are transparent in some of his works through the conventional disguises in which prudent writers of the time were wont to wrap their assaults on orthodoxy. To attack Mohammedanism by arguments which are equally applicable to Christianity was a device for propagating rationalism in days when it was dangerous to propagate it openly.' (*Idea of Progress*, pp. 129–30.)

the hostility it generated.[4]

Among the interests and favourite authors of these lawyers and administrators, we can trace a number of those suspect sources around which Vico had built his dissembling strategies of omissions, silences and expedient condemnations. These were the same favourite group of writers 'as those shared by European men of culture at the end of the century (Gassendi, Descartes, Malebranche, Spinoza, the members of the Royal Society: Machiavelli, Hobbes, Bodin, Cujas, Huet)'.[5] And while the disappointing failure of the Austrian rulers in Naples to lend support to the anti-ecclesiastical forces ultimately led to 'a withdrawal of these men from active politics', the effect on others such as Vico was to breed that caution and art of concealment we have found to be a feature of some aspects of the *Scienza nuova*. This is especially understandable when we bear in mind that 'ecclesiastical censure and the Inquisition remained very serious threats'; and while this was true of the whole period during which Vico worked on the *Scienza nuova*, it was especially so of the period between 1730 and 1740, that is, when Vico was busy on his definitive revisions for his final edition – because the princes who offered dissident intellectuals a certain measure of protection, 'placed in difficulty by the crisis which shook the whole of Italy, partially withdrew their protection'.[6]

Yet in spite of the constant risk of ecclesiastical disapproval, in strictly theoretical terms Vico's compromises tend to be largely superficial. For, although he was clearly unable to express many of his ideas in as direct and forthright a manner as he would have liked, his strategy of concealment was on the whole employed intelligently and effectively. Hence he succeeded in effect in producing a devastating attack on the traditional notion of 'natural law'. In substance, he both absorbed into his theory elements of the conception of 'force' as the basis of legal authority and at the same time undermined any notion of 'eternal' principles of natural justice. His tactic consisted in totally ignoring rather than refuting the major Catholic authorities in the field such as Suárez and Aquinas.

He adopted a similar approach in his inevitable undermining of

---

4. In this connection, Stuart Woolf has written:
The struggle was resumed with particular intensity after 1680 in Naples, where a small group of jurists opposed papal claims of feudal sovereignty over territory in the kingdom. These men of law . . . who were wholly dependent on royal protection and who, between 1690 and 1695, were fiercely persecuted by the Inquisition, turned with hope to Austria and prepared the ground through their writings, for the arrival of Charles Bourbon. ('La storia politica e sociale', p. 61).
5. Ibid., pp. 61–2.
6. Ibid., p. 63.

the doctrine of free-will. Such problems were never, of course, made explicit, but rather were implied in both the thrust and detail of his naturalism. At certain points, however, he adopted a 'camouflaging' technique whereby he actually claimed to be proving the doctrine he was in fact contradicting. But we find here once again a remarkable state of affairs: one in which an author claiming to support a particular Catholic doctrine goes to great lengths to avoid even the mention of the major Catholic authorities in the field.

This apparently wilful neglect is repeated, moreover, in the case of providence, but with the difference that Vico pretends to be inventing a new branch of (civil) theology within which he claims providence ought to be more exhaustively considered. In this way he attempts to justify avoiding a confrontation with the major Catholic authorities on the subject. When it comes to the notion of historical cycles, he even takes the double precaution of ignoring both the pagan originators of the idea and their Christian detractors. He thus avoids bringing out into the open all the doctrinal problems associated with this fundamentally pagan notion.

All the observations which we have examined in some detail in this study are dependent on a willingness to perceive the deep-rooted and systematic naturalism at work in Vico's thinking. Appraisals of the *Scienza nuova* will incline to be misleading if they lose sight of the 'philosophy of nature' which occasions both the weaknesses and strengths of this remarkable work.

The starting point for Vico's far-reaching reflections is to be found in the sphere of law. Here he achieved a striking synthesis between the traditionally dichotomized areas of 'ideal' and 'positive' law. By accommodating all the *realist* elements of 'force', 'struggle' and the general limitations and imperfections to be found in legal systems within a universal pattern of development common to all societies, his concept of the 'natural law of the gentes' overcame this damaging traditional dichotomy, and in the process provided a justification for the rule of law. That is to say, the 'natural law of the gentes' became the rationale for the 'authority' of legal systems since it denoted the appropriateness of the latter to the changing times of which they were a reflection.

The sheer intellectual power of Vico's thought is demonstrated by its extraordinary range. In the first place, the synthesis he achieved between the formerly distinct areas of 'theoretical' and 'historical' legal studies required the creation of a form of historical understanding capable of unifying these otherwise traditionally disparate disciplines. This was a remarkable achievement in its own right, one in which the first steps were taken towards constructing further cross-cultural relationships well beyond the field of law.

But in the second place, besides providing a powerful theoretical stimulus for a long-term cultural renewal, Vico's reflections were also highly pertinent to more contingent issues. His attempt to re-think the theoretical basis of jurisprudence, for instance, and his desire to produce a 'philosophy of authority' take place at a time when 'the pressing problem in the civil life of Naples was that of authority'.[7]

Broadly speaking, a general cultural tension was in evidence during this period in Naples between the inherited naturalism which had been implicit in the thinking of the Investiganti and a 'philosophy of mind' which by contrast stressed the role of rationality. Studies of the period have highlighted the kind of shift which was taking place in legal thinking as a result of such problems and debates. The emphasis which had for some time been placed by progressive juridical thinkers on 'natural' liberties and rights was under threat from a new trend in legal thought which was beginning to stress the idea of 'civil authority'. This latter current emphasized the 'constraints' and 'duties' imposed by law rather than the 'freedoms' it guaranteed. Within this context Doria's *Vita civile* was an important landmark, and expressed a tendency to raise 'mind' (and thus law as one of the creations of 'mind') above 'nature'.

To Vico, as has been abundantly stressed, law was not a creation of the rational mind, and his thought worked entirely in the opposite direction. In Doria, moreover, the emphasis on 'mind' carried with it very marked political overtones. His ideas could be broadly characterized as anti-populist and as amounting to 'a theory of *wisdom*, which aims to correct the "errors of the vulgar herd"'[8] who take their natural inclinations as their guide.

In its stress on law in its naturalistic setting, Vico's theory can be seen as an ideological counterblast to this aristocratic tendency. For the 'senso comune', which is the foundation of his 'natural law of the gentes', clearly brings the 'vulgus' or 'herd' back into the political, social and legal arena. In fact, whether we are looking at the phenomenon of language through the concept of 'natural signification', or at the struggles of lower social groups attempting to gain rights of ownership and 'connubium', Vico's naturalism acts as a consistent corrective to what he sees as the myopic, narrow and anachronistic theoretical horizons of his rivals.

7. De Giovanni, 'Il "De nostri temporis studiorum ratione"', p. 191.
8. Ibid., p. 160.

His theoretical labours, therefore, are embedded in the humus of contemporary problems, but are not overwhelmed by them. What enabled Vico to transcend the provincialism of these local debates was the fact that the particulars of his theory were integrated into the broad sweep of the historicism underlying his 'ideal eternal history'.

We have seen how this 'ideal eternal history' is, in fact, a cosmic organic process embracing a naturalistic and cyclical regenerative mechanism. Its various parts and secondary processes, moreover, are held together within a conational and broadly deterministic framework, thus providing a high level of integration and coherence for his whole scheme. Yet Vico's very success in constructing such a unified theoretical system was achieved only at a price.

The first and most obvious disadvantage resulting from such integration is a certain rigidity in the manner of conceiving historical development. It is reflected, on one level, in the tenacity with which Vico clings to his tripartite scheme of things. But this is in turn part of the general cosmic pessimism so fundamental to his cyclical perspective, which ultimately absorbs historical change into one of the numerous processes of 'nature'. The result is a historicism deprived of its most valuable attribute – a sense of open-endedness. We cannot therefore endorse the extravagant claims made by many critics regarding the modernity of Vico's historicism.

Had he possessed a conception of linear advancement he would have had no inhibitions about expressing it, since he could have ranged himself squarely alongside the orthodox eschatological tradition and even have attacked the pernicious idea of historical cycles, which he in fact espoused. In this connection, we have seen that it is not correct to suppose that a thinker such as Vico, who was aware of advances in particular areas of human enquiry, would automatically think in terms of a *general* and continuing historical progression. If such a conceptual transition had been so easy and natural, we would certainly have expected the notion of historical 'progress' to have emerged in the minds of major scientific innovators such as Newton. Instead 'the world-view of Newton, and by inference that of the century in general, was a static one', and, on examination we find that 'Newton and many of his English contemporaries seem, like the Stoics, to view the cosmos as going through successive cycles.'[9]

The distinction between the notion of a *general* historical progres-

---

9. Kubrin, 'Newton and the Cyclical Cosmos', p. 169.

sion, on the one hand, and advancement in particular fields, on the other, is very important. The evidence suggests that perhaps the major antecedent of the idea of progress was the conception of advancement in knowledge. Given Vico's relative scepticism with regard to man's rational powers, and also his notion of 'ricorsi', it is not difficult to see how far removed he was from conceiving of a general progress in history as a whole.

It is ironic that the more positive qualities of Vico's historicism should have owed so much to his opposition to Cartesianism, within which the doctrine of progress was slowly emerging. We have seen that the empirical aspect of Vico's *Scienza nuova* derives its inspiration from Bacon's conception of scientific induction. It is not fortuitous that 'it was within the Cartesian rather than the Baconian tradition that the dogma of progress made its first full-dress appearances'.[10] In this sense, Vico's opposition to Cartesian rationalism, and his espousal of Baconian empiricism, were ill-fated but also, as we shall see, inevitable.

It was, of course, to be expected that the idea of intellectual progress should eventually be enlarged into a general conception of human progress.[11] Vico's dissent from the enthusiastic appraisal of reason which is entailed in such a transition is well known, and partly explains his distance from the emergent 'unilinear' and 'optimistic' historicism this eventually produced. But there were deeper roots to Vico's opposition to Cartesian rationalism, and, ironically, these were concerned with what he saw as a two-fold attack on history by Descartes and his followers.

It is well known that the pursuit of clear and distinct ideas in philosophy was regarded by the Cartesians as the only worthwhile academic activity, and that history was on the whole regarded as a second-order form of enquiry. Indeed history 'was not expected to strive to follow a strict method, to conform to the rules of a compulsory technique. It was a species of literature.'[12] In addition to this, Descartes saw the study of history almost as a form of subservience to the past, epitomized for him in the method of study which relied upon the texts of 'authorities'. He intended, consequently, to establish a philosophy 'based on rational principles and

10. Baillie, *Belief in Progress*, p. 104.
11. 'The transition was easy. If it could be proved that social evils were due neither to innate and incorrigible disabilites of the human being nor to the nature of things, but simply to ignorance and prejudice, then the improvement of his state, and ultimately the attainment of felicity, would be only a matter of illuminating ignorance and removing errors, of increasing knowledge and diffusing light.' (Bury *Idea of Progress*, p. 128.)
12. Lucien Lévy-Bruhl, 'The Cartesian Spirit and History', pp. 191.

strictly demonstrated. At the same time the method of authority was to disappear.'[13]

Vico thus found himself in opposition to Descartes on two counts as far as history was concerned. He intended to show, first, that a science of history was possible, and then, second, that such a science did not enslave minds into subservience to the past. His response was to seek to raise the study of history to the level of a rigorous and demonstrable science. We will recall that he called this science a 'philosophy of authority', for he was seeking to show, against the Cartesian detractors of the study of history, that an examination of the past is not only a useful, disciplined and worthy theoretical pursuit but that it also reveals a fundamental and coherent rationale for the nature of 'authority'. The study of history did not encourage blind subservience, but rather highlighted the changing relationship between those forces which, in their struggles either to win or retain privileges and rights, helped to shape the course of the 'ideal eternal history'. His opposition to Cartesian rationalism was thus an essential part of his defence of a science of history.

That the idea of progress should have emerged more easily within the anti-historical cultural ethos of Vico's opponents illustrates the complexity and unevenness of development in the history of ideas. But whereas his opposition to Cartesian rationalism cut him off from those currents in which the idea of progress emerged, his contribution to the study of history is nevertheless immense. Vico's remarkable originality lies in the clarity with which he perceived the existence of a matrix of relationships operating within the constantly changing forms of social reality. No thinker before him had seen with such lucidity and depth the fact that a particular epoch is a construction of parallel developments in different spheres – and that historians can use the discoveries they make in one sphere to uncover the characteristics of another. While individual scholars and scientists had certainly contributed much to the advancement and historical understanding of their own disciplines, Vico's genius lies in his unrivalled and strikingly original perception of their interdependence and of their reciprocal interconnections in successive phases of development. Thereafter students of language, of ideas, of myth, of political, social and legal institutions would find common elements and determining features straddling traditional disciplinary boundaries and providing a more profound 'contextual' perspective for each.

13. Ibid., pp. 192–3.

Ironically, we are indebted to Vico's naturalism for this remarkable advance in historical understanding. For it was only because he regarded reality and its changing forms as the expression of a naturalistically structured social organism evolving along a fixed path that he was able to theorize the conception of its various parts developing along a parallel pattern. This pattern, moreover, which he describes in terms of a providential force revolving around certain fixed points, excludes the sense of progressive linear development with which we are today so familiar. His concept of the 'ricorso' is far from being a dispensable appendage. It is an integral and logical part of his naturalistic synthesis of providence and historical necessity; a synthesis which removes any possibility of an open-ended historicism in the *Scienza nuova*, and which, in this respect, depicts a rather 'closed' historical process nearer the pessimistic cosmology of classical origin.

Yet, despite the limitations of his 'ideal eternal history', Vico's discovery of the relatedness of all aspects of human existence in successive phases of its development marks him out as a theoretical innovator of the first order. His originality, therefore, lies more in his understanding of the complexity and of the dynamic features of historical development than in his conception of its overall direction. Great weaknesses and great strength could, and did, coexist in Vico's thought. It may be tempting to hold to a Manichaean conception of the history of ideas, but in reality there are shades of light and darkness along the paths of all those who have enlightened humanity. We must also, if we are to arrive at a balanced and accurate assessment of what remains to be said about the *Scienza nuova*, be prepared sometimes to read strategically between the lines and resist the temptation to force the ambiguities of the work into the confines of our own perspectives. It is in the hope of restoring some of the original sense to Vico's much-glossed historical outlook that the foregoing pages have been written.

Bibliography

(Original dates of publication, where appropriate, are given in parenthesis.)

Editions of Vico's Work

In English
The New Science of Giambattista Vico, translated from the third edition (1744) by T. G. Bergin and M. H. Fisch, Ithaca, N.Y.: Cornell University Press, 1948. Revised edition with an introduction by M. H. Fisch, 1968. Unabridged, including 'Practic of the New Science', Cornell Paperbacks, 1984.

The Autobiography of Giambattista Vico, translated with an introduction and notes by M. H. Fisch and T. G. Bergin, Ithaca, N.Y.: Cornell University Press, 1944. Reprinted, with corrections and supplementary notes: Cornell University Press, Great Seal Books, 1963; Cornell Paperbacks, 1975.

On the Study Methods of Our Time, translated with an introduction and notes by Elio Gianturco, Indianapolis, Ind.: Bobbs-Merrill, 1965.

Vico: Selected Writings, edited and translated by Leon Pompa, Cambridge: Cambridge University Press, 1982.

In Italian
Opere, edited with an introduction and notes by F. Nicolini, Milan and Naples: Ricciardi, 1953.

La Scienza nuova seconda, Giusta l'edizione del 1744 con le varianti dell' edizione del 1730 e di due redazioni intermedie inedite, edited by F. Nicolini, Bari: Laterza, 1953.

Autobiografia, edited by M. Fubini, Turin: Einaudi, 1965.

La scienza nuova prima (1725), edited by F. Nicolini, Bari: Laterza, 1968.

Opere filosofiche, edited by P. Cristofolini, with an introduction by N. Badaloni, Florence: Sansoni, 1971.

Opere giuridiche, edited by P. Cristofolini, with an introduction by N. Badaloni, Florence: Sansoni, 1974.

Bibliography

Secondary Sources

In English

Adams, H. P., *The Life and Writings of Giambattista Vico*, London: Allen and Unwin, 1935.

Attfield, R., *God and The Secular*, Cardiff: University College Cardiff Press, 1978.

Baillie, J., *The Belief in Progress*, Oxford: Oxford University Press, 1950.

Barnouw, J., 'Vico and the Continuity of Science: The Relation of his Epistemology to Bacon and Hobbes', *Isis* 71 (1980), 609–20.

Bedani, G. L. C., 'The Poetic as an Aesthetic Category in Vico's *Scienza Nuova*', *Italian Studies* 31 (1976), 22–36.

Berlin, I., *Vico and Herder*, London: Hogarth Press, 1976.

—— 'Vico and the Ideal of the Enlightenment', *Social Research* 43 (1976), 640–53.

Bultmann, R., *History and Eschatology*, Edinburgh: Edinburgh University Press, 1958.

Burke, P., *Vico*, Oxford: Oxford University Press, 1985.

Bury, J. B., *The Idea of Progress. An Inquiry into its Origin and Growth*, London: Macmillan & Co., 1920.

Caponigri, A. R., *Time and Idea. The Theory of History in G. B. Vico*, Notre Dame, Ind.: University of Notre Dame Press, 1968.

Collingwood, R. G., *The Idea of History*, Oxford: Oxford University Press, 1956.

Copleston, F., *A History of Philosophy*, 8 volumes, New York: Image Books, 1962–7.

Croce, B., *The Philosophy of Giambattista Vico*, trans. R. G. Collingwood, London: Howard Latimer, 1913.

Delumeau, J., *Catholicism Between Luther and Voltaire: A New View of the Counter-Reformation*, London: Burns and Oates, 1977.

De Mauro, T., 'From Rhetoric to Linguistic Historicism', in Tagliacozzo (ed.), *Giambattista Vico: An International Symposium*, pp. 279–95.

Duchesne-Guillemin, J., *The Western Response to Zoroaster*, Oxford: Clarendon Press, 1958.

Fassò, G., 'The Problem of Law and the Historical Origin of the *New Science*', in Tagliacozzo and Verene (eds.), *Giambattista Vico's Science of Humanity*, pp. 3–14.

Fisch, M. H., 'The Academy of the Investigators', in E.A. Underwood (ed.), *Science, Medicine, and History: Essays on the Evolution of Scientific Thought and Medical Practice Written in Honour of Charles Singer*, London: Oxford University Press, 1953, vol. I, pp. 521–63.

Flint, R., *Vico*, Edinburgh: Blackwood, 1901.

From Alexander to Constantine: Passages and Documens Illustrating the History of Social and Political Ideas, 336 BC–AD 337, translated, with introduction, notes and essays by Ernest Barker, Oxford: Clarendon Press, 1956.

Funkenstein, A., 'Natural Science and Social Theory: Hobbes, Spinoza and Vico', in Tagliacozzo and Verene (eds.), *Giambattista Vico's Science of Humanity*, pp. 187–212.

Gillispie, C. C., *Genesis and Geology*, New York: Harper and Row, 1959.

Gilson, É., 'Concerning Christian Philosophy. The Distinctiveness of the Philosophic Order', in Klibansky and Paton (eds.), *Philosphy and History*, pp. 61–76.

Glacken, C. J., *Traces on the Rhodian Shore: Nature and Culture in Western Thought from Ancient Times to the Eighteenth Century*, Berkeley Cal.: University of California Press, 1973.

González, J. L., *A History of Christian Thought*, 3 volumes, Nashville: Abingdon Press, 1975.

Guthrie, W. K. C., *In The Beginning*, London: Methuen, 1957.
A History of Greek Philosophy, 5 volumes, Cambridge: Cambridge University Press, 1962–78.

Haddock, B. A., *Vico's Political Thought*, Swansea: Mortlake Press, 1986.

Hall, Jr, Robert, A., 'G. B. Vico and Linguistic Theory', *Italicum* 18 (1941), 145–54.

Hampshire, S., *Spinoza*, Harmondsworth: Penguin Books, 1970.

Hutton, P. H., 'Vico's Theory of History and the French Revolutionary Tradition', *Journal of the History of Ideas* 37: 2 (1976), 241–56.

Jaki, S. L., *Science and Creation: From Eternal Cycles to an Oscillating Universe*, Edinburgh and London: Scottish Academic Press, 1974.

Joyce, SJ, G. H., 'Providence and the Problem of Evil', in G. H. Joyce, SJ, *Principles of Natural Theology*, London: Longman, Green and Co., 1934, pp. 557–606.

Kirk, G. S., and Raven, J. E. (eds.), *The Presocratic Philosophers*, Cambridge: Cambridge University Press, 1963.

Klibansky, R., and Paton, H. J. (eds.), *Philosophy and History, Essays Presented to Ernst Cassirer*, Oxford: Clarendon Press, 1936.

Kubrin, D., 'Newton and the Cyclical Cosmos: Providence and the Mechanical Philosophy', in C. A. Russell (ed.), *Science and Religious Belief*, London: University of London Press, 1973, pp. 147–69.

Lévy-Bruhl, L., 'The Cartesian Spirit and History', in Klibansky and Paton (eds.), *Philosophy and History*, pp. 191–6.

Lowith, K., *Meaning in History*, Chicago, Ill.: University of Chicago Press, 1949.

Mazlish, B., *The Riddle of History. The Great Speculators from Vico to Freud*, New York: Harper and Row, 1966.

Midgley, E. B. F., *The Natural Law Tradition and the Theory of International Relations*, London: Paul Elek, 1975.

Momigliano, A., 'Vico's "Scienza Nuova": Roman "Bestioni" and Roman "Eroi"', *History and Theory* 5 (1966), 3–23.

Mooney, M., *Vico in the Tradition of Rhetoric*, Princeton, N.J. Princeton University Press, 1985.

Nisbet, R., 'Vico and the idea of Progress', *Social Research* 43 (1976), 625–37.

—— *History of the Idea of Progress*, London: Heinemann, 1980.

Passerin D'Entreves, A., *Natural Law*, London: Hutchinson University Library, 1970.

Pompa, L., *Vico: A Study of the 'New Science'*, Cambridge: Cambridge University Press, 1975.

—— 'Human Nature and the Concept of a Human Science', *Social Research* 43 (1976), 434–45.

—— Imagination in Vico', in Tagliacozzo (ed.), *Vico: Past and Present*, pp. 162–70.

Rattansi, P. M., 'The Social Interpretation of Science in the Seventeenth Century', in P. Mathias (ed.), *Science and Society 1600–1900*, Cambridge: Cambridge University Press, 1972, pp. 1–32.

Richmond, J., *Theology and Metaphysics*, London: SCM Press Ltd, 1970.

Rossi, P., *The Dark Abyss of Time: The History of the Earth and the History of Nations from Hooke to Vico*, trans. Lidia G. Cochrane, Chicago, Ill.: University of Chicago Press, 1984.

Streuver, N. S., 'Vico, Valla and the Logic of Humanist Inquiry', in Tagliacozzo and Verene (eds.), *Giambattista Vico's Science of Humanity*, pp. 173–88.

Tagliacozzo, G. (ed.), *Giambattista Vico: An International Symposium*, Baltimore, Md: Johns Hopkins University Press, 1969.

—— (ed.), *Vico: Past and Present*, Atlantic Highlands, N.J.: Humanities Press, 1981.

—— (ed.), *Vico and Marx: Affinities and Contrasts*, Atlantic Highlands, N.J.: Humanities Press; London: Macmillan, 1983.

Tagliacozzo, G. and Verene, D. P. (eds.), *Giambattista Vico's Science of Humanity*, Baltimore, Md: Johns Hopkins University Press, 1976.

Tagliacozzo, G., Mooney, M. and Verene, D. P. (eds.), *Vico and Contemporary Thought*, Atlantic Highlands, N.J.: Humanities Press, 1979.

Trompf, G. W., *The Idea of Historical Recurrence in Western Thought: From Antiquity to the Reformation*, Berkeley, Cal.: University of California Press, 1979.

Vaughan, F., 'La Scienza Nuova: Orthodoxy and the Art of Writing', *Forum Italicum* 2 (1968), 332–58.

—— *The Political Philosophy of Giambattista Vico*, The Hague: Martinus Nijhoff, 1972.

Verene, D. P., 'Vico's Science of Imaginative Universals and the Philosophy of Symbolic Forms', in Tagliacozzo and Verene (eds.), *Giambattista Vico's Science of Humanity*, pp. 295–317.

—— 'Vico's Philosophy of Imagination', *Social Research* 43 (1976), 410–26.

—— *Vico's Science of Imagination*, Ithaca, N.Y.: Cornell University Press, 1981.

Walsh, W. H., 'The Logical Status of Vico's Ideal Eternal History', in

Tagliacozzo and Verene (eds.), *Giambattista Vico's Science of Humanity*, pp. 141–53.

Watkins, J. W. N., *Hobbes's System of Ideas*, London: Hutchinson and Co. Ltd, 1973.

Webb, C. C. J., *Studies in the History of Natural Theology*, Oxford: Clarendon Press, 1970.

In Italian

Amabile, L., *Il Santo Officio della Inquisizione in Napoli*, 2 volumes, Città di Castello, 1892.

Amerio, F., *Introduzione allo studio di G. B. Vico*, Turin: Società Editrice Internazionale, 1947.

—— 'Sulla vichiana dialettica della storia', in *Omaggio a Vico*, pp. 113–40.

Badaloni, N., *Introduzione a G. B. Vico*, Milan: Feltrinelli, 1961.

—— 'Vico nell' ambito della filosofia europea', in *Omaggio a Vico*, pp. 233–66.

—— *Introduzione a Vico*, Rome-Bari: Laterza, 1984.

Battistini, A., 'Gli studi vichiani di Antonino Pagliaro', *Bollettino del Centro di Studi Vichiani* 7 (1977), 81–112.

—— (ed.) *Vico oggi*, Rome: Armando, 1979.

Bellofiore, L., *La dottrina della provvidenza in G. B. Vico*, Padua: Cedam, 1962.

Cantelli, G., *Vico e Bayle: premesse per un confronto*, Naples: Guida editori, 1971.

—— *Mente corpo linguaggio: Saggio sull' interpretazione vichiana del mito*, Florence: Sansoni, 1986.

Carpanetto, D., *L'Italia nel Settecento*, Turin: Loescher, 1980.

Comparato, V. I., 'Ragione e fede nelle discussioni di C. Grimaldi', in *Saggi e ricerche sul Settecento*, pp. 48–93.

—— *Giuseppe Valletta, un intellettuale napoletano della fine del Seicento*, Naples: Istituto Italiano per gli Studi Storici, 1970.

Corsano, A., *Umanesimo e religione in G. B. Vico*, Bari: Laterza, 1935.

—— *G. B. Vico*, Bari: Laterza, 1956.

—— *Bayle, Leibniz e la storia*, Naples: Guida editori, 1971.

Croce, B., *La filosofia di Giambattista Vico*, Bari: Laterza, 1973.

—— *Storia del regno di Napoli*, Bari: Laterza, 1966.

De Giovanni, B., *Filosofia e diritto in Francesco D'Andrea. Contributo alla storia del previchismo*, Milan: Giuffré, 1958.

—— 'Cultura e vita civile in G. Valletta', in *Saggi e ricerche sul Settecento*, pp. 1–47.

—— 'Il "De nostri temporis studiorum ratione" nella cultura napoletana del primo Settecento', in *Omaggio a Vico*, pp. 141–91.

De Mas, E., *Bacone e Vico*, Turin: Edizioni di Filosofia, 1959.

Fassò, G., *Vico e Grozio*, Naples: Guida editori, 1971.

Finetti, B., *Difesa dell' autorità della Sacra Scrittura contro Giambattista Vico*

(1768), with an introduction by B. Croce, Bari: Laterza, 1936.

Garin, E., 'Appunti per una storia della fortuna di Hobbes nel Settecento italiano', *Rivista critica di storia della filosofia* 17 (1962), 514–27.

—— *Storia della filosofia italiana*, 3 volumes, Turin: Einaudi, 1966.

Giambattista Vico nel terzo centenario della nascita, various authors, Naples: Edizioni Scientifiche Italiane, 1971.

Giannone, P., *Vita scritta da lui medesimo*, (1736–7), ed. S. Bertelli, Milan: Feltrinelli, 1960.

Giordano, P., *Vico filosofo del suo tempo* Padua: Cedam, 1974.

Grimaldi, C., *Memorie di un anticurialista del Settecento* (1734–5), ed. V. I. Comparato, Florence: Leo S. Olschki, 1964.

Iannizzotto, M., *L'Empirismo nella gnoseologia di Giambattista Vico*, Padua: Cedam, 1968.

Labanca, B., *G. B. Vico rispetto ai suoi contemporanei*, Naples: Pierro, 1898.

Marini, C., *Giambattista Vico al cospetto del secolo xix*, Naples: Stamperia Strada Salvatore, 1852.

Mastellone, S., *Pensiero politico e vita culturale a Napoli nella seconda metà del Seicento*, Messina-Florence: D'Anna, 1965.

—— *Francesco D'Andrea politico e giurista (1648–1698). L'Ascesa del ceto civile*, Florence: Leo S. Olschki, 1969.

Mazzarino, S., *Vico, l'annalistica e il diritto*, Naples: Guida editori, 1971.

Melpignano, SJ, A., *L'Anticurialismo napoletano sotto Carlo III*, Rome: Herder, 1965.

Mondolfo, R., *Il 'verum-factum' prima di Vico*, Naples: Guida editori, 1969.

Nicolini, F., *La religiosità di G. B. Vico*, Bari: Laterza, 1949.

—— 'Il Vico e il suo censore ecclesiastico', in Nicolini, *Saggi vichiani*, pp. 281–95.

—— *Saggi vichiani*, Naples: Giannini, 1955.

—— *Vico storico*, ed. F. Tessitore, Naples: Morano, 1967.

Nuzzo, E., *Vico*, Florence: Valecchi, 1974.

Omaggio a Vico, various authors, Naples: Morano, 1968.

Osbat, L., *L'Inquisizione a Napoli. Il processo agli ateisti 1688–1697*, Rome: Edizioni di Storia e Letteratura, 1974.

Paci, E., *Ingens Sylva. Saggio sulla filosofia di G. B. Vico*, Milan: Mondadori, 1949.

Pagliaro, A., *Altri saggi di critica semantica*, Messina-Florence: D'Anna, 1961.

Papini, M., *Arbor Humanae Linguae. L'etimologia di G. B. Vico come chiave ermeneutica della storia del mondo*, Bologna: Cappelli, 1984.

—— *Il geroglifico della storia. Significato e funzione della dipintura nella 'Scienza Nuova' di G. B. Vico*, Bologna: Cappelli, 1984.

Pasini, D., *Diritto, società e stato in Vico*, Naples: Jovene, 1970.

Rak, M., 'Una teoria dell'' incertezza. Note sulla cultura napoletana del secolo XVIII', *Filologia e letteratura* 69, ser. 3 (1969), 233–97.

Rossi, P., *Le sterminate antichità: Studi vichiani*, Pisa: Nistri-Lischi, 1969.

Bibliography

Sabarini, R., *Il tempo in G. B. Vico*, Rome–Milan: Bocca editore, 1954.

Saggi e ricerche sul Settecento, various authors, Naples: Istituto Italiano per gli Studi Storici, 1968.

Semerari, G., 'Intorno all' anticartesianesimo di Vico', in *Omaggio a Vico*, pp. 195–232.

Tessitore, F., *Quaderni contemporanei 2. Giambattista Vico nel terzo centenario dalla nascita*, Naples: Istituto Universitario di Salerno, 1968.

Valletta, G., *Opere filosofiche* (1690–1704), ed. M. Rak, Florence: Leo S. ✓ Olschki, 1975.

Valsecchi, F., *L'Italia nel Settecento, dal 1714 al 1788*, Milan: Mondadori, ✓ 1975.

Verri, P., *Del piacere e del dolore ed altri scritti* (1763–97), ed. R. De Felice, Milan: Feltrinelli, 1964.

Woolf, S. J., 'La storia politica e sociale', in *Storia d'Italia*, vol. iii: *Dal primo Settecento all' unità*, Turin: Einaudi, 1973, pp. 5–508.

Other Sources

Aquinas, St Thomas, *Summa Theologica*. All standard editions of the 3 Parts and Supplement of the *Summa* are in 5 volumes.

Augustine, St, *De Civitate Dei*. *Corpus Christianorum*, Latin series, Vols. 47 and 48, Turnhout: Brepols, 1955.

—— *De Doctrina Christiana*. *Corpus Christianorum*, Latin series, Vol. 32, Turnhout: Brepols, 1962.

—— *City of God*, trans. J. Healey, ed. R. V. G. Tasker, London: J. M. Dent, 1950

Bacon, Francis, *De Dignitate et Augmentis Scientiarum*, in *The Works of Francis Bacon*, 10 volumes, London: J. Johnson, 1803, Vol. 7.

Denzinger, H., *Enchiridion Symbolorum*, Rome: Herder, 1957.

Galilei, Galileo, *Opere*, Milan, Naples: Riccardo Ricciardi, 1953.

Grotius, Hugo, *De Iure Belli et Pacis*, 4 volumes, with an abridged translation by William Whewell, Cambridge: Cambridge University Press, 1853.

Hobbes, Thomas, *Leviathan*, ed. A. R. Waller, Cambridge: Cambridge University Press, 1904.

—— *The English Works*, 11 volumes, ed. Sir William Molesworth, London: Longman, Brown, Green; Longmans, 1839–45.

Justinian, *The Institutes of Justinian*, translated with introduction and notes by Thomas Collett Sandars, London: Longmans, 1962.

Lucretius, *De Rerum Natura*, 3 volumes, edited with translation and commentary by C. Bailey, Oxford: Clarendon Press, 1947.

Origen, *Contra Celsum*, translated with an introduction and notes by Henry Chadwick, Cambridge: Cambridge University Press, 1980.

Plato, *The Republic*, trans. F. M. Cornford, Oxford: Clarendon Press, 1961.

Polybius, *The Histories*, 6 volumes, translated by W. R. Paton, London: William Heinemann; New York: G. P. Putnam's Sons, 1922–7.

Seneca, *Naturales Quaestiones*, 7 Books in 2 volumes, trans. Thomas H. Corcoran, London: Heinemann; Cambridge, Mass: Harvard University Press, 1971–2.

Spinoza, *Ethica*, in *Opera*, Vol. i, Leipzig: Bernhard Tauchnitz, 1843.

—— *Tractatus Theologicus – Politicus*, in *Opera*, Vol. iii, Leipzig Bernhard Tauchnitz, 1846.

Suárez, Francisco, *Tractatus de Legibus ac Deo Legislatore*, 4 books in 10 volumes, Coimbra: Loureyro, 1612.

Bibliographies and Commentaries

In English

The most comprehensive and updated bibliography of works by and on Vico in English is to be found in G. Tagliacozzo, D. P. Verene and V. Rumble, *A Bibliography of Vico in English 1884–1984*, Philosophy Documentation Center, Bowling Green, Ohio: Bowling Green State University, 1986. An updated supplement to this bibliography is to be found in *New Vico Studies*, vol. 3, Atlantic Highlands, N.J.: Humanities Press International, 1985, printed 1987.

In Italian

Croce, B., *Bibliografia vichiana*, with additions by F. Nicolini, 2 volumes, Naples: Ricciardi, 1947–8.

Donzelli, M., *Contributo alla bibliografia vichiana (1948–1970)*, Naples: Guida editori, 1973.

Nicolini, F., *Commento storico alla seconda Scienza Nuova*, 2 volumes, Rome: Edizioni di Storia e Letteratura, 1949–50.

Index

3, 58

- first chap good on theo hist

25-6 censor: rewriting Ⓐ

38 monosyllables

41 "naturalness" at early stages / soghiero 42

46 dispersion before tongue confusion? Ⓐ

49-51 Moses

54 poetry = true = natural narration

Chap 5: against collapse of 3 languages, "aesthet"
   of poetry - good. No aesth in V Ⓐ

79f major gods created naturally, later w reflection ⒶⒶ

99 good on V's slippery movement at flood, etc Ⓐ

Chap 6: right that V fudges, but not a sign of heterodoxy
   Also shows that chron doesn't hold together (p.109)

123 cheat Deno p.93 on animals: not right.

126 interprets ricorso as pres of "species"

136 Takes V's citation of Grotius as approval!

138 noncitation of Thomas prone w big 137-8

147 calls queen St. Aug arg in Desert Jansenist. Possible.
   But see 148 on Richardus

183f rightly criticizes "privileged insight" theory of NS
   and imagination.

194·5 see prov > v.f. good Then conclude V is inductive!

216 right that men don't direct hist, wrong that full doesn't count

222 out on nat theology

226f Aquinas on prov. Aug 228·9

235f Homer: Dante in DC! Ⓐ

242 claims V borrows from Methodius

247 treats V as hist pessimist, cycle contra Aug

260 good on preservation (cf 261)

265f conatus. Take deterministically

Grimaldi

- notes 3, 30-1,

- attacks Rossi, whom I'll have to
  defend. Also Mooney in "Bestia

- B reads him as Epicurean

- Do Mauro or Leibniz's linguistic
  in Tag vol 2.

- must dist nat use from utility

- Cassirer sees naturalism in Ep
  light, not nat right.

- are there ways in which
  is less careful i NSS? Y
  seems more Epic

   · must mention toleration
     tyrants in chap Va
     (Synopsis p6)

- Get Mastellone at BN

· See Opere filosofiche on
   uncertainty of nev, pp. 80°

   · reread whole but chp
   · Affield, Webb Ⓐ
   · Berlizze on prog
   " on cycle, Cristia
     109d-110, Law
     676

   " Papini p.92
     on conatus